Vocabulary
AND
Composition

Through
Pleasurable
Reading

BOOK III

HAROLD LEVINE
Chairman Emeritus of English
Benjamin Cardozo High School, New York

NORMAN LEVINE
Associate Professor of English
City College of the City University of New York

ROBERT T. LEVINE
Professor of English
North Carolina A & T State University

Vocabulary books by the authors

Vocabulary and Composition Through Pleasurable Reading, Books I–VI
Vocabulary for Enjoyment, Books I–III
Vocabulary for the High School Student, Books A, B
Vocabulary for the High School Student
Vocabulary for the College-Bound Student
The Joy of Vocabulary

Vocabulary
AND
Composition
Through
Pleasurable
Reading

BOOK III

SECOND EDITION

When ordering this book please specify *either* R 646 W
or Vocabulary and Composition
Through Pleasurable Reading, Book III, Workbook

AMSCO SCHOOL PUBLICATIONS, INC.
315 Hudson Street / New York, NY 10013

Acknowledgments

Grateful acknowledgment is made to the following sources for having granted permission to reprint copyrighted materials.

David R. Godine, Publisher, Inc. *Selection 11.* From *Hunger of Memory* by Richard Rodriguez, reprinted by permission of David R. Godine, Publisher, Inc. Copyright © 1982 by Richard Rodriguez.

HarperCollins Publishers. *Selection 6.* From *The Good Earth* by Pearl S. Buck, copyright 1931, 1949, 1958 by Pearl S. Buck. Reprinted by permission of HarperCollins Publishers, Inc.

Selection 8. From *Black Boy* by Richard Wright, copyright 1937, 1942, 1944, 1945 by Richard Wright. Reprinted by permission of HarperCollins Publishers, Inc.

Alfred A. Knopf, Inc. *Selection 4.* From *The Autobiography of an Ex-Coloured Man* by James Weldon Johnson, copyright 1927 by Alfred A. Knopf, Inc., and renewed 1955 by Carl Van Vechten. Reprinted by permission of the publisher.

W. W. Norton & Company, Inc. *Selection 10.* From *An American Doctor's Odyssey* by Victor Heiser, copyright 1936, © 1964 by Dr. Victor Heiser. Reprinted by permission of W. W. Norton & Company, Inc.

I. Milo Shepherd. *Selection 1.* From "To Build a Fire," from *Lost Face* by Jack London. Reprinted with the permission of I. Milo Shepherd, Executor.

ISBN 1-56765-043-0
NYC Item 56765-043-X

1 2 3 4 5 6 7 8 9   03 02 01 00 99 98 97

To the Student

What will you achieve by using this revised and enlarged second edition of *Vocabulary and Composition Through Pleasurable Reading, Book III?*

You will learn eleven skills for being a better writer from the eleven distinguished authors whose works are sampled in this book. How do you suppose they themselves learned to write, if not by carefully studying the work of other writers whom they enjoyed and admired? You can do the same.

You will write eleven compositions, some of which you might like to have included in your writing portfolio. In these compositions, you will be putting into use your newly acquired writing skills. For each composition you are asked to write, you will be provided with a model composition to guide you.

You will considerably improve your skills of close reading, critical thinking, and concise writing, especially by doing the exercises that teach these skills in every lesson in the book.

You will add a couple of hundred words to your vocabulary.

You will improve your spelling and wordbuilding skills.

And you will enjoy the selections from the works of the eleven famous authors. These selections are the backbone of the book and the inspiration for everything it has to teach you.

The Authors

For Your Reading Pleasure

from

"To Build a Fire"

by Jack London

It is the time of the Gold Rush. A newcomer, abandoning the main Yukon trail, is making his way up a little-traveled creek. He does not realize it is 107 degrees below freezing.

Empty as the man's mind was of thoughts, he was keenly observant, and he noticed the changes in the creek, the curves and bends and timber jams, and always he sharply noted where he placed his feet. Once, coming around a bend, he shied abruptly, like a startled horse, curved away from the place where he had been ⁵ walking, and retreated several paces back along the trail. The creek he knew was frozen clear to the bottom—no creek could contain water in that arctic winter—but he knew also that there were springs that bubbled out from the hillsides and ran along under the snow and on top of the ice of the creek. He knew that the cold- ¹⁰ est snaps never froze these springs, and he knew likewise their danger. They were traps. They hid pools of water under the snow that might be three inches deep, or three feet. Sometimes a skin of ice half an inch thick covered them, and in turn was covered by the snow. Sometimes there were alternate layers of water and ice skin, ¹⁵ so that when one broke through he kept on breaking through for a while, sometimes wetting himself to the waist.

That was why he had shied in such panic. He had felt the give under his feet and heard the crackle of a snow-hidden ice skin. And to get his feet wet in such a temperature meant trouble and dan- ²⁰ ger. At the very least it meant delay, for he would be forced to stop and build a fire, and under its protection to bare his feet while he dried his socks and moccasins. He stood and studied the creek bed and its banks, and decided that the flow of water came from the

25 right. He reflected awhile rubbing his nose and cheeks, then skirted to the left, stepping gingerly and testing the footing for each step. Once clear of the danger, he took a fresh chew of tobacco and swung along at his four-mile gait.

In the course of the next two hours he came upon several simi-
30 lar traps. Usually the snow above the hidden pools had a sunken, candied appearance that advertised danger. Once again, however, he had a close call; and once, suspecting danger, he compelled the dog to go on in front. The dog did not want to go. It hung back until the man shoved it forward, and then it went quickly across the
35 white, unbroken surface. Suddenly it broke through, floundered to one side, and got away to firmer footing. It had wet its forefeet and legs, and almost immediately the water that clung to it turned to ice. It made quick efforts to lick the ice off its legs, then dropped down in the snow and began to bite out the ice that had formed
40 between the toes. This was a matter of instinct. To permit the ice to remain would mean sore feet. It did not know this. It merely obeyed the mysterious prompting that arose from the deep crypts of its being. But the man knew, having achieved a judgment on the subject, and he removed the mitten from his right hand and helped
45 tear out the ice particles. He did not expose his fingers more than a minute, and was astonished at the swift numbness that smote them. It certainly was cold. He pulled on the mitten hastily, and beat the hand savagely across his chest.

At twelve o'clock the day was at its brightest. Yet the sun was
50 too far south on its winter journey to clear the horizon. The bulge of the earth intervened between it and Henderson Creek, where the man walked under a clear sky at noon and cast no shadow. At half-past twelve, to the minute, he arrived at the forks of the creek. He was pleased at the speed he had made. If he kept it up, he
55 would certainly be with the boys by six. He unbuttoned his jacket and shirt and drew forth his lunch. The action consumed no more than a quarter of a minute, yet in that brief moment the numbness laid hold of the exposed fingers. He did not put the mitten on, but, instead, struck the fingers a dozen sharp smashes against his leg.
60 Then he sat down on a snow-covered log to eat. The sting that followed upon the striking of his fingers against his leg ceased so quickly that he was startled. He had had no chance to take a bite of biscuit. He struck the fingers repeatedly and returned them to the mitten, baring the other hand for the purpose of eating. He
65 tried to take a mouthful, but the ice muzzle prevented. He had forgotten to build a fire and thaw out. He chuckled at his foolishness, and as he chuckled he noted the numbness creeping into the exposed fingers. Also, he noted that the stinging which had first come to his toes when he sat down was already passing away. He
70 wondered whether the toes were warm or numb. He moved them inside the moccasins and decided that they were numb.

He pulled the mitten on hurriedly and stood up. He was a bit frightened. He stamped up and down until the stinging returned into the feet. It certainly was cold, was his thought. That man from

Sulphur Creek had spoken the truth when telling how cold it ⁷⁵ sometimes got in the country. And he had laughed at him at the time! That showed one must not be too sure of things. There was no mistake about it, it *was* cold. He strode up and down, stamping his feet and thrashing his arms, until reassured by the returning warmth. Then he got out matches and proceeded to make a fire. ⁸⁰ From the undergrowth, where high water of the previous spring had lodged a supply of seasoned twigs, he got his firewood. Working carefully from a small beginning, he soon had a roaring fire, over which he thawed the ice from his face and in the protection of which he ate his biscuits. For the moment the cold of space was ⁸⁵ outwitted. The dog took satisfaction in the fire, stretching out close enough for warmth and far enough away to escape being singed.

When the man had finished, he filled his pipe and took his comfortable time over a smoke. Then he pulled on his mittens, settled the ear flaps of his cap firmly about his ears, and took the creek ⁹⁰ trail up the left fork. The dog was disappointed and yearned back toward the fire. This man did not know cold. Possibly all the generations of his ancestry had been ignorant of cold, of real cold, of cold one hundred and seven degrees below freezing point. But the dog knew; all its ancestry knew, and it had inherited the knowl- ⁹⁵ edge. And it knew that it was not good to walk abroad in such fearful cold. It was time to lie snug in a hole in the snow and wait for a curtain of cloud to be drawn across the face of outer space whence this cold came. On the other hand, there was no keen intimacy between the dog and the man. The one was the toil-slave of ¹⁰⁰ the other, and the only caresses it had ever received were the caresses of the whiplash and of harsh and menacing throat sounds that threatened the whiplash. So the dog made no effort to communicate its apprehension to the man. It was not concerned in the welfare of the man; it was for its own sake that it yearned back ¹⁰⁵ toward the fire. But the man whistled, and spoke to it with the sound of whiplashes, and the dog swung in at the man's heels and followed after.

The man took a chew of tobacco and proceeded to start a new amber beard. Also, his moist breath quickly powdered with white ¹¹⁰ his mustache, eyebrows, and lashes. There did not seem to be so many springs on the left fork of the Henderson, and for half an hour the man saw no signs of any. And then it happened. At a place where there were no signs, where the soft, unbroken snow seemed to advertise solidity beneath, the man broke through. It was not ¹¹⁵ deep. He wet himself halfway to the knees before he floundered out to the firm crust.

Exercise 1.1: Close Reading

In the blank space, write the *letter* of the choice that best completes the statement.

1. At no time in the passage did __*d*__.

   (A) the man disregard the dog's welfare
   (B) the dog show concern over its own welfare
   (C) the man show he was afraid
   (D) the dog show concern over the man's welfare

2. According to the passage, the man __*c*__.

   (A) broke through the ice because of carelessness
   (B) lacked skill in building a fire
   (C) was very perceptive
   (D) managed to eat his lunch and feed his dog

3. The reader may conclude that __*b*__.

   (A) the sun was never seen in Henderson Creek
   (B) at lunchtime the man was confident of being able to reach his destination
   (C) firewood was scarce in Henderson Creek
   (D) the man won his dog's obedience through kindness

4. The passage suggests that __*a*__.

   (A) the dog sensed an approaching disaster
   (B) the dog was in all ways superior to the man
   (C) the man would reach his destination by six o'clock
   (D) the dog trusted in the man's judgment

5. As used in line 26, *gingerly* means "__*a*__."

   (A) with extreme caution
   (B) rapidly
   (C) vigorously
   (D) in a confident manner

Going Over the Answers   To get the right answers to questions like those you were just asked, follow one simple rule: *never guess!* The proof for the right answer is in the passage; sometimes it is obvious, and sometimes less than obvious, but it is always there, waiting for you to find it.

   Here are the answers to the reading questions you have just been working on. Carefully note the reasoning in arriving at these answers.

QUESTION 1: *Why the Correct Answer Is D:*

The dog (states lines 104–105) "was not concerned in the welfare of the man." It obeyed him because of compulsion (lines 32–33) and threats (line 103), not love.

Why the Other Answers Are Wrong:

A. The man disregarded the dog's welfare when he compelled it to go over a dangerous stretch of ice (lines 32–33).

B. The dog showed concern for its own welfare by not wanting to go over the suspected pool (line 33); by swiftly removing the ice from its wet legs and toes (lines 33–35); and by staying as close to the fire as safety would permit (lines 86–87). See also lines 91–92, 94–97, and 105–106.

C. The man showed he was afraid when he shied away in panic from a water trap (lines 17–18), and when, fearing for his own safety, he forced the dog to go on in front (lines 32–33). Also, he was "a bit frightened" by the effects of the cold on his feet (lines 72–73).

QUESTION 2: *Why the Correct Answer Is C:*

Line 1 states the man "was keenly observant (perceptive)." Note, too, the examples of the man's powers of observation (perception) in lines 2–3, 18–19, and 23–25.

Why the Other Answers Are Wrong:

A. The man cannot be charged with carelessness because there were no signs of danger at the place where he broke through the ice (lines 111–113).

B. Lines 80–83 describe how skillfully, quickly, and carefully the man built a roaring fire.

D. The man ate his lunch (line 85), but there is no evidence in the passage that he gave any food to this dog.

QUESTION 3: *Why the Correct Answer Is B:*

At 12:30 P.M., according to lines 52–55, the man thought "he would certainly be with the boys by six" if he kept up his speed. In fact, he was so confident of this that he "took his comfortable time over a smoke" (lines 88–89).

Why the Other Answers Are Wrong:

A. At the time of the story, "the sun was too far south on its winter journey to *clear the horizon* (be seen)" in Henderson Creek (lines 49–50). But that does not prove that the sun could not clear the horizon in the other seasons of the year.

C. The man had no trouble getting firewood from the undergrowth in the creek, where he found "a supply of seasoned twigs" (line 82).

D. The man gained the dog's obedience by compulsion (lines 32–34) and threats (lines 106–107), not kindness. See also lines 102–103.

QUESTION 4: *Why the Correct Answer Is A:*

Lines 91–99 and 104 show that when the man left the fire to continue his journey in the bitter cold, the dog felt not only disappointment but also *apprehension* (dread of what might happen).

Why the Other Answers Are Wrong:

B. In some respects the dog was superior. It knew the dangers of "fearful cold," while the man "did not know cold" (lines 92–94). In some respects the man was superior. He could provide fire; the dog could not (lines 80–87).

C. The man felt that if he kept up his pace, "he would certainly be with the boys by six" (lines 54–55), but that was before his accident (lines 113–115) and the considerable delay it would necessarily entail (lines 20–22).

D. The dog showed no faith in the man's judgment when he compelled it to go over a suspicious stretch of ice (lines 32–33), and also when he resumed the journey despite the extreme cold (lines 90–91). The dog "knew it was not good to walk abroad in such fearful cold" (lines 96–97).

QUESTION 5: *Why the Correct Answer Is A:*

The meaning of an unfamiliar word like *gingerly* can sometimes be learned from its *context*—the other words with which it is used. In lines 26–27, the words "testing the footing for each step"—making sure there was enough support for each step before he put his weight on it—suggest that *gingerly* means "with extreme caution."

Why the Other Answers Are Wrong:

B, C, and **D:** "Rapidly," "vigorously," and "in a confident manner" are all inconsistent with the man's "testing the footing for each step" (lines 26–27).

IMPROVING YOUR SENTENCE SKILLS: VARYING SENTENCE BEGINNINGS

We know that a sentence normally starts with the subject:

> **Vegetables** (*subject*) are usually plentiful in summer.

> **Hector** (*subject*) saw Maria on the bus sometimes.

But that does not mean that you should begin *all* of your sentences with the subject. If you do, your writing will be monotonous.

Note that Jack London does not begin all his sentences with the subject:

> [1]**In the course of the next two hours** [prepositional phrase] he came upon several similar traps. [2]**Usually** [adverb] the snow above the hidden pools had a sunken, candied appearance that advertised danger. [3]**Once**

again [adverb], however, he had a close call; and once, suspecting danger, he compelled the dog to go on in front. ⁴**The dog** [subject] did not want to go. ⁵**It** [subject] hung back until the man shoved it forward, and then it went quickly across the white, unbroken surface. ⁶**Suddenly** [adverb] it broke through, floundered to one side, and got away to firmer footing. ⁷**It** [subject] had wet its forefeet and legs, and almost immediately the water that clung to it turned to ice. ⁸**It** [subject] made quick efforts to lick the ice off its legs, then dropped down in the snow and began to bite out the ice that had formed between the toes.

You, too, can make your writing more intesting by varying the beginning of *some* (by no means all) of your sentences. Note the different ways in which the following sentence can begin:

SUBJECT FIRST
Vegetables are usually plentiful in summer.

ADVERB FIRST
Usually vegetables are plentiful in summer.

PREPOSITIONAL PHRASE FIRST
In summer vegetables are usually plentiful.

Exercise 1.2:   Varying Sentence Beginnings

Below are ten sentences that begin with the subject. Rewrite each sentence twice. On line A, begin with an adverb. On line B, begin with a prepositional phrase. Study this sample:

Hector saw Maria on the bus sometimes.

A. **Sometimes** Hector saw Maria on the bus.
B. **On the bus** Hector sometimes saw Maria.

1. Emily needs some help in math occasionally.
   A. _Ocassionally,_
   B. _in math_

2. The best seats have probably been sold by now.
   A. _Probably the best seats have sold by now_
   B. _By now_

3. My grandparents are going south for the winter once again.
   A. _once again_
   B. _for again the winter_

4. It will undoubtedly be cooler at the seashore.
   A. _undoubted_
   B. _at the seashore_

5. You can find good people in our community everywhere.

A. _everywher_

B. _in our community_

6. Ralph unfortunately ended our hopes by striking out.

A. _Unfortunately_

B. _by striking out_

7. They have enough supplies for the rest of the trip anyhow.

A. _For the rest of the trip_

B. _Anyhow_

8. One can often have a good time at family gatherings.

A. _often_

B. _at family gatherings_

9. The Braves have done well in home games lately.

A. _lately_

B. _in home games_

10. Restaurants generally serve brunch on Sundays.

A. _generally_

B. _on Sundays_

Exercise 1.3: Writing a Composition

In a paragraph of about 100 to 125 words, relate an unforgettable incident from your childhood. Here are some suggestions to guide you.

1. Write your first draft on scrap paper, jotting down your thoughts about the incident just as they come to you.

2. Give adequate details. Mention where the incident occurred, how old you were at the time, and who the other people were that were involved. Include any other details that made the incident unforgettable for you.

3. Go over your first draft to make sure not only that you have (*a*) included adequate details, but (*b*) varied your sentence beginnings. Then write the final draft in the space provided.

Sample Paragraph: A Day I Shall Always Remember

I shall never forget the morning there was a fire in the five-story tenement where my family lived on the Lower East Side of Manhattan. Swiftly waking my brother Romero and me—I was then about four—my frail mother, with my infant sister Nina on her shoulder, led us up to the roof, where a crowd of other shivering tenants had already gathered. Fortunately, not too long afterwards, we were allowed to return to our apartments, but I remember that for several days there was a bitter stench of smoke and no heat in the building. My father didn't know what had happened until he returned from work late that night, and when he heard my mother's report, he was thankful all of us were well.

Your Paragraph: A Day I Shall Always Remember

The dayd I shall remember is when I was walking home with my cousens after a bomb threat at a house in my neighborhood. We had to take a detour back. On the way my cousine's and I were attacked by a small but fast dog. One of my cousein & I were able to run away from the dog. However my other two other cousine weren't so lucky They were trapped behind a van. Soon we were able to go home when the owner called off the dog.

LEARNING NEW WORDS

Line	Word	Meaning	Typical Use
101	**caress** (n.) kə-'res	tender or loving touch; light stroking; embrace; kiss	When the affectionate puppy approached me for a *caress*, I gently stroked its back.
56	**consume** (v.) kən-'süm	1. use up	Last night I couldn't watch TV because homework *consumed* most of my time.

		2. eat or drink up; devour	We quickly *consumed* our sandwiches, as we were very hungry.
		3. destroy; do away with	Flames *consumed* the structure before the firefighters arrived.
45	**expose** (*v.*) ik-ʹspōz	uncover; bare to the cold, air, rain, etc.; deprive of shelter; leave unprotected (*ant.* **cover**)	After our swim, we lunched in the shade of our beach umbrella, so as not to *expose* ourselves too much to the sun.
35	**flounder** (*v.*) ʹflaun-dər	struggle awkwardly to move or to obtain footing; proceed clumsily; wallow	When she saw I was *floundering*, the teacher came over to help me.
28	**gait** (*v.*) ʹgāt	manner of walking, running, or moving on foot; pace	I didn't know where Pam was going, but from her leisurely *gait* I could see she was in no hurry.
40	**instinct** (*n.*) ʹin-stiŋkt	1. inborn inclination; natural impulse	Birds do not have to be taught to build a nest; *instinct* tells them how to do it.
		2. natural talent; gift; knack; aptitude	We chose Carolyn to speak for us because she has an *instinct* for saying the right thing.
99	**intimacy** (*n.*) ʹint-ə-mə-sē	state of being *intimate* (closely acquainted or associated); familiarity; close association (*ant.* **unfamiliarity**)	Because of your *intimacy* with Eric—he is your best friend—perhaps you can tell us what he would like as a farewell gift.
102	**menacing** (*adj.*) ʹmen-əs-iŋ	threatening; appearing likely to cause harm; endangering	"I'll teach you a lesson!" he screamed with a *menacing* gesture as if he were going to punch me.
87	**singe** (*v.*) ʹsinj	burn superficially or slightly; scorch	The potholder was *singed* as I removed the pot from the flame, but my fingers were not burned.
66	**thaw** (*v.*) ʹthȯ	1. rid of chilling, numbness, stiffness, or other effects of extreme cold	When they came in from the frost, the youngsters got next to the radiator to *thaw* out fingers and toes.
		2. melt; cause to melt; reverse the effect of freezing (*ant.* **freeze**)	If the ice cream is very hard, let it *thaw*, but not too long, or it will turn to liquid.

Exercise 1.4: Sentence Completion

Enter the choice required by the sentence, as in 1, below.

1. We were shocked when our (*foes, friends*) _friends_ made a menacing move toward us.

2. Is this gait satisfactory, or shall we (*slow down, open the door*) _slow down_ a bit?

3. Put (*out that match, down that knife*) _out that match_ before it singes your fingers.

4. I must have found the spot by instinct, having (*often, never*) _never_ been there before.

5. It is (*dangerous, safe*) _dangerous_ to skate on the lake if the ice is thawing.

6. As Tom was leaving, Dad (*waved good-bye, patted him on the shoulder*) _patted him on the shoulder_ in a parting caress.

7. With Charley at the oars, we began to flounder; he (*could not row, knew how to fish*) _could not row_.

8. Jackie needs another coin for the parking meter as (*none, all*) _all_ of her time has been consumed.

9. Because of his intimacy with the mountain, Jeff was asked to (*lead the way, bring up the rear*) _lead the way_.

10. Your sleeve is (*long, short*) _short_; it exposes too much of the wrist.

Exercise 1.5: Using Fewer Words

Replace the italicized words in each sentence with a single word from the following list. The first replacement has been entered as a sample.

consumed	gait	thawed	caress	exposed
intimacy	menaced	instinct	singed	floundered

1. I *struggled awkwardly* for a moment before regaining my footing. _floundered_

2. The sun *caused* the ice to *melt*. _thaw_

3. Living things have a(an) *inborn inclination* for self-preservation.

instinct

4. The soil was washed away and the roots were *left unprotected*.

exposed

5. Some of the hair on his arm was *burned superficially*.

singed

6. All of our supplies were *used up*.

consumed

7. The mother's *tender touch* calmed the sobbing child.

caress

8. You should have been consulted because of your *close association* with the case.

intimacy

9. We recognized your cousin by her *manner of walking*.

gait

10. The fierce dogs *appeared likely to cause harm to* the letter carrier.

menacing

Exercise 1.6:   Name-the-Person Quiz

Read all the statements in the boxes. Then answer questions 1–10 below. The first answer has been inserted as a sample.

When Ruth saw Ann was having trouble operating the copier, she went over to help. ✓	Betty removed the hamburgers from the freezer and kept them at room temperature for an hour before broiling. ✓

We tried to be friends with Fred, but he always kept pretty much to himself. ✓

Lou moved back a bit from the fireplace after an exploding spark caught him on the wrist. ✓	After hearing a melody just once, Alex could play it on the piano even though he had never had a single lesson. ✓

Mother kissed Nancy and reminded her to write every week. ✓	On his way back from lunch, Harvey was caught in a downpour. ✓	Emily's new shoes prevented her from keeping up with us. ✓

Pat and Barbara had cereal and waffles with syrup; Diane sipped some coffee. ✓	Ron raced through two red lights and paid no attention to a "stop" sign. ✓

1. Who menaced others? _Ron_
2. Who was singed? _Lou_
3. Who did some thawing? _Betty_
4. Who was guided by instinct? _Alex_
5. Whose gait was affected? _Emily_
6. Who received a caress? _Nancy_
7. Who was floundering? _Ann_
8. Who consumed little? _Pat, Charles, Diana_
9. Who was exposed? _Harvey_
10. Who discouraged intimacy? _Fred_

Exercise 1.7:   Synonyms and Antonyms

Fill each blank below with the required word from the following list:

devoured	frozen	pace	threatened	covered
unfamiliarity	wallowed	scorched	aptitude	embrace

1. synonym for *menaced* _threatened_
2. antonym for *intimacy* _unfamiliarity_
3. synonym for *caress* _embrace_
4. synonym for *singed* _scorched_
5. antonym for *thawed* _frozen_
6. synonym for *instinct* _aptitude_
7. synonym for *consumed* _devoured_
8. synonym for *gait* _pace_
9. antonym for *exposed* _covered_
10. synonym for *floundered* _wallowed_

LEARNING SOME DERIVATIVES

Suppose you have just learned that the verb *consume* means "use up." As a result, you should easily be able to recognize that . . .

consumer means "user": Almost everyone is a *consumer* of electricity.

consumption means "use": Our *consumption* of electricity is increasing.

consumable means "able to be used up": Ordinary lightbulbs are *consumable*—they need to be replaced often.

nonconsumable means "not able to be used up": Lighting fixtures are *nonconsumable*— they last for years and years.

Words like *consumer, consuming, consumption, consumable, nonconsumable,* etc., are called **derivatives** because they are derived (formed) from *consume*.

A word like *consume*, from which other words are derived, is called a **root**.

Each capitalized word below is a *root*. The words under it are its *derivatives*.

CARESS (*n.*)	Infants need a parent's *caress*.
caress (*v.*)	Infants need to be *caressed*.
caressing (*adj.*)	Infants need a parent's *caressing* touch.

caressingly (*adv.*)	Infants need to be stroked *caressingly*.
CONSUME (*v.*)	The Japanese *consume* a great deal of fish.
consumer (*n.*)	The Japanese are heavy *consumers* of fish.
consuming (*adj.*)	The Japanese are a fish-*consuming* people.
consumption (*n.*)	The Japanese are known for their fish *consumption*.
consumable (*adj.*)	Paper napkins are *consumable;* they are used once and discarded.
nonconsumable (*adj.*)	A napkin dispenser is *nonconsumable;* it lasts indefinitely.
EXPOSE (*v.*)	District attorneys are supposed to *expose* criminals.
exposer (*n.*)	They are *exposers*.
exposure (*n.*)	The *exposure* of criminals is her responsibility.
exposé (*n.*)	Today's newspapers feature an *exposé* of a public official who has taken bribes.
INSTINCT (*n.*)	Moths are attracted to light by *instinct*.
instinctive (*adj.*)	They have an *instinctive* attraction to light.
instinctively (*adv.*)	Moths *instinctively* fly toward light.
INTIMATE (*adj.*)	We are not on *intimate* terms with the neighbors.
intimately (*adv.*)	We are not *intimately* acquainted with them.
intimacy (*n.*)	We have no *intimacy* with the neighbors.
MENACE (*n.*)	The bully was a *menace* to the younger children.
menace (*v.*)	The bully *menaced* the younger children.
menacing (*adj.*)	He frightened them with *menacing* looks.
menacingly (*adv.*)	He shook his fists at them *menacingly*.
THAW (*v.*)	Floods developed when the snows *thawed* too rapidly.
thaw (*n.*)	The sudden *thaw* caused flooding.

Exercise 1.8: Roots and Derivatives

Fill each blank with the above root or derivative that best fits the meaning of the sentence.

1. We have met the Napolitanos once; we do not know them __*intimately*__ .

2. The icy sidewalk is a(an) __*menace*__ ; two pedestrians have already slipped.

3. To reduce gasoline __*consumption*__ , one should buy a smaller car.

4. A homeless dog needs someone to feed and __*caress*__ him.

5. Infants cry ___*instinctively*___ when they hear sudden loud noises.

6. The reporter won an award for her ___~~intimacy~~ *exposé*___ of the inhumane treatment of elderly people in nursing homes.

7. Too many teenagers are heavy ___*consumer*___s of sweets.

8. For a few days in January, we had a(an) ___*thaw*___ when the temperature rose above freezing.

9. Black clouds approached ___*menacingly*___ from the west.

10. From time to time automobile owners have to replace such ___~~expired~~ *consumable*___ items as tires, spark plugs, and the battery.

IMPROVING YOUR SPELLING: ADDING SUFFIXES

A *suffix* is a sound added to the end of a word to form a new word:

WORD   SUFFIX   NEW WORD

foolish + -ness (state of being) = foolish*ness* (state of being foolish)

Study these suffixes and their meanings:

SUFFIX	MEANING	SAMPLE WORD
-able	able to be	consum*able* (able to be consumed)
-er	one who	consum*er* (one who consumes)
-or	one who	creat*or* (one who creates)
-ist	one who	typ*ist* (one who types)
-ly	in a _____ manner	savage*ly* (in a savage manner)
-ness	state of being	numb*ness* (state of being numb)
-ure	act of	expos*ure* (act of exposing)
-ed	(ending of past participle)	Yesterday we consum*ed* half.
-ing	(ending of present participle)	Today we are consum*ing* the rest.

Adding Suffixes

1. As a rule, do not add or drop a letter when adding a suffix to a word. Keep *all* the letters of the word and *all* the letters of the suffix.

intimate + ly = intimately   sudden + ness = suddenness

usual   + ly = usually   violin + ist = violinist

2. However, if the word ends in silent *e*, drop the *e* before a suffix beginning with a *vowel*. (Remember: *a, e, i, o,* and *u* are *vowels*.)

believe + able = believable   menace + ing = menacing

receive + er = receiver   supervise + or = supervisor

menace + ed = menaced   seize + ure = seizure

Exercise 1.9: Wordbuilding With Suffixes

Complete the following. The first answer has been entered as a sample.

1. expose + ed = **exposed**
2. excuse + able = _excusable_
3. final + ly = _finally_
4. mean + ness = _meanness_
5. erase + ure = _erasure_
6. settle + er = _settler_
7. menace + ing = _menacing_
8. instinctive + ly = _instinctively_
9. dispose + able = _disposable_
10. investigate + or = _investigator_
11. gentle + ness = _gentleness_
12. achieve + ed = _achieved_

13. extreme + ist = _extremist_
14. press + ure = _pressure_
15. replace + ing = _replacing_
16. imitate + or = _imitator_
17. open + ness = _openess_
18. reserve + ist = _reservist_
19. use + able = _usable_
20. freeze + ing = _freezing_
21. hopeful + ly = _hopefully_
22. renew + able = _renewable_
23. immediate + ly = _immediately_
24. manage + er = _Manager_

25. disclose + ure = _disclosure_

Exercise 1.10: Using Fewer Words

State in one word, as in 1, below:

1. able to be endured **endurable**
2. one who receives _receiver_
3. state of being lame _lameness_
4. act of foreclosing _forclosure_
5. present participle of **like** _liking_

6. in an accidental manner _accidentally_
7. able to be compared _comparable_
8. one who buys _buyer_
9. past participle of **arrive** _arrived_
10. state of being drunken _drunkness_

A **_noun_** (_n._) is a word naming a person, animal, place, thing, or condition. In the following passage, the nouns are _London_, _character_, _dog_, _understanding_, and _weather:_

London shows quite clearly that the main **character** is very cruel to the
N   N

dog and has practically no **understanding** of extremely cold **weather**.
N   N   N

An **_adjective_** (_adj._) is a word that modifies (describes) a noun. In the same passage, the adjectives are _main_, _cruel_, _no_, and _cold_.

London shows quite clearly that the **main** _character_ is very **cruel** to the
                                    ADJ   N   ADJ

dog and has practically **no** _understanding_ of extremely **cold** _weather_.
                         ADJ   N   ADJ   N

    main (modifies _character_)   **no** (modifies _understanding_)
    ADJ   N   ADJ   N

    cruel (modifies _character_)   **cold** (modifies _weather_)
    ADJ   N   ADJ   N

A **_verb_** (_v._) is a word that expresses action or a state of being. The verbs in the above passage are _shows_, _is_, and _has_.

A verb usually has a **_subject_** (person or thing spoken of).

London shows quite clearly . . .
N-SUBJ   V

(The noun _London_ is the subject of the verb _shows_.)

The main _character is_ very cruel to the dog and _has_ practically no understanding . . .
        N-SUBJ V   V

(The noun _character_ is the subject of the verb _is_ and also the verb _has_.)

A verb may also have an **_object_** (person or thing that receives the action of the verb).

The main character . . . _has_ practically no _understanding_ . . .
                  V   N-OBJ

(The noun _understanding_ is the object of the verb _has_.)

An **_adverb_** (_adv._) is a word that modifies a verb, an adjective, or another adverb. Adverbs in the following sentence are _quite_, _clearly_, _very_, _practically_, _extremely_.

Reading Selection 1: To Build a Fire

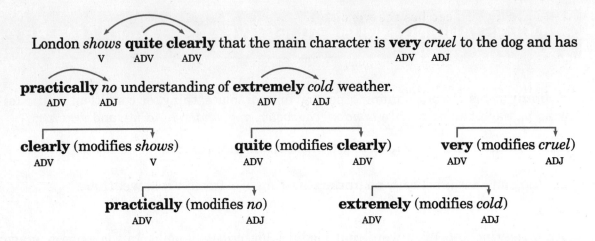

London *shows* **quite clearly** that the main character is **very** *cruel* to the dog and has
    V   ADV   ADV   ADV   ADJ

practically *no* understanding of **extremely** *cold* weather.
 ADV   ADJ   ADV   ADJ

clearly (modifies *shows*)   **quite** (modifies **clearly**)   **very** (modifies *cruel*)
 ADV   V   ADV   ADV   ADV   ADJ

practically (modifies *no*)   **extremely** (modifies *cold*)
 ADV   ADJ   ADV   ADJ

Let us look at the passage once more to review all the parts of speech we have so far discussed.

London shows quite clearly that the main character is very cruel to the dog and
  N   V   ADV   ADV   ADJ   N   V ADV ADJ   N

has practically no understanding of extremely cold weather.
 V   ADV   ADJ   N   ADV   ADJ   N

QUESTION: How can we tell whether a word is a noun, adjective, verb, or adverb?

HINT: Look at the word's *function*—the way it is used in the sentence. Note why *back* is a different part of speech in each of the following sentences.

1. My *back* aches.	*back* is the subject of the verb *aches*	*back* is a noun
2. Al took a *back* seat.	*back* modifies the noun *seat*	*back* is an adjective
3. We *back* our teams.	*back* expresses the action of the subject *We*	*back* is a verb
4. Mary went *back*	*back* modifies the verb *went*	*back* is an adverb

Exercise 1.11: Noun, Adjective, Verb, or Adverb?

State the part of speech of the italicized word, as in 1, below.

1. The days *pass* quickly. (*pass* is a(an) __verb__)
2. This *pass* admits two. (*pass* is a(an) _noun_)
3. The days pass *quickly*. (*quickly* is a(an) _adverb_)
4. Sometimes merchants *lower* their prices. (*lower* is a(an) _verb_)
5. Pat received a *lower* mark. (*lower* is a(an) _adj_)
6. Mother moved the shade *lower*. (*lower* is a(an) _adverb_)

7. The *early* bird catches the worm. (*early* is a(an) _adj_)
8. The guests hardly *knew* each other. (*knew* is a(an) _verb_)
9. The early bird catches the *worm*. (*worm* is a(an) _noun_)
10. The guests *hardly* knew each other. (*hardly* is a(an) _adv._)

from

The Autobiography of Benjamin Franklin

If you could have your choice, would you go to work for a relative or would you prefer someone else as your employer? Why?

My brother had, in 1720 or 21, begun to print a newspaper. It was the second that appeared in America, and was called the *New England Courant*. The only one before it was the *Boston News-Letter*. I remember his being dissuaded by some of his friends from
5 the undertaking, as not likely to succeed, one newspaper being, in their judgment, enough for America. At this time (1771), there are not less than five-and-twenty. He went on, however, with the undertaking, and after having worked in composing the types and printing off the sheets, I was employed to carry the papers through
10 the streets to the customers.

He had some ingenious men among his friends, who amused themselves by writing little pieces for this paper, which gained it credit and made it more in demand, and these gentlemen often visited us. Hearing their conversations, and their accounts of the
15 approbation their papers were received with, I was excited to try my hand among them; but, being still a boy, and suspecting that my brother would object to printing anything of mine in his paper if he knew it to be mine, I contrived to disguise my hand and, writing an anonymous paper, I put it in at night under the door of the
20 printing-house. It was found in the morning and communicated to his writing friends when they called in as usual. They read it, commented on it in my hearing, and I had the exquisite pleasure of finding it met with their approbation, and that, in their different guesses at the author, none were named but men of some charac-
25 ter among us for learning and ingenuity. I suppose now that I was

rather lucky in my judges, and that perhaps they were not really so very good ones as I then esteemed them.

Encouraged, however, by this, I wrote and conveyed in the same way to the press several more papers which were equally approved; and I kept my secret till my small fund of sense for such perfor- 30 mances was pretty well exhausted, and then I discovered it, when I began to be considered a little more by my brother's acquaintance, and in a manner that did not quite please him, as he thought, probably with reason, that it tended to make me too vain. And perhaps this might be one occasion of the differences that we began to have 35 about this time. Though a brother, he considered himself as my master, and me as his apprentice, and accordingly expected the same services from me as he would from another, while I thought he demeaned me too much in some he required of me, who from a brother expected more indulgence. Our disputes were often brought 40 before our father, and I fancy I was either generally in the right, or else a better pleader, because the judgment was generally in my favor. But my brother was passionate, and had often beaten me, which I took extremely amiss; and, thinking my apprenticeship very tedious, I was continually wishing for some opportunity of shorten- 45 ing it, which at length offered in a manner unexpected.*

One of the pieces in our newspaper on some political point, which I have now forgotten, gave offense to the Assembly. He was taken up, censured, and imprisoned for a month, by the speaker's warrant, I suppose because he would not discover his author. I too 50 was taken up and examined before the council; but, though I did not give them any satisfaction, they contented themselves with admonishing me, and dismissed me, considering me, perhaps, as an apprentice who was bound to keep his master's secrets.

During my brother's confinement, which I resented a good deal, 55 notwithstanding our private differences, I had the management of the paper; and I made bold to give our rulers some rubs in it, which my brother took very kindly, while others began to consider me in an unfavorable light, as a young genius that had a turn for libeling and satire. My brother's discharge was accompanied with an 60 order of the House (a very odd one), that "James Franklin should no longer print the paper called the *New England Courant.*"

There was a consultation held in our printing-house among his friends what he should do in this case. Some proposed to evade the order by changing the name of the paper; but my brother see- 65 ing inconveniences in that, it was finally concluded on as a better way to let it be printed for the future under the name of *Benjamin Franklin;* and to avoid the censure of the Assembly, that might fall on him as still printing it by his apprentice, the contrivance was that my old indenture should be returned to me, 70 with a full discharge on the back of it, to be shown on occasion; but to secure to him the benefit of my service, I was to sign new

---

*I fancy his harsh and tyrannical treatment of me might be a means of impressing me with that aversion to arbitrary power that has stuck to me through my whole life. 75

indentures for the remainder of the term, which were to be kept private. A very flimsy scheme it was; however, it was immediately executed, and the paper went on accordingly under my name for several months.

Line 19. *anonymous:* bearing no name; unsigned
Line 31. *discovered:* revealed
Line 60. *satire:* use of ridicule to expose abuses
Line 70. *indenture:* contract binding a person to serve another

UNDERSTANDING THE SELECTION

Exercise 2.1: Close Reading

In the blank space, write the *letter* of the choice that best completes the statement.

1. The passage indicates that young Benjamin Franklin ____.

   (A) never did anything that pleased his brother
   (B) was unusually good at keeping a secret
   (C) did not get along well with his brother
   (D) was glad to see his brother imprisoned

2. James Franklin ____.

   (A) never disregarded the advice of his friends
   (B) showed a lack of courage
   (C) could not control his temper at times
   (D) had no confidence whatsoever in his younger brother's ability

3. At the time the passage was written, ____.

   (A) there were only two newspapers in America
   (B) James Franklin was in prison
   (C) Benjamin Franklin was an apprentice
   (D) the author was most likely in his sixties

4. The author suggests that ____.

   (A) the *New England Courant* succeeded in arousing reader interest
   (B) he learned nothing of value from his brother
   (C) he was not so intelligent as his brother
   (D) from the very beginning his brother knew who was writing the anonymous papers

5. As used in the footnote on page 21, *arbitrary* means "____."

   (A) political
   (B) dictatorial
   (C) physical
   (D) limited

IMPROVING YOUR COMPOSITION SKILLS: USING PARTICIPIAL PHRASES

1. The **present participle** is a verb form ending in -ING: *passing, being, coming, stepping,* etc.

2. The **past participle** is a verb form ending in -ED: *passed, stepped, encouraged, imprisoned,* etc.

> EXCEPTIONS: The past participle of an irregular verb does not end in -ED. For example, the past participle of the irregular verb *ring* is not "ringed" but *rung*. The past participles of *be, come,* and *hear* are, respectively, *been, come,* and *heard*.

Note that when the principal parts of a verb are given—as in a dictionary, for instance—the past participle is always the *last* principal part mentioned: *pass, passing, PASSED; be, being, BEEN; come, coming, COME; hear, hearing, HEARD;* etc.

VERB	PRESENT PARTICIPLE	PAST PARTICIPLE
pass	passing	passed
step	stepping	stepped
encourage	encouraging	encouraged
imprison	imprisoning	imprisoned
ring	ringing	rung
be	being	been
come	coming	come
hear	hearing	heard

3. A participle is an adjective.

Hearing of his brother's imprisonment, Benjamin felt bitter toward the Assembly.

Hearing (modifies *Benjamin*)
ADJ   N

Imprisoned unjustly by the Assembly, James was away from his shop for a whole month.

Imprisoned (modifies *James*)
ADJ   N

4. A **participial phrase** consists of a participle and its modifiers.

> *Hearing of his brother's imprisonment* (participial phrase)
> *Imprisoned unjustly by the Assembly* (participial phrase)

5. A participial phrase is separated from the rest of the sentence by one or two commas.

ONE COMMA if the participial phrase begins the sentence:
Imprisoned unjustly by the Assembly, James was away from his shop for a whole month.

ONE COMMA if the participial phrase ends the sentence:
James was away from his shop for a whole month, *imprisoned unjustly by the Assembly.*

TWO COMMAS if the participial phrase is within the sentence:
James, *imprisoned unjustly by the Assembly,* was away from his shop for a whole month.

6. With participial phrases, you can construct more mature, more interesting sentences.

Jack London did *not* write:

(A) He worked carefully from a small beginning. He soon had a roaring fire.

He wrote:

(B) "*Working carefully from a small beginning* [participial phrase], he soon had a roaring fire."

By beginning with a participial phrase, London immediately made his sentence more interesting, since most sentences begin with the subject. Note also that in *A*, above, the subject *He* is used twice, whereas London, in *B*, used *he* only once, thanks to the participial phrase. Repetition of the subject is usually boring; the participial phrase makes such repetition unnecessary. More important, the participial phrase enabled Jack London to express more effectively in one sentence what a less experienced writer might have said in two.

Likewise, Franklin did *not* write:

I was encouraged, however, by this. I wrote and conveyed in the same way to the press several more papers . . .

He wrote:

"*Encouraged, however, by this* [participial phrase], I wrote and conveyed in the same way to the press several more papers . . . "

Exercise 2.2: Using Participial Phrases to Combine Sentences

Combine the two sentences into one by changing the italicized sentence into a participial phrase. Samples follow:

Lisa inspected the tires. She noticed that one of them was nearly flat.

Inspecting the tires, Lisa noticed that one of them was nearly flat.

Most of the audience left early. *They were disappointed with the performance.*

Most of the audience left early, **disappointed with the performance.**

1. *Pat rushed to join us at our table.* She dropped a whole tray of food.

   _____

   _____

2. The authorities did not imprison Benjamin. *They thought he was merely an apprentice.*

   _____

   _____

3. *We were exhausted by the heat.* We decided to rest awhile in the shade.

   _____

   _____

4. The dog took satisfaction in the fire. *He stretched out close enough for warmth and far enough away to escape being singed.*

   _____

   _____

   _____

5. *I was still a boy.* I suspected that my brother would object to printing anything of mine in his paper.

   _____

   _____

   _____

6. The attendant at the door asked to see our membership cards. *He suspected that we were outsiders.*

   _____

   _____

7. *The coach was discouraged by our failure to win a single game.* He offered to resign.

   _____

   _____

8. *I overheard their conversations.* I was excited to try my hand at writing, too.

   _____

   _____

9. *The musicians were delayed in heavy traffic.* They arrived an hour late.

   _____

10. He skirted to the left. *He stepped gingerly.*

   _____

Exercise 2.3: Positioning Participial Phrases

Rewrite the sentence twice, each time moving the participial phrase to a different position.

SAMPLE: *Convinced that I am a good risk,* my younger brother has decided to lend me five dollars.

    A. My younger brother, **convinced that I am a good risk,** has decided to lend me five dollars.

    B. My younger brother has decided to lend me five dollars, **convinced that I am a good risk.**

1. *Sensing trouble with one of the engines,* the pilot returned to the airport right after takeoff.

    A. _____

    _____

    B. _____

    _____

2. The ex-champion, *determined to regain her title,* will reenter the tournament next spring.

    A. _____

    _____

    B. _____

    _____

3. The veteran senator has called a press conference, *disturbed by rumors about his health.*

    A. _____

    _____

    B. _____

    _____

4. *Hoping to get her operator's license soon,* Lola's mother has enrolled for another driving course.

    A. _____

    _____

    B. _____

    _____

5. The man ahead of me gave up his place in line, *saying that he could not wait.*

    A. _____

    _____

    B. _____

    _____

Exercise 2.4: Varying Sentence Beginnings

In the following paragraph, every sentence begins with the subject. Rewrite the paragraph, making these changes:

S1: Begin with a prepositional phrase.
S2: Begin with an adverb.
S3 and S4: Combine into one sentence ending in a participial phrase.
S5 and S6: Combine into one sentence beginning with a participial phrase.

[1]Shoppers began arriving from the moment the doors opened. [2]A long line soon formed at my checkout counter. [3]The salespeople were busy all day. [4]They tried to help the customers. [5]I was relieved that the sale was at last over. [6]I clocked out forty minutes after closing time.

_____

_____

_____

_____

_____

Exercise 2.5: Writing a Composition

Like Benjamin Franklin, almost all of us have at one time or another had a problem in getting along with another person. In a paragraph of about 100 to 125 words, describe a problem that you have had in getting along with someone. Give adequate details. Be sure to provide the following information:

1. Who was the person you could not get along with?

2. What was there in the behavior of that person that bothered you?

3. To what extent do you feel the other person was to blame for the problem?

4. To what extent may you yourself have possibly been to blame?

Carefully reread your first draft. Make sure (*a*) that you have given enough details so that anyone reading the paragraph will readily understand your problem, and (*b*) that you have begun at least one sentence with a participial phrase.

Sample Paragraph: A Problem in Getting Along

The person I have had trouble getting along with is my younger sister, Maria. Too many times, when I have had my heart set on wearing a certain outfit that I had just washed and ironed, Maria would "borrow" it without my permission, wear it, and bring it back wrinkled and dirty. Her excuse was that she needed it badly because she had to go out. Without asking permission, she sometimes has "borrowed" other things belonging to me, such as my Walkman, and my bracelets and earrings. I hold her entirely responsible for the bad feeling between us. Perhaps I am wrong to let myself be so upset, but the truth is she has really angered me.

Your Paragraph: A Problem in Getting Along

_____

_____

_____

_____

_____

_____

_____

_____

_____

_____

LEARNING NEW WORDS

Line	Word	Meaning	Typical Use
53	**admonish** (*v.*) ad-ˈmän-ish	warn of a fault; reprove gently but seriously	Ever since an instructor *admonished* me for my poor handwriting, I have tried to write more legibly.
	(*ant.* **commend**)		Yesterday he *commended* me on my improvement.
15	**approbation** (*n.*) ˌap-rə-ˈbā-shən	commendation; praise; official approval	Naturally, I was pleased to receive my teacher's *approbation*.
	(*ant.* **disapprobation**)		The President has indicated his *disapprobation* of the bill, declaring that he will veto it if it ever reaches his desk.
74	**arbitrary** (*adj.*) ˌär-bə-ˌtrer-ē	1. not restrained or limited in exercising power; ruling by absolute authority; dictatorial; despotic	Unlike *arbitrary* rulers, who can do as they wish and are accountable to nobody, our President must obey the law and heed the will of the people.
	(*ant.* **legitimate**)		A head of state who is democratically elected is a *legitimate* ruler.

		2. marked by or resulting from the unrestrained or tyrannical use of power	The Constitution protects Americans from *arbitrary* arrest and imprisonment.
49	**censure** (*v.*) 'sen-shər	criticize harshly; find fault with; blame (*ant.* **commend**)	The officer was *censured* for neglect of his duties and fined one month's pay.
76	**flimsy** (*adj.*) 'flim-zē	lacking strength or solidity; weak; inadequate	The unprepared student offered the *flimsy* excuse that he had done his assignment but left it at home.
11	**ingenious** (*adj.*) in-'jē-nyəs	1. clever; original; inventive; resourceful	Some of our most *ingenious* medical researchers are working full time to discover how to cure and prevent cancer.
		2. conceived or done in an original or clever manner	The computer is an *ingenious* electronic apparatus that provides speedy answers to many problems.
59	**libel** (*v.*) 'lī-bəl	injure a person's reputation by a false statement, printed or written; give an unflattering or damaging picture of; defame	The candidate claims he was *libeled* in a pamphlet that referred to him as a "compulsive liar." He is threatening to sue.
55	**resent** (*v.*) ri-'zent	feel or show annoyance or indignation at (a person or act)	Customers who realize they have been overcharged may *resent* it and go elsewhere to do their shopping.
45	**tedious** (*adj.*) 'tēd-ē-əs	tiresome because of length or dullness; wearisome; boring (*ant.* **exciting**)	Realizing that many readers find long descriptive passages *tedious*, Harold began his story with an *exciting* conflict.
34	**vain** (*adj.*) 'vān	excessively proud of one's looks or abilities; conceited (*ant.* **humble**)	Jackie objects to wearing her championship pin; she does not want to be considered *vain*. If I had won the award, I would not be so *humble;* I would wear it.

Exercise 2.6:   Sentence Completion

Enter the choice required by the sentence, as in 1, below.

1. A flimsy structure is (*certain, unlikely*) __unlikely__ to survive a hurricane.
2. Was the trip tedious, or did it (*fascinate, bore*) _____ you?
3. Chris resented the late fee; she felt it was (*fair, excessive*) _____.
4. Brown was libeled when he was called a daring (*base, horse*) _____ stealer.
5. Rosa had an ingenious idea that had (*often, never*) _____ been tried before.
6. Prices were arbitrarily high; there was (*fierce, no*) _____ competition.
7. Maria was commended for her (*unselfishness, forgetfulness*) _____.
8. A (*frown, nod*) _____ is one of the ways by which we indicate approbation.
9. Mark is quite vain; he keeps talking about (*his, your*) _____ achievements.
10. Two employees were admonished for their (*tardiness, honesty*) _____.

Exercise 2.7:   Using Fewer Words

Replace the italicized words with a single word from the following list. See answer to 1, below.

libeled	vain	arbitrary	censured	flimsy
resented	tedious	approbation	admonished	ingenious

1. I *felt indignation at* another person's opening my mail.   __resented__
2. Jerry is *excessively proud of his looks*.   _____
3. My opponent *gave an unflattering picture of* me.   _____
4. Don't expect me to read your composition if it is *tiresome because of its length or dullness*.   _____
5. When she talked about quitting, I *reproved* her *gently but seriously*.   _____
6. The monarch's rule was *marked by a tyrannical use of power*.   _____
7. The guard was *criticized harshly* for absence from his post.   _____
8. I admit that the planning was *done in a clever manner*.   _____
9. Her explanations were regarded as *lacking strength or solidity*.   _____
10. No refund can be made without the manager's *official approval*.   _____

Exercise 2.8: Using Synonyms and Antonyms

A. Avoid repetition by replacing the italicized word with a SYNONYM from the following word list. See 1, below.

admonished	commend	defame	disapprobation	exciting
humble	indignant	legitimate	resourceful	weak

1. Make no libelous remarks. Don't *libel* anyone. _____**defame**_____

2. You have a flimsy case. Your evidence is quite *flimsy*. _____

3. What an ingenious plan! I must say you are *ingenious*. _____

4. You have no cause for resentment. Don't be *resentful*. _____

5. The dean had *warned* me, but I didn't heed her warning. _____

B. Complete the sentence by inserting an ANTONYM of the italicized word from the above word list. See 6, below.

6. The opening scene was *tedious*, but the rest of the play was ___**exciting**___.

7. Some people are quick to *censure* others and rarely _____ anyone.

8. Her ideas met with *approval* from some but _____ from others.

9. _____ heads of state have gradually displaced *arbitrary* rulers.

10. *Vain* champions boast about their victories; _____ ones never do so.

Exercise 2.9: Name-the-Person Quiz

Read all the statements in the boxes. Then answer questions 1 to 10. The first answer has been inserted as a sample.

Enid was able to solve a problem that was baffling the teacher.	Bob took a long time to explain, and he kept repeating himself.	Because of its vague language, Stevens sent back the contract unsigned.

"Where were you?" the manager asked Julie. "We needed you! If you can't get back on time, we can do without you!"

When Mrs. Bradshaw told Philip to stop interrupting me and let me finish my report, he said he was very sorry.

Ben asserted that, beginning immediately, we would have to do things his way, since he is the chairman of the committee.

Catherine explained that she could not make a contribution because she didn't have the right change.

Ralph did not let a day pass without reminding his teammates that last year he was high scorer.

In a letter to the voters before the election, Meredith stated that Pearson had falsified his address.

Ted was annoyed when Blanche revealed his plans without his permission.

1. Who was censured? _____Julie_____
2. Who libeled somebody? _____
3. Who was ingenious? _____
4. Who had a flimsy excuse? _____
5. Who was admonished? _____

6. Who resented something? _____
7. Who was tedious? _____
8. Who acted arbitrarily? _____
9. Who was vain? _____
10. Who withheld approbation? _____

LEARNING SOME DERIVATIVES

Each capitalized word below is a *root*. The words under it are its *derivatives*.

ADMONISH (*v.*)	By a gesture, the teacher *admonished* the restless student.
admonishingly (*adv.*)	*Admonishingly*, the teacher pointed a finger at the restless pupil.
admonition (*n.*)	She gave the restless pupil a look of *admonition*.
admonitory (*adj.*)	She pointed an *admonitory* finger at him.
APPROVE (*v.*)	With a smile, the employer *approved* my request.
approvingly (*adv.*)	When I asked permission to leave earlier she nodded *approvingly*.
approval (*n.*) approbation (*n.*)	I would not have left at 4:30 without her *approval* (or *approbation*).
ARBITRARY (*adj.*)	Knowing that you failed every test and were absent half the time, how can you say that your mark was *arbitrary?*
arbitrarily (*adv.*)	Clearly, your instructor failed you justifiably, not *arbitrarily*.
arbitrariness (*n.*)	You cannot accuse the teacher of *arbitrariness*.

CENSURE (*n.*)	Found guilty of having left his post, the guard now faces *censure*.
censure (*v.*)	He will probably be *censured* for neglect of duty.
censurable (*adj.*)	Leaving one's post without authorization is a *censurable* offense.
FLIMSY (*adj.*)	Examining the furniture, I found that it was *flimsy*.
flimsily (*adv.*)	It was *flimsily* constructed.
flimsiness (*n.*)	Despite its *flimsiness*, the furniture had a high price tag.
INGENIOUS (*adj.*)	That was an *ingenious* repair job.
ingeniously (*adv.*)	You repaired the loose handle by *ingeniously* wedging in a piece of metal.
ingenuity (*n.*)	In making that repair, you showed *ingenuity*.
LIBEL (*n.*)	Fearing lawsuits, editors are careful not to print *libels*.
libel (*v.*)	Editors take pains not to *libel* anyone.
libelous (*adj.*)	They almost never print *libelous* material.
RESENT (*v.*)	Most shoppers *resent* the sales tax.
resentful (*adj.*)	Some are *resentful* because the tax is not based on the ability to pay.
resentfully (*adv.*)	Believing that it is an unfair tax, they pay it *resentfully*.
resentment (*n.*)	The proposal to raise the tax has increased their *resentment*.
TEDIOUS (*adj.*)	Unfortunately, it was a *tedious* ride.
tediously (*adv.*)	Caught in the rush-hour traffic, the bus inched its way *tediously* up the avenue.
tediousness (*n.*) tedium (*n.*)	Some of the passengers sought relief from the *tediousness* (or *tedium*) by gazing at the advertisements; a few dozed.
VAIN (*adj.*)	The twins are very *vain* about their good looks.
vainly (*adv.*)	At every mirror, they will stop *vainly* to admire themselves.
vanity (*n.*)	Obviously, they suffer from *vanity*.

Exercise 2.10: Using Roots and Derivatives

Fill each blank with the above root or derivative that best fits the meaning of the sentence. The first blank has been filled as an example.

1. The puzzle did not require much _____ingenuity_____; it was easy to solve.

2. I warned you not to play with that dog, but you disregarded my _____.

3. The full purchase price will be cheerfully refunded if the merchandise does not meet with your _____.

4. The union leader did not call the strike _____; the members had voted to go on strike.

5. For breaking training rules, an athlete is subject to _____ and dismissal from the team.

6. The chairs were returned because of their _____; they seemed ready to fall apart.

7. His _____ led him to believe that he was the most talented and the best-looking student in the class.

8. Some of the members are _____ because they were not included in the club photograph.

9. If you use a long paragraph to explain something that can be stated in a short sentence, you are writing _____.

10. The publisher advised the author to delete a(an) _____ statement that might have damaged the reputation of a public official.

INTRODUCTION TO ANALOGIES

Word Relationships

BROTHER : RELATIVE

What is the relationship between BROTHER and RELATIVE? Obviously, a BROTHER is a RELATIVE. So, too, are a *sister*, *father*, *mother*, *grandfather*, *grandmother*, *uncle*, *aunt*, *cousin*, etc. RELATIVE, clearly, is the category of which BROTHER is one member.

If we call BROTHER word *A* and RELATIVE word *B*, we may express the BROTHER : RELATIVE relationship by saying "*A* is a member of the *B* category."

Here are some additional pairs of words with an explanation of the relationship in each pair. As above, let us call the first word *A* and the second *B*.

LIBEL : REPUTATION

A LIBEL may damage a person's REPUTATION. To express the LIBEL : REPUTATION relationship, let us say "*A* may damage *B*."

THAW : FLOOD

A THAW may cause a FLOOD. The relationship here is "*A* may cause *B*."

NOD : APPROBATION

A NOD is a way of indicating APPROBATION. The relationship in this pair is "*A* is a sign of *B*."

FLIMSY : STRENGTH

Anything FLIMSY lacks STRENGTH. We may express this relationship as "Anything that is *A* lacks *B*."

To find the relationship between a pair of words, do the same reasoning as described in the paragraphs above. When you have determined the relationship, sum it up in a very short sentence using *A* and *B*, as in the following additional examples:

BLIZZARD : SNOWSTORM	*A* is a severe form of *B*.
MITTEN : HAND	*A* is an item of apparel for *B*.
RESENTMENT : ARBITRARINESS	*A* may result from *B*.
AFFLUENT : MONEY	One who is *A* has plenty of *B*.
NEEDLE : SEW	*A* is used for the action of *B*.
BRAGGART : HUMBLE	*A* lacks the qualities of a *B* person.
CADET : OFFICER	*A* is training to become a *B*.

Exercise 2.11: Matching up Word Pairs With Similar Word Pairs

Match each of the following word pairs with a similar pair in 1 to 11, below. The first match has been made as a sample.

resentment : arbitrariness   needle : sew
mitten : hand   thaw : food
flimsy : strength   affluent : money
libel : reputation   braggart : humble
blizzard : snowstorm   nod : approbation
                    cadet : officer

1. MOCCASIN : FOOT :: _____mitten_____ : _____hand_____

   EXPLANATION: a MOCCASIN is apparel for the FOOT; a *mitten* is apparel for the *hand*.

2. HURRICANE : CROP :: _____ : _____

3. KNIFE : CUT :: _____ : _____

4. TEDIOUS : EXCITEMENT :: _____ : _____

5. CARESS : AFFECTION :: _____ : _____

6. INGENIOUS : CLEVERNESS :: _____ : _____

7. APPRENTICE : MASTER :: _____ : _____

8. CENSURE : ADMONITION :: _____ : _____

9. IMITATOR : CREATIVE :: _____ : _____

10. FALL : INJURY :: _____ : _____

11. FLOUNDERING : IGNORANCE :: _____ : _____

RULE: To change an adjective to an adverb, we usually add *ly*.

ADJECTIVE	SUFFIX		ADVERB
extreme	+ ly	=	extremely
firm	+ ly	=	firmly
equal	+ ly	=	equally

EXCEPTIONS:

1. If the adjective ends in a consonant plus -LE, change the -LE to -LY.

ADJECTIVE	ADVERB
probable	probably
idle	idly
ample	amply

2. If the adjective ends in -Y preceded by a consonant, change Y to I before adding -LY.

ADJECTIVE	SUFFIX		ADVERB
hasty	+ ly	=	hastily
flimsy	+ ly	=	flimsily

3. If the adjective ends in -IC, add AL before attaching -LY.

drastic	+	al	+	ly	=	drastically
scientific	+	al	+	ly	=	scientifically

4. Finally, note the dropping of the **e** in these three special exceptions:

ADJECTIVE	ADVERB
due	duly
true	truly
whole	wholly

Exercise 2.12: Changing Adjectives to Adverbs

Enter the required adverb, as in 1, below.

1. resentful   **resentfully**   6. intimate _____

2. true _____   7. gentle _____

3. unfavorable _____   8. tyrannical _____

4. arbitrary _____   9. tragic _____

5. menacing _____   10. due _____

Exercise 2.13:   Changing Adverbs to Adjectives

Enter the required adjective, as in 1, below.

1. instinctively   __instinctive__   6. wholly   _____

2. happily   _____   7. busily   _____

3. continually   _____   8. democratically   _____

4. comfortably   _____   9. possibly   _____

5. finally   _____   10. ingeniously   _____

Exercise 2.14:   Rephrasing Sentences

A. Rephrase the sentence, changing the italicized word to an adverb.

1. We had *comfortable* seats.   __We were comfortably seated.__

2. Pat was a *heavy* smoker.   _____

3. It is a *gentle* rain.   _____

4. He feels *keen* disappointment.   _____

5. They received *due* punishment.   _____

B. Rephrase the sentence, changing the italicized word to an adjective.

6. It ends *unhappily*.   __It has an unhappy ending.__

7. Are they *amply* protected?   _____

8. I departed *hastily*.   _____

9. Al was *politely* received.   _____

10. Nero ruled *tyrannically*.   _____

IMPROVING YOUR USAGE: AVOIDING UNNECESSARY WORDS

What does Benjamin Franklin mean by *the second* in the following?

> My brother had, in 1720 or 21, begun to print a newspaper. It was the second that appeared in America . . .

Obviously, he means *the second newspaper*. Note that he does not repeat *newspaper* because the context makes it unnecessary.

Exercise 2.15: Avoiding Unnecessary Words

Rewrite sentences 1 to 10 below, leaving out all unnecessary words.

First study these three samples:

> SAMPLE: Our team is the best team in the league.
> **Our team is the best in the league.**

> SAMPLE: It was the only time in my life I had won a door prize.
> **It was the only time I had won a door prize.**

> SAMPLE: The way plumbers are paid is by the hour.
> **Plumbers are paid by the hour.**

1. We had not seen them in a long period of time.

_____

2. No agreement has been reached on the subject of wages.

_____

3. The shortage was greater than we had expected it to be.

_____

4. He certainly was not ugly looking.

_____

5. All of our players are below six feet in height.

_____

6. She was not aware of the fact that you were ill.

_____

7. Do you want me to tell you the real truth?

_____

8. In the period of the Renaissance, there was a renewed interest in learning.

_____

9. The entrance is in the process of being modernized.

_____

10. Down the road is a deserted house in which no one lives.

_____

from

Les Misérables

by Victor Hugo

We are in a quiet town in Southeastern France on an October evening in 1815. As darkness descends, a rumor spreads that a suspicious, dangerous-looking stranger has been seen entering town.

Just as the bishop entered, Madame Magloire was speaking with some warmth. She was talking to *Mademoiselle* upon a familiar subject, and one to which the bishop was quite accustomed. It was a discussion on the means of fastening the front door. It seems that while Madame Magloire was out making provisions for supper, she had heard the news in sundry places. There was talk that an ill-favored runaway, a suspicious vagabond, had arrived and was lurking somewhere in the town, and that some unpleasant adventures might befall those who should come home late that night; and that everyone ought to be careful to shut up, bolt, and bar his house properly, and *secure his door thoroughly*. 5 10

Madame Magloire went on: "We say that this house is not safe at all; and if monseigneur will permit me, I will go and tell the locksmith to come and put the old bolts in the door again. I say we must have bolts, were it only for tonight; for I say that a door which opens by a latch on the outside to the first comer, nothing could be more horrible: and then monseigneur has the habit of always saying 'Come in,' even at midnight. There is no need even to ask leave—" 15

At this moment there was a violent knock on the door. 20

"Come in!" said the bishop.

The door opened. It opened quickly, quite wide, as if pushed by some one boldly and with energy. A man entered. That man, we know already; it was the traveller we have seen wandering about in search of a lodging. He came in, took one step, and paused, leaving the door open behind him. He had his knapsack on his back, his stick in his hand, and a rough, hard, tired, and fierce look in his eyes, as seen by the firelight. He was hideous.

Madame Magloire had not even the strength to scream. She stood trembling with her mouth open. Mademoiselle Baptistine turned, saw the man enter, and started up half alarmed; then, slowly turning back again towards the fire, she looked at her brother, and her face resumed its usual calmness and serenity. The bishop looked upon the man with a tranquil eye.

As he was opening his mouth to speak, doubtless to ask the stranger what he wanted, the man, leaning with both hands on his club, glanced from one to another in turn, and without waiting for the bishop to speak, said in a loud voice:

"See here! My name is Jean Valjean. I am a convict; I have been nineteen years in the galleys. Four days ago I was set free, and started for Pontarlier, which is my destination; during those four days I have walked from Toulon. Today I have walked twelve leagues. When I reached this place this evening I went to an inn, and they sent me away on account of my yellow passport, which I had shown at the mayor's office, as was necessary. I went to another inn; they said: 'Get out!' It was the same with one as with another; nobody would have me. I went to the prison, and the turnkey would not let me in. There in the square I lay down upon a stone; a good woman showed me your house, and said 'Knock there!' I have knocked. What is this place? Are you an inn? I have money; my savings, one hundred and nine francs and fifteen sous which I have earned in the galleys by my work for nineteen years. I will pay. What do I care? I have money. I am very tired—twelve leagues on foot and I am so hungry. Can I stay?"

"Madame Magloire," said the bishop, "put on another plate."

The man took three steps, and came near the lamp which stood on the table. "Stop," he exclaimed; as if he had not been understood, "not that, did you understand me? I am a galley-slave—a convict—I am just from the galleys." He drew from his pocket a large sheet of yellow paper, which he unfolded. "There is my passport, yellow as you see. That is enough to have me kicked out wherever I go. Will you read it? I know how to read, I do. I learned in the galleys. There is a school there for those who care for it. See, here is what they have put in the passport: 'Jean Valjean, a liberated convict, native of ——,' you don't care for that, 'has been nineteen years in the galleys; five years for burglary; fourteen years for having attempted four times to escape. This man is very dangerous.' There you have it! Everybody has thrust me out; will you receive me? Is this an inn? Can you give me something to eat, and a place to sleep? Have you a stable?"

"Madame Magloire," said the bishop, "put some sheets on the bed in the alcove."

Madame Magloire went out to fulfill her orders. The bishop turned to the man: "Monsieur, sit down and warm yourself: we are going to take supper presently, and your bed will be made ready while you sup."

At last the man quite understood; his face, the expression of which till then had been gloomy and hard, now expressed stupefaction, doubt, and joy, and became absolutely wonderful. He began to stutter like a madman,

"True? What! You will keep me? You won't drive me away? a convict! You call me *Monsieur* and don't say 'Get out, dog!' as everybody else does. I thought that you would send me away, so I told you just who I am. Oh! the fine woman who sent me here! I shall have a supper! a bed like other people with mattress and sheets— a bed! It is nineteen years that I have not slept on a bed. You are really willing that I should stay? You are good people! Besides I have money; I will pay well. I beg your pardon, Monsieur Innkeeper, what is your name? I will pay all you say. You are a fine man. You are an innkeeper, an't you?"

"I am a priest who lives here," said the bishop.

"A priest!" said the man. "Oh, noble priest! Then you do not ask any money? You are the curé, an't you? the curé of this big church? Yes, that's it. How stupid I am; I didn't notice your cap."

While speaking, he had deposited his knapsack and stick in the corner, replaced his passport in his pocket, and sat down. Mademoiselle Baptistine looked at him pleasantly. He continued:

"You are humane, Monsieur Curé; you don't despise me. A good priest is a good thing. Then you don't want me to pay you?"

"No," said the bishop, "keep your money. How much have you? You said a hundred and nine francs, I think."

"And fifteen sous," added the man.

"One hundred and nine francs and fifteen sous. And how long did it take you to earn that?"

"Nineteen years."

"Nineteen years!"

The bishop sighed deeply.

The man continued: "I have all my money yet. In four days I have spent only twenty-five sous which I earned by unloading wagons at Grasse. As you are an abbé, I must tell you, we have a chaplain in the galleys. And then one day I saw a bishop; monseigneur, they called him. It was the Bishop of Majore from Marseilles. He is the curé who is over the curés. You see—beg pardon, how I bungle saying it, but for me, it is so far off! you know what we are. He said mass in the center of the place on an altar; he had a pointed gold thing on his head, that shone in the sun; it was noon. We were drawn up in line on three sides, with cannons and matches lighted before us. We could not see him well. He spoke to us, but he was not near enough, we did not understand him. That is what a bishop is."

While he was talking, the bishop shut the door, which he had left wide open. Madame Magloire brought in a plate and set it on the table.

"Madame Magloire," said the bishop, "put this plate as near the fire as you can." Then turning towards his guest, he added: "The night wind is raw in the Alps; you must be cold, monsieur."

Every time he said this word monsieur, with his gently solemn, and heartily hospitable voice, the man's countenance lighted up. *Monsieur* to a convict, is a glass of water to a man dying of thirst at sea. Ignominy thirsts for respect.

130 "The lamp," said the bishop, "gives a very poor light."

Madame Magloire understood him, and going to his bedchamber, took from the mantle the two silver candlesticks, lighted the candles, and placed them on the table.

"Monsieur Curé," said the man, "you are good; you don't despise
135 me. You take me into your house; you light your candles for me, and I haven't hid from you where I come from and how miserable I am."

The bishop, who was sitting near him, touched his hand gently and said: "You need not tell me who you are. This is not my house;
140 it is the house of Christ. It does not ask any comer whether he has a name, but whether he has an affliction. You are suffering; you are hungry and thirsty; be welcome. And do not thank me; do not tell me that I take you into my house. This is the home of no man, except him who needs an asylum. I tell you, who are a traveller,
145 that you are more at home here than I; whatever is here is yours. What need have I to know your name? Besides, before you told me, I knew it."

The man opened his eyes in astonishment: "Really? You knew my name?"

150 "Yes," answered the bishop, "your name is My Brother."

UNDERSTANDING THE SELECTION

Exercise 3.1: Close Reading

In the blank space, write the *letter* of the choice that best completes the statement.

1. The passage indicates that ____.

   (A) Madame Magloire is in no way critical of her employer
   (B) Mademoiselle Baptistine is more easily influenced by Madame Magloire than by her brother
   (C) Jean Valjean mistakes the bishop for an innkeeper
   (D) the bishop's door has never been bolted

2. Jean Valjean ____

   (A) does not give anyone any cause to be afraid of him
   (B) shows gratitude
   (C) gives little information about himself
   (D) insists on sleeping in the stable

3. The bishop ____.

(A) instructs Madame Magloire to shut the door
(B) explains his true rank to Jean Valjean
(C) shows some fear of Jean Valjean
(D) treats Jean Valjean with respect

4. Madame Magloire ____, without being specifically asked to do so.

(A) sends for a locksmith
(B) prepares a bed for Jean Valjean
(C) brings in the silver candlesticks
(D) serves Jean Valjean his dinner

5. The passage indicates that, at the time of the events described, ____.

(A) no convict was given any opportunity to improve himself during his imprisonment
(B) the laws were intended to help only those ex-convicts who showed a sincere desire to be good citizens
(C) it was impossible for any convict to escape from prison
(D) an ex-convict faced tremendous obstacles when he tried to return to society

IMPROVING YOUR COMPOSITION SKILLS: USING THE SIMPLE SENTENCE EFFECTIVELY

1. A simple sentence has only one main clause made up of

a subject, or compound subject, and
a verb, or compound verb.

All of the following are simple sentences:

a. The door opened.
      S   V

SUBJECT: *door*
VERB: *opened*

b. Sue and I disagreed.
  S1   S2   V

COMPOUND SUBJECT: *Sue* and *I*
VERB: *disagreed*

c. The bishop, his sister, and their housekeeper were at home.
    S1   S2   S3   V

COMPOUND SUBJECT: *bishop*, *sister*, and *housekeeper*
VERB: *were*

d. Madame Magloire brought in a plate and set it on the table.
         S   V1   V2

SUBJECT: *Madame Magloire*
COMPOUND VERB: *brought* and *set*

e. He came in, took one step, and paused.
    S   V1   V2   V3

SUBJECT: *He*
COMPOUND VERB: *came*, *took*, and *paused*

f. The man and his dog sat by the fire and warmed themselves.
    S1   S2 V1   V2

COMPOUND SUBJECT: *man* and *dog*
COMPOUND VERB: *sat* and *warmed*

2. You can expand a simple sentence by adding one or more prepositional phrases.

SIMPLE SENTENCE	WITH PREPOSITIONAL PHRASE(S)
There was a violent knock.	*At this moment* there was a violent knock *on the door*.
She stood trembling.	She stood trembling *with her mouth open*.

3. Another way to expand a simple sentence is to add one or more participial phrases.

SIMPLE SENTENCE	WITH PARTICIPIAL PHRASE(S)
He came in, took one step, and paused.	He came in, took one step, and paused, *leaving the door open behind him*.
She recovered her balance and continued down the icy pavement.	She recovered her balance and continued down the icy pavement, *stepping gingerly* and *testing the footing for each step*.

4. A series of short simple sentences can have a choppy effect.

CHOPPY	MORE EFFECTIVE
He opened his wallet. He took out a dollar.	He opened his wallet and took out a dollar.
Suddenly the dog broke through. It floundered to one side. It got away to firmer footing.	Suddenly the dog broke through, floundered to one side, and got away to firmer footing.

Exercise 3.2: Using *and* to Combine Choppy Simple Sentences

Using *and* only once, combine each group of choppy simple sentences into a more effective simple sentence. Note the examples in 4, above.

1. I woke up. I shut off the alarm.

_____

2. Madame Magloire brought in a plate. She set it on the table.

_____

3. They packed their belongings. They paid their bill. They left.

_____

_____

4. Then he pulled on his mittens. He settled the ear flaps of his cap firmly about his ears. He took the creek trail up the left fork.

_____

_____

_____

5. The bishop welcomed the stranger. He invited him to dinner. He offered him lodging.

_____

_____

Exercise 3.3: Ending With a Participial Phrase to Avoid Choppiness

Combine each group of choppy simple sentences into a simple sentence ending in a participial phrase. Note the following:

CHOPPY: He came in. He took one step. He paused. He left the door open behind him.

SMOOTH: He came in, took one step, and paused, **leaving the door open behind him.**

1. I ran upstairs. I found my swimsuit. I rushed down to join my waiting friends. I forgot to take a towel.

_____

_____

_____

2. Joan brought the water to a boil. She added the ingredients. She reduced the flame. She stirred the pot.

_____

_____

_____

3. Audrey rose to her feet. She recovered her racket. She walked off the court. She limped slightly.

_____

_____

_____

4. She signaled for a left turn. She got into the turning lane. She stopped at the intersection. She waited for a chance to make a safe turn.

_____

_____

_____

5. The pitcher checked the runner at first. He took a short windup. He fired the ball over the plate. He tried to catch the outside corner.

_____

_____

_____

Exercise 3.4:   Using a Participial Phrase at Other Places in the Sentence

In combining the following sentences, use *and*, but also change the italicized words to a participial phrase. Note these samples:

SAMPLE: *The merchant was encouraged by his success.* He opened two new stores. He staffed them with experienced salespeople.

Encouraged by his success, the merchant opened two new stores and staffed them with experienced salespeople.

SAMPLE: I entered the library. *I noticed Mary.* I went over to chat with her.

I entered the library and, **noticing Mary,** went over to chat with her.

1. *We arrived at the theater early.* We found a space in the parking lot. We purchased tickets. We bought some refreshments.

_____

_____

_____

2. They packed their belongings. *They gave no reason for their sudden change of plan.* They paid their bill. They left.

_____

_____

_____

3. The train glided from the station. *It picked up speed.* It passed the town limits. It entered the open country.

_____

_____

_____

4. *Harvey started down the stairs.* He heard the telephone ring. He returned to his room.

_____

_____

_____

5. Madame Magloire understood him. *She went to his bedchamber.* She took from the mantel the two silver candlesticks. She lighted the candles. She placed them on the table.

_____

_____

_____

_____

Exercise 3.5: Using a Prepositional Phrase to Combine Simple Sentences

Rewrite as one simple sentence, reducing the italicized words to a prepositional phrase.

SAMPLE: Madame Magloire stood trembling. *She had her mouth open.*

Madame Magloire stood trembling **with her mouth open.**

SAMPLE: *It was the end of the quarter.* The team returned to the bench exhausted.

At the end of the quarter, the team returned to the bench exhausted.

1. I awoke early. *I was in a bad mood.*

_____

2. Your batting average has gone up. *It is above .300.*

_____

3. *She spoke from the back of the room.* She answered the question clearly.

_____

_____

4. *It was nine o'clock.* He left the meeting abruptly. *He had a look of resentment.*

_____

_____

5. The temperature has dropped. *It is below freezing.*

_____

_____

Exercise 3.6: Rewriting a Paragraph to Eliminate Choppiness

The paragraph below, consisting of seventeen short simple sentences that all begin with the subject, is obviously very choppy. Rewrite the paragraph, reducing it to six smoother simple sentences, by making these changes:

I. Combine S1, S2, and S3, reducing S2 and S3 to participial phrases.

II. Combine S4, S5, and S6, reducing S5 and S6 to prepositional phrases.

III. Rewrite S7 so that it begins with an adverb.

IV. Combine S8, S9, S10, and S11, reducing S9, S10, and S11 to participial phrases.

V. Rewrite S12 so that it begins with a prepositional phrase. Then combine it with S13, reducing S13 to a prepositional phrase.

VI. Combine S14, S15, S16, and S17, reducing S15, S16, and S17 to participial phrases.

[1]Many of my classmates work part-time. [2]They earn spending money for themselves. [3]They perform services that people in the community need. [4]Tricia and Manuel wait on hungry customers. [5]They work in a fast-food restaurant. [6]Their hours are from 4 P.M. to 7 P.M. [7]The restaurant is usually very crowded at that time. [8]Randy and Paul work in a supermarket. [9]They stock the shelves. [10]They bag groceries. [11]They round up shopping carts from the parking lot. [12]Mary, Yolanda, and Pat do babysitting on weekends. [13]They work in the neighborhood. [14]Mike and Roger do outdoor work. [15]They mow lawns. [16]They trim shrubs. [17]They shovel snow.

_____

_____

_____

_____

_____

_____

_____

_____

_____

_____

_____

_____

_____

_____

_____

_____

Varying Sentence Length

A paragraph whose sentences are all of about equal length can be very monotonous. Note how Victor Hugo made his writing more interesting by varying the length of his sentences:

[1]The door opened. [2]It opened quickly, quite wide, as if pushed by someone boldly and with energy. [3]A man entered. [4]That man, we know already; it was the traveller we have seen wandering about in search of a lodging. [5]He came in, took one step, and paused, leaving the door open behind him. [6]He had his knapsack on his back, his stick in his hand, and a rough, hard, tired, and fierce look in his eyes, as seen by the firelight. [7]He was hideous.

The lengths of the seven sentences in the above paragraph are, respectively, 3, 14, 3, 19, 14, 28, and 3 words.

The very short simple sentences can have a dramatic effect. Notice how Hugo created suspense by skillful positioning of S1 and S3, each consisting of only three words.

Especially effective is the very short simple sentence coming immediately after one or more relatively long sentences. A good example of this is S7, which climactically sums up the paragraph in the three words: *He was hideous.*

In this paragraph, Hugo depended on variety of sentence length rather than of sentence opening to make his writing interesting. Note that every sentence except S4 opens with the subject. There is a reason for this: Hugo wanted to rivet our attention on the man. Evidence of this is the fact that S4 begins with the object *That man.* If it had started with the subject *we* (*We already know that man*), it would have taken our attention momentarily away from the man he was describing.

Exercise 3.7: Writing a Composition

You find yourself in an embarrassing situation. A classmate has borrowed five dollars from you, promising to repay you the next day, but has not done so. Three days have passed without a word from the classmate about the loan. Finally, you decide you must bring up the subject.

In a paragraph of about 75 words, explain what you would say to the classmate. Your aim is to recover the money without hurting your relationship with this classmate—if possible.

After your first draft, vary the length of your sentences if you have not already done so. Then write your final draft in the space below.

Final Draft: Request for Repayment of a Loan

_____

_____

_____

_____

_____

_____

_____

_____

LEARNING NEW WORDS

Line	Word	Meaning	Typical Use
141	**affliction** (*n.*) ə-ˈflik-shən	anything causing continued mental or physical suffering; distress; woe; calamity	Drug addiction is a terrible *affliction*.

Reading Selection 3: Les Misérables   49 (*ant.* **consolation, solace**) | Mona was upset by her failure in chemistry, but her A's in world history and English were a *consolation* to her.

144 **asylum** (*n.*)
ə-'sī-ləm

inviolable place of refuge; shelter; protection; sanctuary

To avoid prosecution, the accused swindler fled to Mexico, but the authorities there refused to grant him *asylum*.

127 **countenance** (*n.*)
'kaůnt-ən-əns

1. expression on a person's face that shows feelings or character; face; visage; appearance

Have you ever noticed how Lita's *countenance* lights up when you pay her a compliment?

2. appearance or expression seeming to approve; encouragement; support; sanction

If the courts took no action against those who destroy public property, they would be giving *countenance* to vandalism.

97 **despise** (*v.*)
di-'spīz

look down on with contempt; scorn; disdain; loathe

(*ant.* **appreciate**)

Many fans are fickle; they appreciate a team when it wins but *despise* it when it loses.

28 **hideous** (*adj.*)
'hid-ē-əs

horribly ugly; repulsive; frightful

(*ant.* **attractive**)

The witch was thought to have the power of turning *attractive* young people into *hideous* monsters.

127 **hospitable** (*adj.*)
'häs-ˌpit-ə-bəl

1. showing *hospitality* (friendliness and kindness to guests and strangers)

Bruno always gives us a warm welcome when we visit him; he is very *hospitable*.

2. open; receptive

Many inventors were laughed at when they first explained their discoveries because people usually are not *hospitable* to new ideas.

(*ant.* **inhospitable**)

When we were not served after sitting at a table for twenty minutes, I complained to the manager about our *inhospitable* reception.

97 **humane** (*adj.*)
hyü-'mān

showing sympathy and consideration for other human beings or for animals; humanitarian; benevolent

When the flood victims began to arrive, the *humane* residents of our neighborhood gave them asylum in their homes.

(*ant.* **barbarous, inhumane, inhuman**)

To have shut our doors to these afflicted people would have been *barbarous*.

64	**liberate** (*v.*) ˈlib-ə-ˌrāt	set at liberty; release from bondage or imprisonment; free; release	As they advanced across Europe, American troops *liberated* country after country from Nazi occupation.
6	**sundry** (*adj.*) ˈsən-drē	various and diverse; miscellaneous; several	People stayed away from the polls for *sundry* reasons: they were busy; the weather was bad; they didn't think their vote would make any difference; they were not interested; etc.
34	**tranquil** (*adj.*) ˈtraŋ-kwəl	free from agitation or disturbance; calm; peaceful; serene (*ant.* **troubled**)	A counselor tries to liberate *troubled* students from their fears so that they may work with a *tranquil* mind.

APPLYING WHAT YOU HAVE LEARNED

Exercise 3.8:   Sentence Completion

Enter the choice required by the sentence, as in 1, below.

1. Seeing our plight, humane motorists stopped to (*observe, help*) _____**help**_____ us.

2. The winds (*howled, moderated*) _____; it was a tranquil night.

3. The (*homeless, hungry*) _____ need asylum.

4. Troops boarded the plane to liberate the (*hijackers, hostages*) _____.

5. The winner was despised by some of his (*rivals, admirers*) _____.

6. (*Christmas, Greeting*) _____ cards are sold for sundry occasions.

7. (*Kindness, Sleeplessness*) _____ is no affliction.

8. Inhospitable hosts make their guests feel (*relaxed, uneasy*) _____.

9. The newscaster's countenance was unobserved by the (*TV, radio*) _____.

10. The sign is hideous, but Ed considers it (*beautiful, repulsive*) _____.

Exercise 3.9:   Using Fewer Words

Replace the italicized words with a single word from the following list. See answer to 1, below.

countenance	sundry	despise	hideous	affliction
hospitable	asylum	humane	liberate	tranquil

1. How can you *look down with contempt at* your own brother?

1. ___despise___

2. Churches and embassies have often served as a(an) *inviolable place of refuge* for fugitives.

2. _____

3. The builder offered *various and diverse* reasons for the delay.

3. _____

4. The scenery is beautiful and the people are *kind to guests and strangers*.

4. _____

5. For millions, the principal *cause of continued suffering* is poverty.

5. _____

6. The new ruler hastened to *release from imprisonment* all who had been arrested for political reasons.

6. _____

7. That coat has a(an) *horribly ugly* fur collar.

7. _____

8. The sea that day was *without agitation or disturbance*.

8. _____

9. In his *facial expression*, there was nothing to suggest anxiety.

9. _____

10. Most people will contribute because they are *sympathetic to other human beings*.

10._____

Exercise 3.10: Using Synonyms and Antonyms

A. Replace the italicized word with a SYNONYM from the following list. See 1, below.

appreciate	attractive	barbarous	miscellaneous	receptive
release	sanctuary	solace	troubled	visage

1. People satisfied with things as they are may not be *hospitable* to change.

___receptive___

2. I recognized the familiar *countenance* of a classmate.

_____

3. How can you remember all these *sundry* details?

_____

4. An abandoned barn offered *asylum* from the storm.

_____

5. She wanted to *liberate* the caged bird.

_____

B. Complete the sentence by inserting an ANTONYM of the italicized word from the above list. See 6, below.

6. Her room was decorated in *hideous* colors.

___attractive___

7. Did the prisoners receive *humane* treatment?

_____

8. At that moment you had a *tranquil* expression.

_____

9. Who says I really *despise* our coach?

_____

10. Work is the *affliction* of many people.

_____

Exercise 3.11: Name-the-Person Quiz

Read all the statements in the boxes. Then answer questions 1 to 10. The first answer has been inserted as a sample.

After deserting to the British, Benedict Arnold was denounced as a traitor.	Despite his many troubles, Richard appeared calm and relaxed.	For six weeks, Jeffers fed a hawk that was unable to fly.

Johnny fetched water, carried coal, swept, helped with the making of ale, and worked in the shop.

In the cave lived Polyphemus, a huge giant with a single eye in the middle of his forehead.	When Roberta's expensive new bicycle was stolen, she did not report the matter to the authorities.

Hunted by the police, Valjean escaped with his adopted daughter to a convent, where he lived peacefully for a time.

Did you know that Jackson, who won the speech prize, was once a stutterer?	After serving nine months of his three-year sentence, Williams was released on parole.	When the old king visited his daughter Regan, she did not make him feel welcome.

1. Who did sundry chores?   **Johnny**

2. Who was humane?   _____

3. Who overcame an affliction?   _____

4. Who was despised?   _____

5. Who gave countenance to crime?   _____

6. Who was liberated?   _____

7. Who found asylum?   _____

8. Who was inhospitable?   _____

9. Who seemed tranquil?   _____

10. Who was hideous?   _____

LEARNING SOME ROOTS AND DERIVATIVES

Each capitalized word below is a *root*. The words under it are its *derivatives*.

AFFLICT (*v.*)   Many young people are *afflicted* with shyness.

affliction (*n.*)   Shyness is a common *affliction* among young people.

COUNTENANCE (n.)	Our Constitution gives no *countenance* to tyranny.
countenance (v.)	Our Constitution does not *countenance* tyranny.
DESPISE (v.)	We *despise* cowardice.
despicable (adj.)	To us, cowardice is *despicable*.
despicably (adv.)	Cowards behave *despicably*.
HIDEOUS (adj.)	The monster looked *hideous*.
hideously (adv.)	He grinned *hideously*.
hideousness (n.)	Despite his *hideousness*, the children were fascinated by him.
HOST (n.)	On our arrival, we were welcomed by the *host* and *hostess*.
hostess (n.)	
hospitable (adj.)	We received *hospitable* treatment.
hospitably (adv.)	We were treated *hospitably*.
hospitality (n.)	We were shown the warmest *hospitality*.
HUMANE (adj.)	Sailors have a reputation for being *humane*.
humanely (adv.)	They respond swiftly and *humanely* when a distressed vessel calls for help.
humaneness (n.)	Responding to an SOS is an act of *humaneness*.
LIBERATE (v.)	Simon Bolivar was able to *liberate* much of South America from Spanish rule.
liberation (n.)	After the *liberation* of Colombia, Bolivar was elected its first president.
liberator (n.)	Bolivar is regarded as one of the world's great *liberators*.
SUNDRY (adj.)	She had finished her shopping, except for some *sundry* items like paper napkins, dental floss, and nail polish.
sundries (n.)	On the notions counter you will find thread, needles, ribbon, buttons, and similar *sundries*.
TRANQUIL (adj.)	After the operation, the patient had a *tranquil* night.
tranquilly (adv.)	She slept *tranquilly*.
tranquility (n.)	There was absolute *tranquility* in her countenance.
tranquilize (v.)	Medication was administered to *tranquilize* the patient.
tranquilizer (n.)	The patient was given a *tranquilizer*.

Exercise 3.12: Using Roots and Derivatives

Fill each blank with the above root or derivative that best fits the meaning of the sentence. The first blank has been filled as an example.

1. On July 14, the people of France celebrate their ___liberation___ from tyranny.

2. An oil spill soiled the white sands of the beaches and turned beauty into _____.

3. Millions in the tropics are _____ with malaria.

4. A heavy truck lumbered down the avenue, shattering the morning _____.

5. The townspeople looked down on the ex-convict; in their eyes he was _____.

6. On our next visit we got a very cool reception; there was no evidence of the usual _____.

7. Get into the habit of coming on time, as most employers do not _____ lateness.

8. At vending machines in public places, you can purchase combs, toothpaste, pens, and other _____.

9. Complaints have been received that the inmates in some institutions are not being _____ treated.

10. George Washington, who led the successful struggle for independence, was hailed as a(an) _____.

IMPROVING YOUR ANALOGY SKILLS

Exercise 3.13: Answering Analogy Questions

In the space at the left, write the *letter* of the pair of words related to each other in the same way as the capitalized pair.

Sample:

_____ INNKEEPER : SHELTER

    (A) fireplace : warmth   (D) cabdriver : transportation
    (B) mother : protection   (E) food : grocer
    (C) pilot : plane

Solution:

The first step is to find the relationship in the capitalized pair INNKEEPER : SHELTER. Since an INNKEEPER is in the business of providing SHELTER, the relationship here is "A is a person who provides B for a fee."

The next step is to analyze the five suggested pairs to see which pair most nearly has the same relationship as INNKEEPER : SHELTER.

    (A) *fireplace : warmth.* A *fireplace* provides *warmth*, but a *fireplace* is not a business person.

    (B) *mother : protection.* A *mother* provides *protection*, but not for a fee.

    (C) *pilot : plane.* A *pilot* does not provide a *plane*.

(D) *cabdriver : transportation.* A *cabdriver* provides *transportation* for a fee. This looks good, but let's check out pair E.

(E) *food : grocer. Food* is provided by a *grocer* for money. Had the order been reversed (*grocer : food*), this too would have been a correct answer.

Correct Answer: D.

With the above discussion to guide you, enter your answers to 1 to 5, below:

_____ **1.** LIBERATOR : BONDAGE

(A) medicine : pain   (D) jury : guilt
(B) reporter : news   (E) rest : weariness
(C) teacher : ignorance

_____ **2.** HOSPITALITY : GUEST

(A) dinner : hostess   (D) dues : member
(B) asylum : enemy   (E) sympathy : patient
(C) employee : wages

_____ **3.** HIDEOUS : UGLY

(A) enormous : large   (D) lukewarm : hot
(B) pretty : ordinary   (E) tardy : late
(C) small : tiny

_____ **4.** AFFLICTION : SUFFER

(A) ambition : hesitate   (D) failure : discouragement
(B) success : rejoice   (E) weariness : travel
(C) courage : tremble

_____ **5.** SERENE : AGITATION

(A) inhumane : cruelty   (D) sea : waves
(B) humble : vanity   (E) troubled : anxiety
(C) greed : generous

REVIEWING BASIC CONCEPTS: THE COMMA AND THE PARTICIPIAL PHRASE

A. 1. A comma sets off a participial phrase beginning a sentence.

Wondering which way to turn next, the puzzled driver stopped to consult his map.

2. A comma sets off a participial phrase ending a sentence.

The puzzled driver stopped to consult his map, *wondering which way to turn next.*

3. Two commas set off a participial phrase in the interior of a sentence.

The puzzled driver, *wondering which way to turn next,* stopped to consult his map.

B. However, note that *no commas* are used in the following:

Drivers *wondering which way to turn next* are a menace.

EXPLANATION: If the participial phrase is *essential*—that is, if the sentence makes no sense without it—*no commas* are used.

In the above sentence **B,** the participial phrase *wondering which way to turn next* is essential. Take it away and you have the absurd statement, *Drivers are a menace.*

In all the other sentences with the participial phrase *wondering which way to turn next* (**A**), the participial phrase is **nonessential.** Take it away, and in all three instances you are left with the perfectly logical statement, *The puzzled driver stopped to consult his map.*

Remember NOT to set off a participial phrase with commas if it is *essential* to the meaning of the sentence.

Exercise 3.14: Setting off Participial Phrases With Commas

In the following sentences, if the participial phrase is nonessential, insert whatever commas are needed. If essential, insert no commas.

1. All students   *failing the final examination*   must repeat the course.
2. *Turned down by one college after another*   Mona is planning to go to work.
3. There were no seats for ticket-holders   *arriving late.*
4. No contestant   *eliminated in the preliminaries*   can remain in the tournament.
5. The performer   *responding to the cheers*   emerged for a second round of applause.
6. She stayed home all afternoon   *hoping for a call from her friend.*
7. People   *afflicted with poor vision*   need corrective lenses.
8. We chatted on the steps of the library   *waiting for the doors to open.*
9. Vehicles   *damaged beyond repair*   should be scrapped.
10. *Returning home*   I met a friend of yours.

SPELLING REVIEW: WHEN TO USE *-ABLE* or *-IBLE*, and *-ABILITY* or *-IBILITY*

A. *-ABLE* or *-IBLE?*

QUESTION: Should you use *-able* or *-ible* to complete *imagin _ _ _ _?*

HINT: If you know there is an *-ation* word beginning with the letters *imagin*—for example—*imagination*, use *-able.*

CORRECT SPELLING: **imaginable**

Note that, because nouns like *presentation, application, irritation,* and *adoration* exist, the corresponding adjectives are spelled *presentable, applicable, irritable,* and *adorable.*

EXCEPTION: *sensible* ends in *-ible,* despite the existence of *sensation.*

B. Except for the hint in **A,** above, there is no easy way to tell whether an adjective ends in -ABLE or -IBLE. Therefore, study the following:

Frequently Used -ABLE Adjectives

acceptable	conceivable	disposable	miserable
advisable	consumable	excusable	perishable
applicable	dependable	hospitable	predictable
available	desirable	imaginable	presentable
believable	despicable	intolerable	probable

Frequently Used -IBLE Adjectives

convertible	feasible	invisible	plausible
digestible	flexible	irresistible	possible
divisible	horrible	legible	responsible
edible	incredible	negligible	sensible
eligible	inexhaustible	permissible	terrible

C. The suffix -ABLE or -IBLE does *not* change when a prefix is added or removed.

un + predict*able* = unpredict*able* improb*able* – im = prob*able*

ir + respons*ible* = irrespons*ible* inexhaust*ible* – in = exhaust*ible*

D. *-ABILITY or -IBILITY?*

Nouns ending in -ABILITY come from adjectives ending in -ABLE. Nouns ending in -IBILITY come from adjectives ending in -IBLE.

ADJECTIVE	NOUN
advisable	advisability
responsible	responsibility

Exercise 3.15:   Using *-ABLE* or *-IBLE*

Below are some adjectives with either *-able* or *-ible* omitted. Write the complete adjective in the space provided.

SAMPLE: undepend   **undependable**

1. unavail	_____	**11.** nonconsum	_____
2. indigest	_____	**12.** convert	_____
3. miser	_____	**13.** inconceiv	_____
4. imposs	_____	**14.** inexcus	_____
5. horr	_____	**15.** resist	_____
6. despic	_____	**16.** indivis	_____
7. unbeliev	_____	**17.** neglig	_____
8. dispos	_____	**18.** improb	_____
9. sens	_____	**19.** unpresent	_____
10. inhospit	_____	**20.** leg	_____

Exercise 3.16: Using *-ABILITY* or *-IBILITY*

Below are some nouns with either *-ability* or *-ibility* omitted. Write the complete noun in the space provided.

SAMPLE: imposs **impossibility**

1. elig _____
2. poss _____
3. applic _____
4. intoler _____
5. feas _____
6. unpredict _____
7. insens _____
8. undepend _____
9. cred _____
10. accept _____

11. digest _____
12. inflex _____
13. vis _____
14. implaus _____
15. present _____
16. irresist _____
17. inexhaust _____
18. undesir _____
19. permiss _____
20. perish _____

from

The Autobiography of an Ex-Coloured Man

by James Weldon Johnson

A boy tells of his first love—and of meeting a stranger who turns out to be a close relative.

She was my first love, and I loved her as only a boy loves. I dreamed of her, I built air castles for her, she was the incarnation of each beautiful heroine I knew; when I played the piano, it was to her, not even music furnished an adequate outlet for my pas-
5 sion; I bought a new notebook and, to sing her praises, made my first and last attempts at poetry. I remember one day at school, after we had given in our notebooks to have some exercises corrected, the teacher called me to her desk and said: "I couldn't correct your exercises because I found nothing in your book but a
10 rhapsody on somebody's brown eyes." I had passed in the wrong notebook. I don't think I have ever felt greater embarrassment in my whole life than I did at that moment. I was ashamed not only that my teacher should see this nakedness of my heart, but that she should find out that I had any knowledge of such affairs. It did
15 not then occur to me to be ashamed of the kind of poetry I had written.

Of course, the reader must know that all of this adoration was in secret; next to my great love for this young lady was the dread that in some way she would find it out. I did not know what some
20 men never find out, that the woman who cannot discern when she is loved has never lived. It makes me laugh to think how successful I was in concealing it all; within a short time after our duet all of the friends of my dear one were referring to me as her "little sweetheart," or her "little beau," and she laughingly encouraged it.
25 This did not entirely satisfy me; I wanted to be taken seriously. I

60

had definitely made up my mind that I should never love another woman, and that if she deceived me I should do something desperate—the great difficulty was to think of something sufficiently desperate—and the heartless jade, how she led me on!

So I hurried home that afternoon, humming snatches of the violin part of the duet, my heart beating with pleasurable excitement over the fact that I was going to be near her, to have her attention placed directly upon me; that I was going to be of service to her, and in a way in which I could show myself to advantage—this last consideration has much to do with cheerful service.—The anticipation produced in me a sensation somewhat between bliss and fear. I rushed through the gate, took the three steps to the house at one bound, threw open the door, and was about to hang my cap on its accustomed peg of the hall rack when I noticed that that particular peg was occupied by a black derby hat. I stopped suddenly and gazed at this hat as though I had never seen an object of its description. I was still looking at it in open-eyed wonder when my mother, coming out of the parlour into the hallway, called me and said there was someone inside who wanted to see me. Feeling that I was being made a party to some kind of mystery, I went in with her, and there I saw a man standing leaning with one elbow on the mantel, his back partly turned toward the door. As I entered, he turned and I saw a tall, handsome, well-dressed gentleman of perhaps thirty-five; he had advanced a step toward me with a smile on his face. I stopped and looked at him with the same feelings with which I had looked at the derby hat, except that they were greatly magnified. I looked at him from head to foot, but he was an absolute blank to me until my eyes rested on his slender, elegant polished shoes; then it seemed that indistinct and partly obliterated films of memory began, at first slowly, then rapidly, to unroll, forming a vague panorama of my childhood days in Georgia.

My mother broke the spell by calling me by name and saying: "This is your father."

"Father, father," that was the word which had been to me a source of doubt and perplexity ever since the interview with my mother on the subject. How often I had wondered about my father, who he was, what he was like, whether alive or dead, and, above all, why she would not tell me about him. More than once I had been on the point of recalling to her the promise she had made me, but I instinctively felt that she was happier for not telling me and that I was happier for not being told; yet I had not the slightest idea what the real truth was. And here he stood before me, just the kind of looking father I had wishfully pictured him to be; but I made no advance toward him; I stood there feeling embarrassed and foolish, not knowing what to say or do. I am not sure but that he felt pretty much the same. My mother stood at my side with one hand on my shoulder, almost pushing me forward, but I did not move. I can well remember the look of disappointment, even pain, on her face; and I can now understand that she could expect nothing else but that at the name "father" I should throw myself into

his arms. But I could not rise to this dramatic, or, better, melodramatic, climax. Somehow I could not arouse any considerable feeling of need for a father. He broke the awkward tableau by saying:
80 "Well, boy, aren't you glad to see me?" He evidently meant the words kindly enough, but I don't know what he could have said that would have had a worse effect; however, my good breeding came to my rescue, and I answered: "Yes, sir," and went to him and offered him my hand. He took my hand into one of his, and, with
85 the other, stroked my head, saying that I had grown into a fine youngster. He asked me how old I was; which, of course, he must have done merely to say something more, or perhaps he did so as a test of my intelligence. I replied: "Twelve, sir." He then made the trite observation about the flight of time, and we lapsed into an-
90 other awkward pause.

My mother was all in smiles; I believe that was one of the happiest moments of her life. Either to put me more at ease or to show me off, she asked me to play something for my father. There is only one thing in the world that can make music, at all times and under
95 all circumstances, up to its general standard; that is a hand-organ, or one of its variations. I went to the piano and played something in a listless, half-hearted way. I simply was not in the mood. I was wondering, while playing, when my mother would dismiss me and let me go; but my father was so enthusiastic in his praise that he
100 touched my vanity—which was great—and more than that; he displayed that sincere appreciation which always arouses an artist to his best effort, and, too, in an unexplainable manner, makes him feel like shedding tears. I showed my gratitude by playing for him a Chopin waltz with all the feeling that was in me. When I had fin-
105 ished, my mother's eyes were glistening with tears; my father stepped across the room, seized me in his arms, and squeezed me to his breast. I am certain that for that moment he was proud to be my father. He sat and held me standing between his knees while he talked to my mother. I, in the meantime, examined him
110 with more curiosity, perhaps, than politeness. I interrupted the conversation by asking: "Mother, is he going to stay with us now?" I found it impossible to frame the word "father"; it was too new to me; so I asked the question through my mother. Without waiting for her to speak, my father answered: "I've got to go back to New
115 York this afternoon, but I'm coming to see you again." I turned abruptly and went over to my mother, and almost in a whisper reminded her that I had an appointment which I should not miss; to my pleasant surprise she said that she would give me something to eat at once so that I might go. She went out of the room
120 and I began to gather from off the piano the music I needed. When I had finished, my father, who had been watching me, asked: "Are you going?" I replied: "Yes, sir, I've got to go to practise for a concert." He spoke some words of advice to me about being a good boy and taking care of my mother when I grew up, and added that he
125 was going to send me something nice from New York. My mother called, and I said good-bye to him and went out. I saw him only once after that.

Exercise 4.1: Close Reading

In the blank space, write the *letter* of the choice that best completes the statement.

1. The narrator implies that the girl he loved _____.

   (A) did not take him seriously
   (B) did not know he loved her
   (C) had never had a boyfriend
   (D) told him she did not love him

2. The narrator _____.

   (A) was impolite to his father
   (B) was overjoyed to see his father
   (C) found nothing to like in his father
   (D) vaguely remembered that in early childhood he had seen his father

3. The passage indicates that the mother _____.

   (A) was not proud of her son
   (B) was entirely pleased with the way her son behaved when she introduced his father
   (C) was overjoyed at the father's visit
   (D) withheld no information from her son

4. The passage suggests that the father had no _____.

   (A) appreciation of musical talent
   (B) love whatsoever for the mother
   (C) intention of living with the mother and son
   (D) dependable source of income

5. The narrator believes that _____.

   (A) girls are heartless
   (B) he would have been very unhappy if his father had stayed
   (C) artists perform best when appreciated
   (D) not every woman can tell when someone is in love with her

IMPROVING YOUR COMPOSITION SKILLS: BUILDING COMPOUND SENTENCES FROM SIMPLE SENTENCES

A. A *compound sentence* combines two or more simple sentences connected usually by *and, but, or, yet, for,* or some other conjunction.

SIMPLE SENTENCES

My mother called.
I said good-bye to him and went out.

COMPOUND SENTENCE

My mother called, *and* I said good-bye to him and went out.

B. Use a comma before the conjunction, unless the sentences are very short, as in the following:

The door opened.
A man entered.

The door opened *and* a man entered.

C. When three or more simple sentences are combined, a conjunction introduces the last one, and the sentences are separated by commas.

Jane won.
Peggy was a close second.
Marie finished third.

Jane won, Peggy was a close second, *and* Marie finished third.

D. Use the conjunctions *but* and *yet* to connect sentences with contrasting ideas.

I've got to go back to New York this afternoon.
I'm coming to see you again.

I've got to go back to New York this afternoon, *but* I'm coming to see you again.

The action consumed no more than a quarter of a minute.
In that brief moment the numbness laid hold of the exposed fingers.

The action consumed no more than a quarter of a minute, *yet* in that brief moment the numbness laid hold of the exposed fingers.

E. Use the conjunction *or* before a probable result or an alternative statement.

Stay in line.
You will lose your turn

Stay in line, *or* you will lose your turn.

You may come to our court.
We will play on yours.

You may come to our court, *or* we will play on yours.

F. Use the conjunction *for* (meaning "because") before a statement offered as a reason.

All the gas stations were closed.
It was past midnight.

All the gas stations were closed, *for* it was past midnight.

G. Instead of a conjunction, you may use a semicolon [;] to connect simple sentences that contrast sharply, or that you wish to present as a single thought.

This did not entirely satisfy me.
I wanted to be taken seriously.

This did not entirely satisfy me; I wanted to be taken seriously.

The situation is critical.
It is a matter of life and death.

The situation is critical; it is a matter of life and death.

Exercise 4.2: Combining Simple Sentences Into a Compound Sentence

Combine each group of simple sentences into a compound sentence, using an appropriate conjunction or a semicolon, plus a comma wherever necessary.

1. The bus lurched forward. I nearly lost my balance.

2. A cool wind was blowing. The water was quite warm.

_____

3. Use a potholder. You will burn your fingers.

_____

4. You are humane, Monsieur Curé. You don't despise me.

_____

5. My mother stood at my side with one hand on my shoulder, almost pushing me forward. I did not move.

_____

_____

_____

6. The sky darkened. There was a flash of lightning. Rain began to fall.

_____

_____

_____

7. The night wind is cold in the Alps. You must be cold, monsieur.

_____

_____

8. There was no mail delivery. It was a national holiday.

_____

_____

9. There did not seem to be many springs on the left side of the Henderson. For half an hour the man saw no signs of any.

_____

_____

_____

10. She called. I was out.

_____

H. Some simple sentences may be connected by a semicolon plus a **_conjunctive adverb_** (an adverb that connects).

The following are some conjunctive adverbs:

however	therefore	then	accordingly
nevertheless	consequently	instead	otherwise

Anderson may win the election.
He has a long way to go.

Anderson may win the election; *however*, he has a long way to go.

You must show your registration card.
You will not be admitted.

You must show your registration card; *otherwise*, you will not be admitted.

Note that a conjunctive adverb introducing a statement is usually preceded by a semicolon and followed by a comma:

; however,
; otherwise,

Exercise 4.3: Using Conjunctive Adverbs in Compound Sentences

Combine each pair of simple sentences into a compound sentence, using an appropriate conjunctive adverb, as in 1, below.

1. Eleven inches of snow has already fallen. All schools will be closed today.

   Eleven inches of snow has already fallen; therefore, all schools will be closed

   today.

2. Morgan is getting his raise. He is still complaining.

3. The program originally scheduled for this time has been canceled. We bring you a special report from Washington, D.C.

4. They must pay their rent. They may be evicted.

5. Awakening at 4:30 A.M., Chris started to get out of bed. Noticing the time, she promptly went back to sleep.

Exercise 4.4: Writing a Composition

An aunt or uncle in a distant city has surprised you by sending you a $100 gift certificate for your birthday. Write him or her a thank-you note of about 100 words.

Here are some matters you may wish to mention:

1. Your delight on receiving this handsome gift on your birthday.

2. An account of what you plan to do with the money.

3. Your appreciation of the relative's thoughtfulness and generosity.

Begin your note with the salutation (*Dear Aunt Martha* or *Dear Uncle Henry*), and end with the closing (*Your nephew* or *Your niece*).

Important: Use at least one compound sentence in the final draft.

Final Draft: A Thank-You Note

_____

_____

_____

_____

_____

_____

_____

_____

_____

_____

_____

_____

_____

_____

_____

_____

_____

_____

LEARNING NEW WORDS

Line	Word	Meaning	Typical Use
17	**adoration** (*n.*) ˌad-ə-ˈrā-shən	act of *adoring* (loving fervently); devoted love; worship	In "How Do I Love Thee?" Elizabeth Barrett expressed her *adoration* of Robert Browning, but she did not show him the poem until after their marriage.

(*ant.* **detestation, loathing**)

Most nations have expressed their *detestation* of nuclear warfare, and their leaders are working to ban the use of atomic weapons.

35	**anticipation** (*n.*) an-ˌtis-ə-ˈpā-shən	act of *anticipating* (looking forward); picturing beforehand a future event; expectation	The candidate was overconfident; he had prepared an acceptance speech in *anticipation* of winning the nomination.
36	**bliss** (*n.*) ˈblis	perfect happiness; joy; ecstasy	After their first meeting, Romeo and Juliet plan to marry, for they can imagine no greater *bliss* than to be with each other.
		(*ant.* **anguish***)*	They take a long time in saying good night in order to postpone the *anguish* of parting.
78	**climax** (*n.*) ˈklī-ˌmaks	highest or most intense point in the development of something; culmination	For me, the *climax* of the exercises came when I was called to the platform to receive my diploma.
105	**glisten** (*v.*) ˈglis-ən	shine with subdued light, as from a wet surface; sparkle; glitter	After the shower, the moist leaves *glistened* in the sun.
97	**listless** (*adj.*) ˈlist-ləs	showing no interest or inclination in exerting oneself; languid; spiritless (*ant.* **eager**)	If you make only a *listless* attempt to find work, you will probably remain unemployed.
55	**obliterate** (*v.*) ə-ˈblit-ə-ˌrāt	destroy all trace of; make undecipherable; blot out; erase	We emerged from the surf, leaving footprints in the sand, but the next wave *obliterated* them.
56	**panorama** (*n.*) ˌpan-ə-ˈram-ə	1. picture unrolled before a spectator, giving the impression of a continuous view	This history course offers a *panorama* of ancient times.
		2. full and unobstructed view of an extensive area	From the top of the hill, you can get a *panorama* of the entire district.
		3. range	In a day's work, a police officer often deals with a wide *panorama* of problems, from the pursuing of suspected criminals to the rescuing of a trapped kitten.

61	**source** (*n.*) 'sòrs	1. place or person from which something comes, arises, or is obtained; origin; beginning; cause	They are working to trace the rumor to its *source*, but as of the moment they do not know who started it.
		(*ant.* **outcome**)	A neighbor recounted the *source* of the quarrel between the sisters, as well as its *outcome*.
		2. beginning, or point of origin, of a stream or river	The Nile has its *source* in Lake Victoria.
89	**trite** (*adj.*) 'trīt	used or occurring so often as to have lost freshness and force; lacking originality; stale	To be interesting, avoid *trite* expressions like "Time flies" or "Haste makes waste"; say something *original*.
		(*ant.* **original, fresh**)	

APPLYING WHAT YOU HAVE LEARNED

Exercise 4.5:   Sentence Completion

Enter the choice required by the sentence, as in 1, below.

1. She sat in class listlessly, as if deeply (*bored, interested*) __**bored**__.
2. The (*furnace, mine*) _____ is a source of coal.
3. The turnout is below our anticipation; (*many, few*) _____ seats are vacant.
4. Be original; (*use, avoid*) _____ trite expressions.
5. Suspects feel it would be bliss to be (*convicted, exonerated*) _____.
6. Use the (*blackboard, eraser*) _____ to obliterate the answer.
7. Prolonged (*cheers, boos*) _____ show a crowd's adoration of a performer.
8. You cannot get a panorama of a parade from a (*peephole, rooftop*) _____.
9. The dew glistened like (*diamonds, fog*) _____.
10. Public interest in the trial mounted steadily, reaching its climax with the news that the jury had (*begun, ended*) its _____ deliberations.

Reading Selection 4: The Autobiography of an Ex-Coloured Man   **69**

Exercise 4.6:   Using Fewer Words

Replace the italicized words with a single word from the following list. See answer to 1, below.

trite   adoration   panorama   bliss   obliterate
anticipation   climax   glisten   listless   source

1. At the *most intense point* of the storm, we had sixty-mile-an-hour winds.   _____climax_____

2. Avoid expressions that are *used so often as to have lost freshness.*   _____

3. *Picturing beforehand a future event* can make a person nervous.   _____

4. The helper you sent was *uninterested in exerting himself.*   _____

5. How can the plumber possibly repair the leak before finding the *place from which it comes?*   _____

6. By her humaneness, the Queen won the *devoted love* of her people.   _____

7. Time can *blot out* the lessons of the past.   _____

8. This shampoo will make your hair *shine with subdued light.*   _____

9. Few people achieve the *perfect happiness* they seek.   _____

10. Our balcony seats gave us a(an) *full and unobstructed view* of the stage.   _____

Exercise 4.7:   Using Synonyms and Antonyms

A. Replace the italicized word with a SYNONYM from the following list, as in 1, below.

loathing   ecstasy   range   erase   eager
expectation   cause   culmination   original   glitter

1. See how the dog's eyes *sparkle* when you pat its head.   _____glitter_____

2. An earthquake can *obliterate* whole towns and villages.   _____

3. The dean has a wide *panorama* of responsibilities.   _____

4. He sat by the telephone in *anticipation* of your call.   _____

5. It looks as if the dispute is nearing its *climax.*   _____

B. Replace the italicized word with an ANTONYM from the vocabulary list.

6. What was the *outcome* of the complaint?   _____

7. It was a moment of *anguish.*   _____

8. For her former friend, she has the greatest *adoration.*   _____

9. That was a very *trite* remark. _____

10. When I explained the job to him, he seemed *listless*. _____

Exercise 4.8:   Name-the-Person Quiz

Read all the statements in the boxes. Then answer questions 1 to 10.

By the time Simpson arrived, the main event of the evening was over.	With cleaning fluid, Shirley removed all traces of the grease stain.	Shakespeare can teach us a great deal about human nature.

Helen concluded by repeating what the other candidates had said: "If elected, I will do my best."

Everyone took notes except Sherwood, who showed little interest and even dozed occasionally.	Patricia expected a difficult test, and she got one.

For Joan, the seashore was a paradise.	When Eric stepped into the sun, there were beads of perspiration on his brow.

Mark acquainted us with a broad stretch of the coastline.	Marie Curie was Geraldine's idol; she worshiped her.

1. Who was trite? _____

2. Who found bliss? _____

3. Who missed a climax? _____

4. Who is a source? _____

5. Who was listless? _____

6. Who obliterated something? _____

7. Whose face glistened? _____'s

8. Whose anticipation was correct? _____'s

9. Who presented a panorama? _____

10. Who aroused adoration? _____

LEARNING SOME ROOTS AND DERIVATIVES

Each capitalized word below is a *root*. The words under it are its *derivatives*.

ADORE (*v.*)   The children *adore* the puppies.

adorable (*adj.*)   The puppies are *adorable*.

adorably (*adv.*)	They play *adorably*.
adoration (*n.*)	They win the *adoration* of all who see them.
ANTICIPATE (*v.*)	The merchant *anticipated* a busy week.
anticipatory (*adj.*)	In an *anticipatory* move, he took on extra salespeople.
anticipation (*n.*)	Contrary to his *anticipation*, business was light.
BLISS (*n.*)	Looking back, he realized that his childhood years had been a period of *bliss*.
blissful (*adj.*)	They were *blissful* years.
blissfully (*adv.*)	He was then *blissfully* ignorant of the problems that lay ahead.
CLIMAX (*n.*)	The *climax* came when the jury brought in the verdict.
climactic (*adj.*)	It was a *climactic* moment.
climactically (*adv.*)	The words "not guilty" *climactically* ended the long trial.
LISTLESS (*adj.*)	Extremely hot weather makes me *listless*.
listlessly (*adv.*)	When the temperature is in the nineties, I go about my work *listlessly*.
listlessness (*n.*)	As the weather cools, my *listlessness* disappears.
OBLITERATE (*v.*)	Heavy traffic *is obliterating* the line between the lanes.
obliteration (*n.*)	You can still tell where the line is, for the *obliteration* is not complete.
PANORAMA (*n.*)	The book provides an excellent *panorama* of World War II.
panoramic (*adj.*)	The book provides a *panoramic* account of the war.
TRITE (*adj.*)	Avoid *trite* expressions.
tritely (*adv.*)	Instead of *tritely* saying, "First and foremost, let's hear from Frank," it is better to say, "First, let's hear from Frank."
triteness (*n.*)	"First" is free of *triteness*.

Exercise 4.9: Using Roots and Derivatives

Fill each blank with the above root or derivative that best fits the meaning of the sentence. The first blank has been filled as an example.

1. You could tell they were not interested because when we asked them to join us they responded _____listlessly_____.

2. The child was a nuisance, but in his parents' eyes he was _____.

3. A community newspaper deals mainly with local events; it does not usually offer _____ coverage of the news.

4. Try to _____ what your problems will be and devise plans to solve them.

5. Make your writing more forceful by ridding it of _____.

6. Some rave about basketball or football; others _____ ballet or the opera.

7. The struggle is intensifying and is about to enter its _____ phase.

8. They accuse us of _____ and say that we have no spirit.

9. Bob was unhappy with farm life; it was not the _____ experience that he had anticipated.

10. The earthquake and tidal wave resulted in the _____ of the villages on the offshore islands.

REVIEW OF SPELLING RULES FOR TURNING VERBS INTO NOUNS

A. Three suffixes for turning verbs into nouns are -ION, -ATION, and -URE. They all have the same meaning: "act or result of."

VERB	+	SUFFIX	=	NOUN
anticipate	+	ion	=	anticipa*tion* (act or result of anticipating)
afflict	+	ion	=	afflic*tion* (act or result of being afflicted)
adore	+	ation	=	ador*ation* (act or result of adoring)
consider	+	ation	=	considera*tion* (act or result of considering)
expose	+	ure	=	expos*ure* (act or result of exposing)
press	+	ure	=	press*ure* (act or result of pressing)

REMINDER: If the verb ends in silent *e* (as in *anticipate*, *adore*, and *expose*, above), drop the *e* before adding -ION, -ATION, and -URE because these suffixes begin with a vowel.

Exercise 4.10: Adding Suffixes

Turn the following verbs into nouns by adding -ION, -ATION, or -URE. The first three entries have been made as samples.

1. discuss _____discussion_____   **4.** liberate _____

2. imagine _____imagination_____   **5.** construct _____

3. seize _____seizure_____   **6.** expose _____

7. civilize _____   14. confess _____
8. appreciate _____   15. obliterate _____
9. erase _____   16. disclose _____
10. infect _____   17. observe _____
11. perspire _____   18. attract _____
12. impress _____   19. enclose _____
13. pollute _____   20. inspire _____

B. By dropping the suffixes -ION, -ATION, and -URE, we may turn nouns into verbs.

NOUN	–	SUFFIX	=	VERB
transact*ion*	–	ion	=	transact
confront*ation*	–	ation	=	confront
press*ure*	–	ure	=	press

If a silent *e* was dropped when the noun was formed, it must be put back into the verb.

NOUN	–	SUFFIX			=	VERB
pollut*ion*	–	ion	+	e	=	pollut*e*
ador*ation*	–	ation	+	e	=	ador*e*
expos*ure*	–	ure	+	e	=	expos*e*

Exercise 4.11: Dropping Suffixes

Turn each of the following nouns into a verb by dropping its suffix. The first three entries have been made as samples.

1. contribution _____contribute_____   11. conservation _____
2. inspection _____inspect_____   12. foreclosure _____
3. resignation _____resign_____   13. expiration _____
4. exaggeration _____   14. prediction _____
5. exploration _____   15. vexation _____
6. composure _____   16. injection _____
7. separation _____   17. forfeiture _____
8. expression _____   18. expectation _____
9. interpretation _____   19. action _____
10. sensation _____   20. elevation _____

IMPROVING YOUR COMPOSITION SKILLS: ELIMINATING TRITE EXPRESSIONS

1. *The Nature of Trite Expressions*

Most of us are familiar with trite expressions because they are so very common. When we hear or see the beginning of such an expression, we can usually foretell the rest of it.

You yourself must know this from personal experience. For example, when you hear "*Last but . . . ,*" you can anticipate "*not least*" before the speaker has uttered the words.

When you read "*Out of a clear . . . ,*" you can be reasonably sure that "*blue sky*" is coming.

If you use trite expressions, your audience will be able to anticipate what you are going to say. They may lose interest and pay less attention. You will bore them. To keep them alert, you must avoid trite expressions, especially in your writing.

2. *Trite Expressions in Conversation*

In everyday conversation, a trite expression can occasionally serve a purpose. For example, the father got himself momentarily out of an embarrassing situation by making "the trite observation about the flight of time" (lines 88–89). He probably said "How time flies!" but the author chose not to bore us by quoting this trite comment.

3. *Eliminating Triteness From Writing*

When you revise your written work, look for trite expressions and replace them with natural and direct language of your own. Here are some examples:

TRITE EXPRESSION	SUGGESTED REPLACEMENT
at this point in time	now
beat about the bush	evade the issue, stall
by a rare stroke of good fortune	luckily
by the skin of one's teeth	barely
dime a dozen	readily available
do a land-office business	do a brisk business
first and foremost	first
fresh as a daisy	refreshed
frightened out of one's wits	shocked
gentle as a lamb	very gentle
go down to defeat	lose
It is an honor and a privilege for me . . .	I am pleased . . .
last but not least	finally
light as a feather	very light
out of a clear blue sky	unexpectedly
plain as the nose on your face	very plain
quick as a flash	quickly
selling like hotcakes	selling very quickly
strong as an ox	very strong
to all intents and purposes	practically speaking
with flying colors	brilliantly
with head bloody but unbowed	determined to fight on

Reading Selection 4: The Autobiography of an Ex-Coloured Man   75

Exercise 4.12:   Replacing Trite Expressions

Rewrite each sentence, eliminating the trite expression. If you do not wish to use the "suggested replacement" (above), create one of your own.

SAMPLE: Partners were a dime a dozen.
Partners were **readily available.**
or
There were **plenty of partners.**

1. The tickets are selling like hotcakes.
   _____

2. I awoke feeling fresh as a daisy.
   _____

3. At this point in time, we must cut expenses.
   _____

4. To all intents and purposes, we lost the game in the first quarter.
   _____
   _____

5. Stop beating about the bush.
   _____

6. It is an honor and a privilege for me to present the next speaker.
   _____
   _____

7. Quick as a flash she returned the serve.
   _____

8. First and foremost, the rent must be paid.
   _____

9. The bundle was light as a feather.
   _____

10. In early April, tax accountants do a land-office business.
    _____
    _____

Exercise 4.13: Revising a Paragraph to Eliminate Triteness

In the following paragraph of six sentences, there are eight trite expressions. Rewrite the paragraph, replacing those expressions.

[1]In the last of the ninth, trailing by a run, we went to the plate with heads bloody but unbowed. [2]However, after our two heavy hitters struck out, it was plain as the nose on your face that we were going to go down to defeat. [3]Then Hennessey, by a rare stroke of good luck, tapped a slow roller to the mound and by the skin of his teeth beat the throw to first. [4]In this crisis the manager frightened us out of our wits by calling on Kowalski to pinch-hit. [5]The lad is inexperienced but strong as an ox. [6]He came through with flying colors, clouting the first pitch over the centerfield fence.

_____

_____

_____

_____

_____

_____

_____

_____

_____

_____

_____

_____

_____

_____

Review I.1: Composition

Rewrite each paragraph in the space provided, following the instructions below.

Emergency

[1]I am usually careful. [2]Once in a while I do something very foolish. [3]I accidentally locked myself out of my car, for example, last Thursday. [4]It happened in the shopping center. [5]To make matters worse, I had neglected to turn off the motor. [6]The engine was beginning to overheat. [7]I tried to raise the hood. [8]It was locked from the inside. [9]I frantically paced from door to door. [10]I tugged at the handles. [11]I talked to myself.

INSTRUCTIONS FOR FIRST PARAGRAPH

Combine S1 and 2 into a compound sentence.
Combine S3 and 4 into a simple sentence beginning and ending with a prepositional phrase.
Combine S5 and 6 into a compound sentence.
Combine S7 and 8 into a compound sentence.
Find an adverb in S9 and make it the first word. Then combine S9, 10, and 11 into a simple sentence, reducing S10 and 11 to participial phrases.

_____
_____
_____
_____
_____
_____
_____
_____
_____
_____
_____

[12]A shopper saw my predicament. [13]She came over to help. [14]She advised me to call my home. [15]She directed me to the nearest telephone. [16]My brother, fortunately, had not yet left for work. [17]He arrived in ten minutes. [18]He brought my second set of keys. [19]I uttered a sigh of relief. [20]I unlocked the door. [21]I shut off the motor.

Combine S12 and 13 into a simple sentence, reducing S12 to a participial phrase.
Combine S14 and 15 into a simple sentence.
Rearrange S16 to begin with an adverb.
Combine S17 and 18, reducing S18 to a participial phrase.
Reduce S19 to a prepositional phrase and combine it with S20 and 21 into a simple sentence.

_____
_____
_____
_____
_____
_____
_____
_____
_____

[22]I now carry duplicate car keys. [23]I keep them in my wallet.

INSTRUCTIONS FOR FINAL PARAGRAPH

Combine S22 and 23 into a simple sentence, reducing S23 to a prepositional phrase.

_____
_____

Review I.2:   Correct Usage

Each item below offers four different ways of expressing the same idea. Which is the correct way? Write the *letter* of your answer on the line at the left.

_____ 1. (A) Our rolls are sold out and we will have a fresh supply in the morning.
(B) Our rolls are sold out, but we will have a fresh supply in the morning.
(C) Our rolls are sold out, we will have a fresh supply in the morning.
(D) Our rolls are sold out, and we will have a fresh supply in the morning.

_____ 2. (A) The odds were in our favor, however we went down to defeat by a score of 5–4.
(B) The odds were in our favor: however, we went down to defeat by a score of 5–4.
(C) The odds were in our favor, however, we lost by a score of 5–4.
(D) The odds were in our favor; however, we lost, 5–4.

_____ 3. (A) Crowds flocked to the beaches, attracted by the fine weather.
(B) Crowds flocked to the beaches. Attracted by the fine weather.
(C) Crowds flocked to the beaches; attracted by the fine weather.
(D) Crowds flocked to the beaches attracted by the fine whether.

_____ 4. (A) All dresses, selling for $19.95 and up, have been drasticly reduced.
(B) All dresses, selling for $19.95 and up, have been drastically reduced.
(C) All dresses selling for $19.95 and up have been drastically reduced.
(D) All dresses selling for $19.95 and up, have been drasticly reduced.

_____ **5.** (A) The outcome was wholely different from what we had hoped it would be.

　　(B) The outcome was wholely different. From what we had hoped.

　　(C) The outcome was wholly different from what we had hoped it would be.

　　(D) The outcome was wholly different from what we had hoped.

Review I.3:　Vocabulary and Spelling

Each line defines a missing word. Find that word in the list at the bottom of the exercise, complete its spelling, and insert it in the WORD column.

DEFINITION　　　　　　　　　　　　　　　　　　　　WORD

1. released from bondage　　　　　　　　　_____

2. most intense point　　　　　　　　　　　_____

3. felt indignation at　　　　　　　　　　　_____

4. manner of walking　　　　　　　　　　　_____

5. lacking strength or solidity　　　　　　_____

6. destroyed all trace of　　　　　　　　　_____

7. close association　　　　　　　　　　　_____

8. showing sympathy for other humans　　_____

9. picturing beforehand a future event　　_____

10. done in an original manner　　　　　　_____

11. official approval　　　　　　　　　　　_____

12. full, unobstructed view　　　　　　　　_____

13. devoted love　　　　　　　　　　　　　_____

14. burned slightly　　　　　　　　　　　　_____

15. shone with subdued light　　　　　　　_____

16. anything causing continued suffering　_____

17. gave a false and damaging picture of　_____

18. proceeded clumsily　　　　　　　　　　_____

19. tender or loving touch　　　　　　　　　_____

20. criticized harshly　　　　　　　　　　　_____

_ _ ISTENED	CAR _ _ _
ANT _ _ _ PATION	LIB _ _ _ TED
_ _ _ ORAMA	INT _ _ _ CY
FL _ _ _ DERED	_ _ _ MAX
AF _ _ _ CTION	S _ _ GED
ADO _ _ TION	CENS _ _ _ D
ING _ _ _ OUS	H _ _ _ NE
_ _ SENTED	OBLI _ _ _ ATED
AP _ _ _ BATION	_ _ IMSY
G _ _ T	LIB _ _ _ D

Review I.4:   Synonyms and Antonyms

For each italicized word, write a SYNONYM in column A and an ANTONYM in column B. Choose all synonyms and antonyms from the list at the bottom of the exercise.

SYNONYM

Column A

ANTONYM

Column B

Column A		Column B
_____	1. *boring* movie	_____
_____	2. *stale* expression	_____
_____	3. *conceited* person	_____
_____	4. full of *ecstasy*	_____
_____	5. *repulsive* creature	_____
_____	6. *loathed* by everyone	_____
_____	7. *spiritless* applicant	_____
_____	8. *benevolent* treatment	_____
_____	9. knew the *origin*	_____
_____	10. deserved to be *blamed*	_____

anguish	censured	hideous	outcome
appreciated	commended	humane	source
attractive	despised	humble	tedious
barbarous	eager	listless	trite
bliss	exciting	original	vain

Review I.5:   Name-the-Situation Quiz

Each sentence below describes a situation that can be summed up in one word. Select that word from the list below, and insert it in the space provided.

instinct	tranquility	tedium	ingenuity
arbitrariness	libel	hideousness	thaw
hospitality	exposure	admonition	liberation

1. _____ There is peace and quiet on our floor now that the noisy neighbors have moved.

2. _____ During their ordeal on the raft, the survivors had no protection from the sun, wind, and rain.

3. _____ A homeowner came out after the game started and told us to keep off the grass.

4. _____ After calling for a vote, the moderator said my motion was defeated without even bothering to count the hands.

5. _____ At 8:53 the pigeons were released from the coop.

6. _____ Some workers on an assembly line perform the same monotonous operation over and over, day in and day out.

7. _____ With the temperature rising, the lake was closed to skaters for the afternoon.

8. _____ The earthworms turned away from the sun and disappeared underground.

9. _____ One sentence in the article suggests that my candidate belongs in a mental institution.

10. _____ Out-of-town students were lodged with local families who had volunteered as hosts for the weekend.

Review I.6:   Making Writing Concise (Using Fewer Words)

Express the thought of each of the following sentences in no more than four words as in 1, below.

1. We have a dislike for those who are excessively proud of their looks or abilities.
   We dislike vain people.
   _____

2. Avoid using expressions that have been used so much that they have lost their force or freshness.
   _____

3. There are times when every one of us shows no interest or inclination to exert himself or herself.
   _____

4. Residents enjoy surroundings that are free from agitation or disturbances of any kind.
   _____

5. The people who live next door to us show sympathy and consideration not only for other human beings but also for animals.
   _____

6. People who keep inns are at all times friendly and kind to guests and strangers.
   _____

Review I.7:   Analogies

At the left, write the *letter* of the pair of words related to each other in the same way as the words of the capitalized pair.

_____ 1. SOURCE : RIVER

   (A) seed : crop   (D) intermission : play
   (B) contents : book   (E) evening : day
   (C) dessert : dinner

   HINT: A SOURCE is the place where a RIVER begins.

_____ 2. CLIMAX : EVENT

    (A) rung : ladder   (D) departure : journey
    (B) cause : effect   (E) peak : mountain
    (C) rut : road

_____ 3. TRITE : ORIGINALITY

    (A) clever : ingenuity   (D) loyal : patience
    (B) flimsy : solidity   (E) menacing : alarm
    (C) rude : discourtesy

_____ 4. LIKE : ADORE

    (A) demand : ask   (D) admonish : censure
    (B) hate : dislike   (E) burn : singe
    (C) refuse : consent

_____ 5. OBLITERATION : IDENTIFY

    (A) hesitation : delay   (D) expulsion : graduate
    (B) fatigue : recover   (E) listlessness : eager
    (C) thrift : save

_____ 6. LISTLESS : VOLUNTEER

    (A) timid : hesitate   (D) patient : wait
    (B) stubborn : yield   (E) vain : boast
    (C) reasonable : compromise

_____ 7. ADORABLE : ENCHANT

    (A) monotonous : bore   (D) injurious : benefit
    (B) unpleasant : delight   (E) immaculate : repel
    (C) stable : upset

_____ 8. EXPOSURE : PROTECTION

    (A) employment : wages   (D) experience : knowledge
    (B) success : prestige   (E) discouragement : hope
    (C) independence : freedom

_____ 9. HAPPINESS : BLISS

    (A) agony : pain   (D) panic : doubt
    (B) fear : terror   (E) selfishness : generosity
    (C) devotion : obedience

_____ 10. GAIT : WALKING

    (A) snow : skiing   (D) weight : dieting
    (B) lungs : breathing   (E) oar : rowing
    (C) style : writing

    HINT: GAIT is a manner of WALKING.

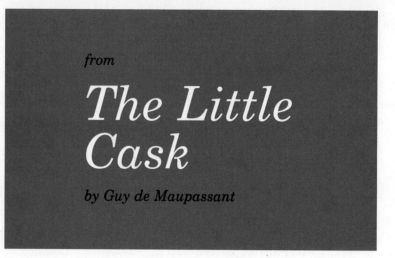

from

The Little Cask

by Guy de Maupassant

*What happens to people who allow the acquisition of property and
money to become the dominant passion of their lives?*

M. Chicot, the innkeeper of Epreville, stopped his cart in front of
the farmhouse of Mother Magloire. He was a jovial fellow, about
forty years old, ruddy and corpulent, and he gave the impression
of being crafty. He hitched his horse to the gatepost and entered
5 the court.

M. Chicot owned property adjoining the old woman's land, and,
for a long time, he had coveted hers. Many times he had tried to
buy it, but Mother Magloire obstinately refused to sell.

"I was born here, and here I shall die," she always said.

10 He found her outside her door paring potatoes. She was sev-
enty-two years old, dried up, lined and bent, but untiring as a
young girl. Chicot gave her a friendly clap on the back and then sat
down on a stool beside her.

"Well, Mother, and how's your health, still fine?"

15 "Not so bad, and yours, Master Prosper?"

"Oh, a few aches; outside of that, pretty fair."

"Well, that's good!"

And she said nothing more. Chicot watched her doing her task.
Her fingers, bent, knotted, hard as crabs' claws, seized the grayish
20 tubercles in one hand like pincers, and quickly turned them around,
paring off long strips of peel with the blade of an old knife which she
held in the other hand. When the potato had become entirely yellow,
she would throw it in a pail of water. Three daring chickens crept
one after the other as far as the hem of her skirts to pick up the par-
25 ings, and then scuttled off, carrying their booty in their beaks.

84

Chicot seemed troubled, hesitating, anxious, as if he had something on his mind that he did not wish to say. Finally he remarked, "Tell me, now, Mother Magloire, this farm of yours—don't you ever want to sell it to me?"

"Certainly not. You can make up your mind on that score. What I have said, I mean, so let's not refer to the matter again."

"All right, only I think I have devised a scheme which we shall both like."

"What is it?"

"Just this: you can sell me the farm and retain it just the same. You don't understand? Just listen to this."

The old woman stopped paring her vegetables and looked at the innkeeper attentively from under her shaggy eyebrows. He continued:

"Let me explain. I shall give you a hundred and fifty francs every month. Do you understand? Every month! I shall bring here in my wagon thirty crowns. And it won't make the least bit of difference to you, not the least! You will stay in your home; you won't trouble yourself with me; you won't do anything for me: you will only take my money. How does that appeal to you?"

He looked at her with a happy, good-natured expression but the old woman glanced back at him with distrust, as if she were searching for some trap.

"It is all right as far as I can see, but," she asked, "you don't think it is going to get the farm for you, do you?"

"Don't you worry about that. You will stay here just as long as God Almighty is willing that you should live. You will stay in your own home, only you will sign a paper before a notary, that, after you are finished with the farm, it will come to me. You have no children—only a few nephews who have scarcely any hold on you. Is that all right for you? You keep your property during your life, and I give you thirty crowns a month. It is all gain for you."

The old woman was still surprised and puzzled, but inclined to accept. She replied:

"I don't say 'no,' but I want to think it over. Come back sometime next week and we will talk it over. I will give you my answer then."

Chicot went away as happy as a king who had just conquered an empire.

Mother Magloire kept thinking about it. She did not sleep that night, and for four days she was in a fever of hesitation. She detected something in the offer which was not to her advantage, but the thought of thirty crowns a month, of all that beautiful jingling money that would come to roll around in her apron pocket, which would fall as if from Heaven, without any effort on her part, filled her with covetousness. Then she went to hunt for a notary and tell him her case. He advised her to accept Chicot's proposition, but to ask for fifty crowns instead of thirty because her farm was worth sixty thousand francs at the lowest estimate.

"If you live fifteen years," the notary said, "in that way he will pay even then only forty-five thousand."

The old woman trembled at the thought of fifty crowns a month,

but she was still suspicious, fearing a thousand unforseen tricks, and she stayed till evening asking questions, unable to make up her mind to leave. Finally she gave the notary instructions to draw
80 up the deed, and went home with her head in a whirl, just as if she had drunk four jugs of new cider.

When Chicot came to get her answer, she took a lot of persuading and declared she could not make up her mind what to do, but all the time she was distracted by the idea that he might not con-
85 sent to give the fifty crowns a month. Finally, when he became insistent, she told him what she wanted for her farm.

He looked surprised and disappointed, and refused. Then, in order to win him over, the old woman began to argue on the probable duration of her life.
90 "I can't have but five or six years more to live. Here I am nearly seventy-three and none too hearty at that. The other evening I thought I was going to die. It seemed to me that my soul was being dragged out of my body and I could scarcely crawl to my bed." But Chicot didn't let himself be taken in.
95 "Come, now," he said, "old woman, you are as solid as a church bell. You will live to be a hundred at least. You will see me buried, I'm sure."

They spent the whole day in discussion, but as the old woman would not give in, the innkeeper finally consented to give her the
100 fifty crowns a month. They signed the deed the next day, and Mother Magloire drew out ten crowns from her wine jug.

Three years rolled by. The old woman lived as if protected by a charm. She seemed not to have aged a day, and Chicot was in despair. It seemed to him that he had been paying this rent for fifty
105 years, and that he had been tricked, cheated, ruined. From time to time he paid a visit to the old farmer woman, as in July we go into the fields to see if the wheat is ripe enough to harvest. She received him with a malicious gleam in her eye. One would say that she was congratulating herself on the good trick she had played on him,
110 and he would quickly get back into his wagon murmuring, "You won't die then, you old brute!"

He didn't know what to do. When he saw her, he wanted to strangle her. He hated her with a ferocious, crafty hatred, with the hatred of a peasant who has been robbed, and he began to think of
115 ways to get rid of her.

Line 3. *ruddy:* having a healthy, reddish color
Line 38. *shaggy:* covered with long, coarse, tangled hair

Exercise 5.1: Close Reading

In the blank space, write the *letter* of the choice that best completes the statement.

1. According to the passage, _____.

   (A) M. Chicot is a generous man
   (B) Mother Magloire has no deception in her heart
   (C) unlike Mother Magloire, Chicot is greedy
   (D) both the innkeeper and the old woman are greedy

2. At the moment that the agreement is signed, _____.

   (A) Chicot believes that Mother Magloire will surely outlive him
   (B) Mother Magloire believes she has only five or six years to live
   (C) Mother Magloire expects to live considerably more than five or six years
   (D) Chicot thinks Mother Magloire will live to be a hundred

3. Of the following statements, the one that does NOT express the speaker's true feelings is _____.

   (A) "It is all right as far as I can see"
   (B) "The other evening I thought I was going to die"
   (C) "You won't die then, you old brute"
   (D) "I was born here, and here I shall die"

4. The passage offers no proof that _____.

   (A) Mother Magloire needs money
   (B) a crown is worth five francs
   (C) Mother Magloire raises chickens
   (D) Chicot drives a horse-drawn wagon

5. Chicot is planning to _____.

   (A) demand the return of his money
   (B) commit murder
   (C) let the agreement run its course
   (D) ask the old woman to release him from their agreement

IMPROVING YOUR COMPOSITION SKILLS: USING ADJECTIVES

If you were to say that "The Little Cask" is about a man and a woman, you would be behaving as if there were no adjectives.

Fortunately, adjectives do exist, and Maupassant has made good use of them. As a result, we know that the story is about

> *a jovial, forty-year-old, ruddy, corpulent, crafty* man

and

> *a seventy-two-year-old, dried-up, lined, bent,* but *untiring* woman.

All of the italicized words above are adjectives. Without adjectives it would be very hard to communicate.

QUESTION A: *What is an adjective?*

(*a*) An **adjective** is a word that modifies (gives more specific information about) a noun or pronoun.

shaggy eyebrows   (adjective *shaggy* modifies noun *eyebrows*)
she was still *suspicious*   (adjective *suspicious* modifies pronoun *she*)

(*b*) An adjective usually answers one of the following questions:

QUESTION	ANSWER
What kind?	*shaggy* eyebrows
Which one?	*this* farm of yours
How much?	a *long* time
How many?	*no* children

(*c*) *Words that are usually nouns are sometimes used as adjectives.*

clean *apron*   (*apron* is a noun)
in her *apron* pocket   (*apron* is an adjective modifying the noun *pocket*)

Exercise 5.2: Recognizing Adjectives

Look back to the passage beginning on page 84 to find the adjectives that modify the following nouns. Write those adjectives in the spaces provided.

SAMPLE:

Line 2   . . . a **jovial** *fellow* . . .

1. Line 12   . . . a _____ *clap* . . .
2. Line 16   . . . a _____ *aches* . . .
3. Line 19   Her *fingers*, _____, _____, _____ as crabs' claws . . .
4. Line 21   . . . _____ *strips* of peel . . .
5. Line 21   . . . an _____ *knife* . . .
6. Line 22   . . . in the _____ *hand.*
7. Line 22   . . . the *potato* had become entirely _____ . . .
8. Line 23   _____ _____ *chickens* . . .
9. Line 26   *Chicot* seemed _____, _____, _____ . . .
10. Line 58   The _____ *woman* was still _____ and _____ . . .

QUESTION B: *In what positions are adjectives used?*

(*a*) The usual position is before the word modified.

shaggy eyebrows
ADJ

ferocious, *crafty* hatred
ADJ ADJ

(*b*) The next most frequent position is in the predicate, after a form of the verb *be* (*is*, *are*, *was*, *were*, etc.) or some other linking verb, such as *become*, *seem*, *look*, *appear*, *taste*, and *sound*.

She was still *suspicious*.
LV ADJ

He looked *surprised* and *disappointed*.
LV ADJ ADJ

(*c*) Occasionally, an adjective comes immediately after the word it modifies. Such adjectives are set off by commas since they interrupt the natural flow of thought.

The hero, *tall*, *dark*, and *handsome*, falls in love with the rancher's daughter.
   ADJ ADJ   ADJ

The swimmer, *exhausted*, collapsed on reaching shore.
     ADJ

Exercise 5.3: Changing the Position of Adjectives

Change the position of the adjectives as required by the column headings. Three positions are possible, but only one is given. Supply the other two.

ADJECTIVE BEFORE NOUN	ADJECTIVE AFTER LINKING VERB	ADJECTIVE AFTER NOUN
Sample:		
The *exhausted* swimmer collapsed on reaching shore.	The swimmer was **exhausted.** He collapsed on reaching shore.	The swimmer, **exhausted,** collapsed on reaching shore.
1. The *furious* customer demanded that her money be refunded.	_____ _____ _____ _____	_____ _____ _____ _____
2. _____ _____ _____	Their defense was *alert* and *stubborn*. It gave us few scoring opportunities.	_____ _____ _____

3. _____ _____ Our protests, *loud* and *per-*
  _____ _____ *sistent*, are beginning to
  _____ bring results.
  _____

4. The *outnumbered* defend- _____ _____
ers cannot hold out much _____ _____
longer. _____ _____
  _____ _____
  _____ _____

5. _____ Your cousin seems *cheerful* _____
  _____ but *pale.* She has obviously _____
  _____ not yet recovered from the
  _____ flu. _____
  _____ _____
  _____

Important. Compare the following:

> (*a*) Sometimes I feel like a *motherless* child.
> (*b*) Sometimes I feel like a child *without a mother.*
> (*c*) Sometimes I feel like a child *who has lost her mother.*

Note that the idea of the adjective *motherless* in sentence *a* can be expressed also through the prepositional phrase *without a mother* in sentence *b*, or the clause *who has lost her mother* in sentence *c*.

QUESTION A: *What is a clause?*

A **clause** is a group of words containing a subject and a verb and forming a part of a sentence. Note that sentence *c* above has two clauses:

> Sometimes *I feel* like a child *who has lost* her mother.
>   S V   S   V

The first clause would be a complete sentence if it stood alone: *Sometimes I feel like a child.* Therefore, it is an **independent clause.**

The second clause—*who has lost her mother*—cannot stand by itself as a sentence; it DEPENDS on the rest of the sentence to complete its meaning. It is a **dependent clause.**

QUESTION B: *What is an adjective clause?*

An **adjective clause** is a clause that does the work of an adjective. In the sentence "Sometimes I feel like a child who has lost her mother," *who has lost her mother* is an adjective clause. Like an adjective, it modifies the noun *child.*

Note that an adjective clause is always a dependent clause; it cannot stand by itself as a sentence.

QUESTION C: *How is an adjective clause introduced?*

The pronouns *who*, *which*, and *that* introduce adjective clauses.

Who refers only to people.
Which refers only to things.
That refers either to people or things.

Sometimes I feel like a child *who* (or *that*) has lost her mother.
These are not the books *which* (or *that*) we ordered.

Note that the pronoun *which* or *that* is sometimes omitted:

These are not the books we ordered.

Exercise 5.4: Using Prepositional Phrases and Adjective Clauses

Express the italicized adjective in column I as a *prepositional phrase* in column II and as an *adjective clause* in column III.

Column I ADJECTIVE	Column II PREPOSITIONAL PHRASE	Column III ADJECTIVE CLAUSE
Samples:		
They gave a *flawless* performance.	They gave a performance **without a flaw.**	They gave a performance **which (or that) had no flaw.**
She is a *wise* woman.	She is a woman **of wisdom.**	She is a woman **who (or that) is wise.**
1. We need an *experienced* coach.		
2. Give me the *end* slice.		
3. A *merciless* foe was at our door.		
4. Do you have an *air-conditioned* room?		

5. This is Chicot, the *Epre- ville* innkeeper.

_____ _____

_____ _____

_____ _____

6. Sue likes *low-heeled* shoes.

_____ _____

_____ _____

_____ _____

7. He is not a *wealthy* man.

_____ _____

_____ _____

_____ _____

8. Is it an *important* rea- son?

_____ _____

_____ _____

_____ _____

9. We are engaged in an *endless* struggle.

_____ _____

_____ _____

_____ _____

10. I chose the *middle* one.

_____ _____

_____ _____

_____ _____

Exercise 5.5: Writing a Composition

Who do you think will win out—the innkeeper, the old woman, or neither?

In a paragraph of about 75 to 100 words, state your prediction and support it with rea- sons. Note (1) that sample paragraph below offers an opinion in its very first sentence, and (2) that all the other sentences present *reasons* to support that opinion.

Suggestion: In your final draft, include an example of (*a*) an adjective that follows the noun it modifies, or (*b*) a prepositional phrase that functions as an adjective.

Sample Paragraph: A Prediction

In my opinion, Mother Magloire will win out. Her health is excellent, and she is enjoying life as never before. M. Chicot, impatient and greedy, is on the verge of a nervous breakdown because he is afraid the old woman will outlive him. The hate he bears her is slowly destroying him. He may think up new schemes to outsmart her, but she will not be caught off guard because she is a woman of caution. His situation looks hopeless.

Your Paragraph: A Prediction

_____
_____
_____
_____
_____
_____
_____
_____
_____

LEARNING NEW WORDS

Line	Word	Meaning	Typical Use
6	**adjoining** (_adj._) ə-ˈjȯin-iŋ	touching or bounding at a point or line; bordering; contiguous; adjacent	The motel offered to accommodate our family in one large room, or in two _adjoining_ rooms with a connecting door.
3	**corpulent** (_adj._) ˈkȯr-pyə-lənt	having a large bulky body; stout; obese; portly	Among the famine victims, even those who had been _corpulent_ looked thin and starved.
		(_ant._ **spare, lean**)	Most youngsters with a _spare_ figure should have no trouble getting through the narrow opening in the fence.
7	**covet** (_v._) ˈkəv-ət	1. enviously desire something belonging to another person; envy	The envious are never content because they _covet_ what others possess.
		2. eagerly wish for	My brother is being promoted to captain, a rank that he has long _coveted._
4	**crafty** (_adj._) ˈkraf-tē	skillful at deceiving others; cunning; sly	The _crafty_ boxer tried to end each round near his own corner so that his foe would lose precious seconds of rest.

32	**devise** (*v.*) 'dē-vīz	form in the mind; invent; concoct; formulate	The town's supervisor *devised* a plan to enable it to meet its expenses without raising taxes.
107	**harvest** (*v.*) 'här-vəst	to gather in, as a crop; reap	If farmers plant turnips in midsummer, they should be able to *harvest* them before the first frost.
2	**jovial** (*adj.*) 'jō-vē-əl	full of good humor; jolly; merry	Since my companions kept telling jokes and laughing heartily, I was in a very *jovial* mood.
108	**malicious** (*adj.*) mə-'lish-əs	feeling or showing *malice* (ill will); spiteful; malevolent	Whenever Curtis was ill or unlucky, it delighted the *malicious* neighbor who had a grudge against him.
8	**obstinately** (*adv.*) 'äb-stə-nət-lē	in an *obstinate* (stubborn) manner; stubbornly; unyieldingly; doggedly (*ant.* **pliably**)	The stranger occupying my seat *obstinately* refused to leave until I returned with the usher. Our opponents thought the weather was threatening, but when we said we were ready to play, they *pliably* acceded to our wishes.
35	**retain** (*v.*) ri-'tān	keep possession of; hold; keep (*ant.* **relinquish**)	The champion must win tonight to retain the title. If elected to Congress, the candidate will have to *relinquish* his post as mayor; he cannot *retain* both positions.

APPLYING WHAT YOU HAVE LEARNED

Exercise 5.6: Sentence Completion

Which of the two choices correctly completes the sentence? Write the *letter* of the correct answer in the space provided.

1. If you retain your position, you may _____.

    A. have to look for another job   B. get a raise in January

2. Some malicious person has just _____ knocked over the trash basket.

    A. accidentally   B. deliberately

3. The king felt _____, since no one coveted his throne.

    A. secure   B. insecure

4. When people devise things, they perform a(an) _____ activity.

    A. underhanded   B. mental

5. The United States and _____ are adjoining nations.

    A. Mexico   B. Argentina

6. She was too crafty to _____.

    A. deceive us   B. disclose her next move

7. He was _____ so much weight that he was becoming corpulent.

    A. gaining   B. losing

8. Farmers usually need extra _____ to harvest their crops.

    A. hands   B. seed

9. A small minority of the strikers obstinately _____ the signing of the contract.

    A. approved   B. opposed

10. Alex would not stop _____, but the rest of us were jovial.

    A. laughing   B. complaining

Exercise 5.7: Making Writing More Concise by Using Fewer Words

Replace the italicized words with a single word from the following list. See 1, below.

devise	retain	adjoining	malicious	obstinately
harvest	jovial	corpulent	covet	crafty

1. Our host was *full of good humor.*   <u>   jovial   </u>

2. You were certainly *showing ill will* when you invented lies about me.   _____

3. Marcie's parents own property *bounding* the Baker estate *at one point.*   _____

4. My clever opponent guessed my plan of attack even before I was able to *form* it *in my mind.*   _____

5. Is it time to *gather in* the crops?   _____

6. Why should anyone *enviously desire* your job?   _____

7. A guard *with a large bulky body* blocked the doorway.   _____

8. Frank was supposed to *keep possession of* the jeep.   _____

9. He had a reputation for being *skillful in deceiving others.*   _____

10. The defenders resisted *in a stubborn manner.*   _____

Exercise 5.8: Using Synonyms and Antonyms

A. Avoid repetition by replacing the italicized word or expression with a SYNONYM from the following list. See 1, below.

harvest	relinquish	lean	adjacent	spiteful
pliable	crafty	devise	gloomy	renounce

1. Several of us gathered at our ailing neighbor's farm to help him *gather in* his crop.   _____ **harvest** _____

2. He may be *skillful at deceiving* others, but he cannot deceive us.   _____

3. They bear no one any malice; they are not *malicious.*   _____

4. I was able to *formulate* a plan, but it is not yet in its final form.   _____

5. If 313 is locked, join us in 315, the *adjoining* room.   _____

B. Complete the sentence by inserting an ANTONYM of the italicized word from the above list. See 6, below.

6. The prince who used to *covet* the throne is now ready to _____ that ambition.   _____ **renounce** _____

7. Yesterday you were *jovial;* today you are _____.   _____

8. The *corpulent* comedian looked disapprovingly at his companion's _____ figure.   _____

9. We may *retain* some gains, but we may have to _____ others.   _____

10. Our opponents were *obstinate* at first, refusing to make concessions, but they eventually became _____.   _____

Exercise 5.9: Name-the-Person Quiz

Read all the statements in the boxes. Then enter the required names in sentences 1 to 10, below.

Gail was seen tearing down her opponent's campaign posters.	Catherine realized that Morris was interested in her only for her money.	Stella returned George's presents but kept his letters.

Henry insisted on having his own way and refused to compromise.	Leaving Maria in the bank, Joe went next door to the bakery while Agnes telephoned from the pharmacy across the street.

The *Monitor,* the first armored ship with a revolving gun turret, was designed by inventor John Ericsson.	Marty paid the grower for the privilege of picking his own berries from the field.

> Alan looked as if he had poor cards; in reality, he held four aces.

> As his waistline kept expanding, Mr. Green made frequent trips to the tailor for alterations.

> Carmelita wore a big smile and entertained the guests with witty remarks all through the evening.

1. _____ was in a jovial mood.
2. _____ coveted wealth.
3. _____ was growing corpulent.
4. _____ behaved obstinately.
5. _____ and _____ were in adjoining places.
6. _____ devised something of great importance.
7. _____ was malicious.
8. _____ did some harvesting.
9. _____ retained something.
10. _____ was crafty.

LEARNING SOME DERIVATIVES

Each capitalized word below is a *root*. The words under it are its *derivatives*.

ADJOIN (*v.*)	Maine *adjoins* New Hampshire.
adjoining (*adj.*)	Maine and New Hampshire are *adjoining* states.
CORPULENT (*adj.*)	If Falstaff were to lose a hundred pounds, he would still seem *corpulent*.
corpulence (*n.*)	No Shakespearean character surpasses Falstaff in *corpulence*.
COVET (*v.*)	Many nations *covet* America's power.
covetous (*adj.*)	They are *covetous* of her natural resources.
covetously (*adv.*)	They eye her industrial output *covetously*.
covetousness (*n.*)	America's standard of living excites their *covetousness*.
CRAFTY (*adj.*)	Your rival is known to be *crafty*.
craftily (*adv.*)	His offer to help may be part of a *craftily* devised scheme.
craftiness (*n.*)	He has a reputation for *craftiness*.

HARVEST (*n.*)	Fortunately, the storm struck two weeks after the peak of the *harvest*.
harvest (*v.*)	By that time practically the entire crop had been *harvested*.
JOVIAL (*adj.*)	The employer was in a *jovial* mood at the luncheon.
joviality (*n.*)	Her employees shared her *joviality* because they had received bonuses.
jovially (*adv.*)	At parting, they *jovially* wished each other a happy holiday.
MALICE (*n.*)	When Lola recommended me, she did it out of *malice*.
malicious (*adj.*)	She was being *malicious* when she said I could do a better job.
maliciously (*adv.*)	She *maliciously* wanted to see me burdened with the extra typing.
OBSTINATE (*adj.*)	Everyone voted to postpone the trip except Carole; she was *obstinate*.
obstinately (*adv.*)	She *obstinately* insisted on going, in spite of the weather.
obstinacy (*n.*)	We did not give in to her *obstinacy*.
RETAIN (*v.*)	Most temporary employees were dismissed, but two were *retained*.
retention (*n.*)	Maria and Ernest had been recommended for *retention* because of their fine work.

Exercise 5.10:   Using Roots and Derivatives

Fill each blank with the above root or derivative that best fits the meaning of the sentence.

1. Eric pretended illness so _____ that everyone felt sorry for him.

2. Melons are now plentiful because the _____ has been good.

3. During the night, someone _____ overturned garbage cans that had been put out for collection.

4. Some people with emotional problems tend to overeat, and this in turn may result in _____.

5. Alice wishes she could have a coat like mine, and when I wear it she is filled with _____.

6. The legislature wants to abolish the sales tax, but the governor favors its _____.

7. On the right, we are next to our old neighbors, the Browns, and on the left we _____ the Johnsons, who have just moved in.

8. Grandpa was in a jolly mood; he greeted everyone _____.

9. There would have been no quarrel if not for Andy's _____; he wanted to sit next to the window, as usual.

10. My partner is not spiteful; he has no _____ against anyone.

Exercise 5.11: Analogies

At the left, write the *letter* of the pair of words related to each other in the same way as the words of the capitalized pair.

_____ 1. CONCOCT : DEVISE

    (A) retain : relinquish   (B) expose : cover
    (C) harvest : reap   (D) admonish : commend
    (E) thaw : freeze

_____ 2. OBSTINATE : PLIABLE

    (A) malicious : spiteful   (B) barbarous : humane
    (C) conceited : vain   (D) resourceful : clever
    (E) ecstatic : blissful

_____ 3. TRITE : FRESHNESS

    (A) authorized : approval   (B) tedious : boredom
    (C) hideous : ugliness   (D) flimsy : solidity
    (E) libelous : defamation

_____ 4. COVETOUS : ENVY

    (A) inventive : ingenuity   (B) tranquil : agitation
    (C) arbitrary : democracy   (D) malevolent : good will
    (E) inhospitable : friendliness

_____ 5. SINGE : BURN

    (A) crush : suppress   (B) slam : strike
    (C) devour : eat   (D) obliterate : destroy
    (E) moisten : wet

SPELLING REVIEW: TURNING NOUNS INTO ADJECTIVES

A. You can change some nouns to adjectives by **dropping a suffix.**

1. *Dropping -NESS*

NOUN	–	SUFFIX	=	ADJECTIVE
covetousness	–	ness	=	covetous
ripeness	–	ness	=	ripe
happiness	–	ness	=	happy

2. *Dropping -ITY*

joviality	–	ity	=	jovial
insanity	–	ity	=	insane

B. You can change some nouns to adjectives by **adding a suffix.**

1. *Adding -FUL*

NOUN	+	SUFFIX	=	ADJECTIVE
beauty	+	ful	=	beautiful
care	+	ful	=	careful

2. *Adding -LESS*

care	+	less	=	careless
pity	+	less	=	pitiless

3. *Adding -OUS*

peril	+	ous	=	perilous
victory	+	ous	=	victorious

4. *Adding -Y*

health	+	y	=	healthy
ice	+	y	=	icy
onion	+	y	=	oniony

C. You can change some nouns to adjectives by **changing a suffix.**

1. *Changing -ANCE or -ANCY to -ANT*

NOUN		ADJECTIVE
abundance	→	abundant
vacancy	→	vacant

2. *Changing -ENCE or -ENCY to -ENT*

corpulence	→	corpulent
urgency	→	urgent

D. Note the spelling irregularities of the following:

awe + ful = awful (silent *e* dropped even though suffix begins with a consonant)

joy + ful = joyful
joy + less = joyless } (*y* does not become *i*)

malice + ous = malicious (after *c*, *e* changes to *i* before *-ous*)

garlic + y = garlicky (*k* inserted before *-y*)

fog + y = foggy
mud + y = muddy } (final consonant doubled before a suffix)

Exercise 5.12: Turning Nouns into Adjectives

Part 1. Complete the following, as in 1, below:

NOUN	ADJECTIVE	NOUN	ADJECTIVE
1. importance	**important**	11. wealth	
2. mud		12. garlic	
3. friendliness		13. success	
4. danger		14. fog	
5. glory		15. urgency	
6. insistence		16. joviality	
7. silver		17. penny	
8. malice		18. truancy	
9. awe		19. juice	
10. solidity		20. hesitancy	

Part 2. From each noun, form (*a*) a -FUL adjective and (*b*) a -LESS adjective.

NOUN	-FUL ADJECTIVE	-LESS ADJECTIVE
color	**colorful**	**colorless**
1. pain		
2. mercy		
3. fruit		
4. power		
5. shame		
6. harm		
7. use		
8. flavor		
9. pity		
10. hope		

Part 3. Turn these adjectives into nouns.

ADJECTIVE	NOUN	ADJECTIVE	NOUN
1. odorous		5. muddy	
2. affluent		6. joyous	
3. insane		7. extravagant	
4. plentiful		8. hard	

9. spicy	_____	**15.** negligent	_____
10. valueless	_____	**16.** awful	_____
11. poisonous	_____	**17.** self-reliant	_____
12. vacant	_____	**18.** ignorant	_____
13. watery	_____	**19.** foggy	_____
14. malicious	_____	**20.** corpulent	_____

USING ADJECTIVES EFFECTIVELY

Compare *A* and *B:*

   (A) He felt *a sense of inferiority.*
   (B) He felt *inferior.*

The adjective *inferior* in *B* does the work of four words in *A: a sense of inferiority.* As a result, *B* is briefer, more direct, and more effective.

   Compare *C* and *D:*

   (C) We are pursuing a course *that is full of peril.*
   (D) We are pursuing a *perilous* course.

The adjective *perilous* replaces *that is full of peril* (five words), making *D* preferable.

Exercise 5.13:   Concise Writing

Rewrite the sentence, replacing the italicized words with an adjective.

1. Your fingers are *as cold as ice.*

_____

2. He usually comes in with a breath *that smells of garlic.*

_____

3. At the moment, I am *without power to do anything.*

_____

4. When Marie sees your Honor Society pin, she will be *filled with covetousness.*

_____

5. These pears are ripe and *full of flavor.*

_____

6. We sailed beneath a moon *that shone like silver.*

_____

7. Before the test I felt *a sense of insecurity*.

_____

8. They met with foes *that showed no mercy*.

_____

9. The dentist assured me that the drilling would be *free of pain*.

_____

10. Do you like soups *that have the flavor of onions?*

_____

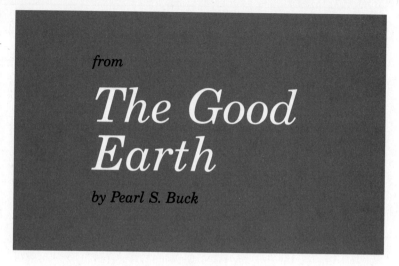

from

The Good Earth

by Pearl S. Buck

In the past Wang Lung, through hard labor and wise management, has been able to grow more than enough food for his family. But now there is famine in the land, and there is nothing to eat.

The extreme gnawing in his stomach which he had had at first was now past and he could stir up a little of the earth from a certain spot in one of his fields and give it to the children without desiring any of it for himself. This earth they had been eating
5 in water for some days—goddess of mercy earth, it was called, because it had some slight nutritious quality in it, although in the end it could not sustain life. But made into a gruel it allayed the children's craving for a time and put something into their distended, empty bellies. He steadfastly would not touch the few
10 beans that O-lan still held in her hand, and it comforted him vaguely to hear her crunching them, one at a time, a long time apart.

And then, as he sat there in the doorway, giving up his hope and thinking with a dreamy pleasure of lying upon his bed and sleep-
15 ing easily into death, someone came across the fields—men walking toward him. He continued to sit as they drew near and he saw that one was his uncle and with him were three men whom he did not know.

"I have not seen you these many days," called his uncle with loud
20 and affected good humor. And as he drew nearer he said in the same loud voice, "And how well you have fared! And your father, my elder brother, he is well?"

Wang Lung looked at his uncle. The man was thin, it is true, but not starved, as he should be. Wang Lung felt in his own shriveled

body the last remaining strength of life gathering into a devastat- 25
ing anger against this man, his uncle.

"How you have eaten—how you have eaten!" he muttered
thickly. He thought nothing of these strangers or of any courtesy.
He saw only his uncle with flesh on his bones, still. His uncle
opened wide his eyes and threw up his hands to the sky. 30

"Eaten!" he cried. "If you could see my house! Not a sparrow even
could pick up a crumb there. My wife—do you remember how fat
she was? How fair and fat and oily her skin? And now she is like a
garment hung on a pole—nothing but the poor bones rattling
together in her skin. And of our children only four are left—the 35
three little ones gone—gone—and as for me, you see me!" He took
the edge of his sleeve and wiped the corner of each eye carefully.

"You have eaten," repeated Wang Lung dully.

"I have thought of nothing but of you and of your father, who is
my brother," retorted his uncle briskly, "and now I prove it to you. 40
As soon as I could, I borrowed from these good men in the town a
little food on the promise that with the strength it gave me I would
help them to buy some of the land about our village. And then I
thought of your good land first of all, you, the son of my brother.
They have come to buy your land and to give you money—food— 45
life!" His uncle, having said these words, stepped back and folded
his arms with a flourish of his dirty and ragged robes.

Wang Lung did not move. He did not rise nor in any way recognize the men who had come. But he lifted his head to look at them
and he saw that they were indeed men from the town, dressed in 50
long robes of soiled silk. Their hands were soft and their nails long.
They looked as though they had eaten and blood still ran rapidly
in their veins. He suddenly hated them with an immense hatred.
Here were these men from the town, having eaten and drunk,
standing beside him whose children were starving and eating the 55
very earth of the fields; here they were, come to squeeze his land
from him in his extremity. He looked up at them sullenly, his eyes
deep and enormous in his bony, skull-like face.

"I will not sell my land," he said.

His uncle stepped forward. At this instant the younger of Wang 60
Lung's two sons came creeping to the doorway upon his hands and
knees. Since he had so little strength in these latter days the child
at times had gone back to crawling as he used in his babyhood.

"Is that your lad?" cried the uncle, "the little fat lad I gave a
copper to in the summer?" 65

And they all looked at the child and suddenly Wang Lung, who
through all this time had not wept at all, began to weep silently,
the tears gathering in great knots of pain in his throat and rolling
down his cheeks.

"What is your price?" he whispered at last. Well, there were 70
these three children to be fed—the children and the old man. He
and his wife could dig themselves graves in the land and lie down
in them and sleep. Well, but here were these.

And then one of the men from the city spoke, a man with one eye
blind and sunken in his face, and unctuously he said, 75

"My poor man, we will give you a better price than could be got in these times anywhere for the sake of the boy who is starving. We will give you . . ." he paused and then said harshly, "we will give you a string of a hundred pence for an acre!"

80 Wang Lung laughed bitterly. "Why, that," he cried, "that is taking my land for a gift. Why, I pay twenty times that when I buy land!"

"Ah, but not when you buy it from men who are starving," said the other man from the city. He was a small, slight fellow with a 85 high thin nose, but his voice came out of him unexpectedly large and coarse and hard.

Wang Lung looked at the three of them. They were sure of him, these men! What will not a man give for his starving children and his old father! The weakness of surrender in him melted into an 90 anger such as he had never known in his life before. He sprang up at the men as a dog springs at an enemy.

"I shall never sell the land!" he shrieked at them. "Bit by bit I will dig up the fields and feed the earth itself to the children and when they die I will bury them in the land, and I and my wife and 95 my old father, even he, we will die on the land that has given us birth!"

He was weeping violently and his anger went out of him as suddenly as a wind and he stood shaking and weeping. The men stood there smiling slightly, his uncle among them, unmoved. This talk 100 was madness and they waited until Wang's anger was spent.

And then suddenly O-lan came to the door and spoke to them, her voice flat and commonplace as though every day such things were.

"The land we will not sell, surely," she said, "else when we return 105 from the south we shall have nothing to feed us. But we will sell the table and the two beds and the bedding and the four benches and even the cauldron from the stove. But the rakes and the hoe and the plow we will not sell, nor the land."

There was some calmness in her voice which carried more 110 strength than all Wang Lung's anger, and Wang Lung's uncle said uncertainly, "Will you really go south?"

At last the one-eyed man spoke to the others and they muttered among themselves and the one-eyed man turned and said,

"They are poor things and fit only for fuel. Two silver bits for the 115 lot and take it or leave it."

He turned away with contempt as he spoke, but O-lan answered tranquilly.

"It is less than the cost of one bed, but if you have the silver give it to me quickly and take the things."

120 The one-eyed man fumbled in his girdle and dropped into her outstretched hand the silver and the three men came into the house and between them they took out the table and the benches and the bed in Wang Lung's room first with its bedding, and they wrenched the cauldron from the earthen oven in which it stood. 125 But when they went into the old man's room Wang Lung's uncle stood outside. He did not wish his older brother to see him, nor did

he wish to be there when the old man was laid on the floor and the bed taken from under him. When all was finished and the house was wholly empty except for the two rakes and the two hoes and the plow in one corner of the middle room, O-lan said to her hus- 130 band.

"Let us go while we have the two bits of silver and before we must sell the rafters of the house and have no hole into which we can crawl when we return."

And Wang Lung answered heavily, "Let us go." 135

But he looked across the fields at the small figures of the men receding and he muttered over and over, "At least I have the land— I have the land."

Line 8. *distended:* swollen; bloated

UNDERSTANDING THE SELECTION

Exercise 6.1:   Close Reading

In the blank space, write the *letter* of the choice that best completes the statement or answers the question.

1. Wang Lung's uncle _____.

    (A) says that he has not eaten
    (B) is still fat
    (C) has been able to get food
    (D) looks starved

2. Which of the following statements about the city men is untrue? _____

    (A) They are well fed.
    (B) They are not neat.
    (C) They want to profit from the suffering of others.
    (D) They do not want to buy anything but land.

3. The adjective that best describes O-lan, as she is portrayed in the passage, is _____.

    (A) realistic
    (B) pessimistic
    (C) emotional
    (D) unconcerned

4. The passage suggests that _____.

    (A) Wang Lung would not have sold his land under any circumstances
    (B) the one-eyed man is the spokesman for the men from the city
    (C) O-lan is getting no nourishment whatsoever
    (D) goddess-of-mercy earth can keep a person from starving to death

5. The person whom the uncle seems to fear most is _____.

(A) his wife
(B) his older brother
(C) Wang Lung
(D) the one-eyed man

IMPROVING YOUR COMPOSITION SKILLS: USING ADJECTIVE CLAUSES

1. *The Adjective Clause as a Tool for Combining Sentences*

When you look over the first draft of something that you have written, you will often find it desirable to combine two sentences with the help of an adjective clause.

Pearl Buck, in describing O-lan, did *not* write:

> There was some calmness in her voice. This calmness carried more strength than all Wang Lung's anger.

She wrote:

> "There was some calmness in her voice *which carried more strength than all Wang Lung's anger.*"

By using the adjective clause "which . . . anger," the author was able to express the two thoughts in a single forceful sentence.

2. *Who, whom, and whose in Adjective Clauses*

Who is used as a subject.

> "Ah, but not when you buy it from men *who* are starving . . ."

(*who* is the subject of the verb *are starving*)

Whom is used

(*a*) as an object of a verb.

> ". . . with him [his uncle] were three men *whom* he did not know."

(*whom* is the object of the verb *did know;* the subject of *did know* is *he*)

(*b*) as an object of a preposition.

> The uncle could hardly recognize the lad to *whom* he had given a coin last summer.

(*whom* is the object of the preposition *to*)

Whose indicates ownership.

> "Here were these men from the town, having eaten and drunk, standing beside him *whose* children were starving . . ."

(*whose*—literally, "of whom"—shows to whom the children belong)

Exercise 6.2: Using An Adjective Clause to Combine Two Sentences

Combine the two sentences by changing one of them to an adjective clause introduced by *who*, *whom*, *whose*, *which*, or *that*. Study the following samples:

Denise surprised me with a birthday cake. She had baked the cake herself.

Denise surprised me with a birthday cake **that (or which) she had baked herself.**

The infant is being cared for by relatives. His parents were injured in an automobile accident.

The infant, **whose parents were injured in an automobile accident**, is being cared for by relatives.

1. At the scene she talked to a bystander. The bystander had witnessed the accident.

_____

_____

2. Finally we succeeded in finding the driver. His car was blocking our driveway.

_____

_____

3. The article discusses two threats to our environment. These threats up to now have received little notice.

_____

_____

_____

4. Waiting for you to come down, I spoke to your neighbor. Her dog had just bitten a passerby.

_____

_____

_____

5. An off-duty police officer gave chase to the two suspects. The officer was in civilian clothes at the time.

_____

_____

_____

6. Angela and Horace will be here tonight. You met them at the last dance.

_____

_____

7. Apparently the investigators have new information about the case. They cannot make this information public at present.

_____

_____

_____

8. He steadfastly would not touch the few beans. O-lan still held these few beans in her hand.

_____

_____

_____

9. Luckily, Dr. Cortesi will be back from vacation tomorrow. My parents have a great deal of confidence in her.

_____

_____

_____

10. Just before retiring, my brother thought he smelled smoke. My brother sleeps in an upstairs bedroom.

_____

_____

_____

Exercise 6.3: Using an Adjective Clause to Combine Three Sentences

Combine each set of three sentences by changing *two* of them as directed.

SAMPLE: Wang Lung is a farmer.
He lives in China.   [adjective clause]
He has a wife and three children.   [prepositional phrase]

Wang Lung is a farmer who lives in China with his wife and three children.

Note that the second sentence has been changed to an adjective clause (*who lives in China*) and the third to a prepositional phrase (*with his wife and three children*).

SAMPLE: He sprang to his feet.   [participial phrase]
He shrieked at the men.
They wanted to rob him of his land.   [adjective clause]

Springing to his feet, he shrieked at the men who wanted to rob him of his land.

The first sentence has been changed to a participial phrase (*Springing to his feet*) and the third to an adjective clause (*who wanted to rob him of his land*).

1. O-lan is a sensible woman.
   She can deal with the strangers.   [adjective clause]
   She does not lose her temper.   [prepositional phrase]

   _____

   _____

   _____

2. She borrowed my scraper.   [participial phrase]
   She removed the thin layer of ice.
   It had formed on her windshield.   [adjective clause]

   _____

   _____

   _____

3. He realized he had missed the bus.   [participial phrase]
   He hailed a cab.
   It had just discharged a passenger.   [adjective clause]

   _____

   _____

   _____

4. Erica can get us the refreshments.
   Her father is in the food business.   [adjective clause]
   She can get them at wholesale prices.   [prepositional phrase]

   _____

   _____

   _____

5. I took my father's car.   [participial phrase]
   I went to pick up my brother.
   He had just telephoned from the station.   [adjective clause]

   _____

   _____

   _____

6. New York City is a tourist attraction.
   It draws millions of visitors.   [adjective clause]
   They come from all parts of the world.   [prepositional phrase]

   _____

   _____

   _____

7. My cousin Roger is staying with us.
You do not know him.   [adjective clause]
He is coming for the Thankgiving weekend.   [prepositional phrase]

_____

_____

_____

8. Chicot was an innkeeper.
His heart was set on a piece of property.   [adjective clause]
It belonged to an elderly woman.   [participial phrase]

_____

_____

_____

9. We were attracted by the sound of music.   [participial phrase]
We came out to watch the marchers.
They were parading up the avenue.   [adjective clause]

_____

_____

_____

10. The Parkside Inn is a popular restaurant.
It serves anything from a snack to a complete meal.   [adjective clause]
It is open from noon to midnight.   [prepositional phrase]

_____

_____

_____

Exercise 6.4:   Writing a Composition

In a paragraph of about five or six sentences, describe a noteworthy event that took place in or out of class. Briefly explain what happened, where and when it happened, who was involved, and why the event was noteworthy. Here are some further hints for making your paragraph effective:

1. Include at least two adjective clauses.
2. Begin at least one sentence with a participial phrase.
3. Begin at least one sentence with a prepositional phrase.
4. End the paragraph with a short simple sentence.

Study the following:

Sample Paragraph: An Unusual Happening

[1]Arlene, who sits next to me in my English class, made an excellent report yesterday. [2]Accompanied on the guitar by my friend Steven, she sang several ballads about life in nineteenth-century America. [3]Before the lesson, she distributed the words of "Sweet Betsy From Pike," "The Erie Canal," "John Henry," and other ballads that she had photocopied. [4]With the words before us, we were able to sing along with Arlene. [5]We had a wonderful time.

ANALYSIS: There is an adjective clause in S1 (*who . . . class*) and another in S3 (*that . . .*). S2 begins with a participial phrase (*Accompanied . . . Steven*). S3 begins with a prepositional phrase (*Before . . . lesson*), as does S4 (*With . . . us*). S5 is a short simple sentence.

Your Paragraph: An Unusual Happening

_____

_____

_____

_____

_____

_____

_____

LEARNING NEW WORDS

Line	Word	Meaning	Typical Use
20	**affected** (*adj*) ə-ˈfekt-əd	not natural or genuine; falsely assumed; pretended	I can assure you her tears were real, not *affected;* she is no hypocrite.
7	**allay** (*v.*) ə-ˈlā	make less severe; calm; relieve; alleviate	Before the test papers were distributed, I was afraid of failing, but a quick look at the questions *allayed* my fears.
	(*ant.* **intensify**)		My fears would have been *intensified* if the test had involved topics that I had not studied.

8	**craving** (*n.*) 'krā-viŋ	great desire or longing; yearning (as for food, drink, etc.)	To rid yourself of excess weight, you must overcome your *craving* for sweets.
1	**extreme** (*adj.*) ik-'strēm	very great or greatest; utmost; excessive	A dentist usually anesthetizes a sensitive tooth before drilling; otherwise, the patient may suffer *extreme* pain.
1	**gnawing** (*n.*) 'nȯ-iŋ	persistent pain, esp. in the stomach, resembling that caused by teeth that *gnaw* (bite away bit by bit); pang	A *gnawing* in a person's stomach may be caused by a lack of food or by a guilty conscience.
6	**nutritious** (*adj.*) nu̇-'trish-əs	of value as food; providing nourishment; nourishing	Milk is far more *nutritious* than soda.
137	**recede** (*v.*) ri-'sēd	move back or away; withdraw; become more distant (*ant.* **advance**)	It is relaxing to lie on the beach and to watch the waves *advancing* and *receding*.
24	**shrivel** (*v.*) 'shriv-əl	shrink and become or make wrinkled; wither	Bodies may *shrivel* from famine, disease, or old age.
57	**sullenly** (*adv.*) 'səl-ən-lē	in a *sullen* (resentfully silent) manner; resentfully; gloomily (*ant.* **cheerfully**)	Feeling that he had been unjustly criticized, the students sat *sullenly* through the rest of the discussion, making no further contributions. If he had received a compliment, he would, of course, have *cheerfully* continued to participate.
7	**sustain** (*v.*) sə-'stān	give support or relief to; supply with *sustenance* (food); nourish; support	An airlift of food and supplies *sustained* the beleaguered inhabitants until the siege was lifted.

APPLYING WHAT YOU HAVE LEARNED

Exercise 6.5: Sentence Completion

Which of the two choices makes the sentence correct? Write the *letter* of the correct answer in the space provided.

1. As people or objects recede, they appear ____.

   A. larger   B. smaller

2. The ____ in ticket sales has allayed our financial worries.

   A. lag   B. spurt

3. Something I had said or done must have ____ you, since you greeted me sullenly.

   A. displeased   B. pleased

4. A ____ for a first speeding offense is not an extreme punishment.

   A. year in jail   B. $100 fine

5. Since you have a nutritious diet, you cannot be called ____.

   A. undernourished   B. overweight

6. The once plump body was now as shriveled as a ____.

   A. prune   B. plum

7. The host's affected friendliness convinced us that we ____.

   A. would not be unwelcome   B. ought not to stay long

8. ____ regions sustain life.

   A. Fertile   B. Desert

9. Gnawing is usually associated with ____ stomach.

   A. a full   B. an empty

10. ____ expresses a craving for one's homeland.

    A. "Oh, to be in England,
       Now that April's there."
          —Robert Browning's "Home Thoughts From Abroad"

    B. "I wish I may never hear of the United States again!"
          —Edward Everett Hale's "The Man Without a Country"

Exercise 6.6: Using Synonyms and Antonyms

A. Avoid repetition by replacing the italicized word or expression with a SYNONYM from the following list.

moderate	advance	pang	nourishing	wither
sustain	cheerful	genuine	intensify	craving

1. Oh! how we yearned for a cool refreshing drink; we would
   have given anything to satisfy that *yearning*.   _____

2. Fruits and vegetables are much more *nutritious* than
   potato chips, which have little nutritional value.   _____

3. Like the gnawings of hunger, the *gnawings* of conscience
are painful and persistent.   _____s

4. The shriveling leaves sprang to life after the rain; without the rain they would have continued to *shrivel*.   _____

5. At 21, instead of working to support themselves, they
expected their parents would continue to *support* them.   _____

    B. Complete the sentence by inserting an ANTONYM of the italicized word from the
above list.

6. Raymonde, who is usually _____ and sociable,
remained *sullen* throughout the evening.   _____

7. Many expected stock prices to *recede* after their sharp
gains, but they continued to _____.   _____

8. It was hard to tell whether the regrets expressed by some
neighbors at our moving were _____ or *affected*.   _____

9. A few senators who had been *extreme* in their opposition
to the bill gradually assumed a more _____ attitude.   _____

10. Adults who seek to *allay* a child's fears must be tactful;
otherwise, they may _____ those fears.   _____

Exercise 6.7: Name-the-Person Quiz

Read all the statements in the boxes. Then enter the required names in sentences 1
to 10, below.

When Valerie said "Hi," Stella just stared at her.	Loretta can hardly believe that her yearning for ice cream is a thing of the past.

You wouldn't recognize Lenny; his face is lined, and he has lost nearly thirty pounds.

Barry who used to play leading roles, is now lucky if he gets a small part.

Willa pretended to feel very sorry when her sister Gail's applications for admission to college were turned down.

Alfredo thought he had broken his nose, but the X-rays showed no fracture.

Lucille would never have become a nurse if her brother had not helped with the tuition.

Elton gave up his hunger strike when the pangs became unbearable.

Like you, Harriet failed the quiz, but she did not decide for that reason to become a school dropout.

For breakfast, Terry ordered Danish pastry and black coffee, Nat had an orange and a bowl of oatmeal, and Alison asked for jelly doughnuts and tea.

1. _____ seemed to know what is most nutritious.
2. _____ received affected sympathy.
3. _____ reacted sullenly.
4. _____'s fears were allayed.
5. _____ was sustained.
6. _____ overcame a craving.
7. _____ has receded from the limelight.
8. _____ avoided an extreme course of action.
9. _____ experienced gnawing.
10. _____ has shriveled.

Exercise 6.8:   Concise Writing (Using Fewer Words)

Replace the italicized words in each sentence below with a single word from the following list.

affected	wither	utmost	sullen	sustain
gnawing	yearning	withdraw	alleviate	nourishing

1. I greeted them, but they remained *resentfully* silent. _____
2. Chewing gum is not *of value as food.* _____
3. At times she speaks with a(an) *falsely assumed* Boston accent. _____
4. As the clouds *move away,* the sun will reappear. _____
5. The strong sun caused the fallen leaves to *shrink and become wrinkled.* _____
6. Shirley has a(an) *great desire* for popularity. _____
7. Randy complained of a(an) *persistent pain* in his stomach. _____
8. Can't you say something to *make* our doubts *less severe?* _____
9. We must *give support to* the flood victims until the emergency is over. _____
10. She mixed the ingredients with *very great* care. _____

Each capitalized word below is a *root*. The words under it are its *derivatives*.

AFFECT (*v.*)	Arnold, who has studied acting, can *affect* a British accent.
affected (*adj.*)	His *affected* speech can make strangers think that he is British.
affectation (*n.*)	After achieving the desired effect, he drops the *affectation* and talks like you and me.
CRAVE (*v.*)	To quit smoking is not easy, for you must give up what you *crave*.
craving (*n.*)	But millions of others have overcome their *craving* for cigarettes.
EXTREME (*adj.*)	Even if you are very calm, you may in a moment of anger do something *extreme*, like punching your opponent.
extreme (*n.*)	In a moment, violent anger can make you go from one *extreme* to the other.
extremely (*adv.*)	If you strike someone, it is a sign that you are *extremely* upset.
extremity (*n.*)	Do not resort to such a violent *extremity;* try to remain calm.
extremist (*adj.*)	Most taxpayers would like to see taxes lowered; few take the *extremist* position of wanting to abolish them altogether.
GNAW (*v.*)	With their sharp teeth, rodents can *gnaw* through wood.
gnawing (*n.*)	A guilty person may feel the *gnawings* of conscience.
NUTRIENT (*n.*)	Among the *nutrients* that our bodies need are protein, calcium, iron, and vitamins.
nutriment (*n.*)	You can get more *nutriment* from whole wheat bread than from white bread.
nutritious (*adj.*)	Whole wheat bread is more *nutritious.*
nutritiously (*adv.*)	Everyone can benefit from *nutritiously* planned meals.
nutrition (*n.*)	If you have studied *nutrition*, you know that fresh foods are usually more nourishing than canned or frozen ones.
nutritionist (*n.*)	The patients' meals are planned by a *nutritionist.*
RECEDE (*v.*)	The hairline in males usually *recedes* as baldness begins to set in.
recess (*n.*)	A *recess*, or "coffee break," allows you to withdraw from your work for a brief period of relaxation.
recession (*n.*)	In a *recession*, there is a slowdown in business, and many people lose their jobs.
recessive (*adj.*)	Since we are trying to improve foreign trade, an increased tax on imports at this time would be a *recessive* move.

SHRIVEL (*v.*)	Have you ever watched paper *shrivel* in a fire?
shriveled (*adj.*)	The wind scattered the *shriveled* leaves.
SULLEN (*adj.*)	The *sullen* child made no reply to any of our questions.
sullenly (*adv.*)	His lips remained *sullenly* sealed.
sullenness (*n.*)	Since he did not utter a word, we could not learn the cause of his *sullenness*.
SUSTAIN (*v.*)	Our government, in time of recession, tries to *sustain* the families of the unemployed.
sustainable (*adj.*)	Unemployment of 10% or more of the work force would not be *sustainable* for a long period.
sustenance (*n.*)	One of the forms of *sustenance* provided to the jobless is unemployment insurance.

Exercise 6.9:   Using Roots and Derivatives

Fill each blank with the above root or derivative that best fits the meaning of the sentence.

1. If everyone were to take a(an) _____ at the same time, the work in the shop would come to a standstill.

2. Please leave. There is nothing that I _____ more than to be left alone.

3. _____ is the science dealing with the nourishment of living beings.

4. Ruth resented my ignoring her at the dance, and that, I learned, was the reason for her _____.

5. Josefina can entertain us with her impersonations of several celebrities; she knows how to _____ their manner of speaking.

6. Newsphotos from the drought area show relief supplies being distributed to the _____ but grateful survivors.

7. During a(an) _____, there is usually an increase in the number of bankruptcies.

8. When the ground is frozen, squirrels sometimes _____ the bark of trees.

9. Unless sales improve, we may be driven to the _____ of going out of business.

10. I can carry quite a few books, but George tried to burden me with a load that was not _____.

SPELLING REVIEW: TURNING VERBS INTO ADJECTIVES

Increase your store of adjectives by getting some of them from verbs.

A. You can form an adjective by adding -ING to a verb.

VERB	ADJECTIVE
starve + ing =	starving

"What will not a man give for his *starving* children and his old father!"

An -ING adjective is also called a *present participle*.

Spelling Reminders:

1. Drop silent *e* before adding -ING.
   starve + ing = starving
   freeze + ing = freezing

2. Change *ie* to *y* before adding -ING.
   die + ing = dying
   tie + ing = tying

B. You can also form an adjective by adding -ED to a regular verb.

VERB	ADJECTIVE
starve + ed =	starved

"The man was thin . . . but not *starved* . . ."

An -ED adjective formed from a verb is also known as a *past participle*.

Spelling Reminders:

1. Drop silent *e* before adding -ED.

   starve + ed = starved
   increase + ed = increased

2. If the verb ends in *y preceded by a consonant*,
   change the *y* to *i* before adding -ED.

   worry + ed = worried
   satisfy + ed = satisfied

3. Do *not* change the *y if it is preceded by a vowel*.

   annoy + ed = annoyed
   decay + ed = decayed

C. If the verb is irregular—for example, *break, broke, broken*—you cannot add -ED. Instead, use the last principal part—*broken*—as an adjective.

   Don't step on the *broken* glass!   (break, broke, **broken**)
   We skated on the *frozen* lake.   (freeze, froze, **frozen**)
   Can you help the *lost* child?   (lose, lost, **lost**)

The last principal part is, of course, a past participle.

D. Note how Pearl Buck formed adjectives from verbs in the following sentence:

   Wang Lung felt in his own *shriveled* body the last *remaining* strength of life gathering into a *devastating* anger against this man, his uncle.

shriveled (from the verb *shrivel*) is an
adjective modifying the noun *body*

remaining (from the verb *remain*) is an
adjective modifying the noun *strength*

devastating (from the verb *devastate*) is an
adjective modifying the noun *anger*

Exercise 6.10: Forming Adjectives Ending in *-ing* and *-ed*

Part 1. For each verb at the left, form an -ING adjective to modify the noun in column A, and an -ED adjective (or its equivalent) to modify the noun in column B.

VERB	COLUMN A	COLUMN B
charge	a **charging** bull	**charged** batteries

1. boil   the _____ kettle   _____ potatoes
2. write   _____ paper   a _____ notice
3. devastate   _____ hatred   the _____ area
4. tie   the _____ run   _____ shoelaces
5. decay   a _____ building   _____ tree trunks
6. embarrass   an _____ moment   an _____ look
7. speak   _____ engagements   the _____ word
8. lose   a _____ battle   a _____ cause
9. spend   a _____ spree   _____ funds
10. encourage   _____ news   an _____ team

Part 2. Complete the sentence by supplying an adjective formed from the verb in parentheses.

SAMPLE: Let us make a **renewed** effort. (*renew*)

1. Alice has made a _____ recovery. (*surprise*)
2. Joe's _____ enthusiasm convinced many, but not all. (*affect*)
3. With his _____ breath, he cursed his fate. (*die*)
4. The _____ player was helped from the field. (*injure*)
5. We walked into the face of a _____ wind. (*bite*)
6. The bulletin is not so _____ as had been feared. (*alarm*)
7. There was no strength in his _____ arm. (*shrivel*)
8. Their _____ figures grew smaller and smaller. (*recede*)
9. It is hard for a _____ tongue to speak the truth. (*lie*)
10. She drove home in a _____ snowstorm. (*blind*)

Exercise 6.11: Analogies

At the left, write the *letter* of the pair of words related to each other in the same way as the words of the capitalized pair.

_____ **1.** CRAVING : DESIRE

    (A) pittance : amount   (B) blunder : mistake
    (C) scratch : wound   (D) trickle : stream
    (E) snack : meal

_____ **2.** ALLAY : SEVERE

    (A) embellish : attractive   (B) update : modern
    (C) multiply : numerous   (D) downgrade : important
    (E) extend : lengthy

_____ **3.** SULLEN : CHEERFUL

    (A) vain : conceited   (B) caressing : affectionate
    (C) attractive : repulsive   (D) listless : languid
    (E) tolerable : sustainable

_____ **4.** HUNGRY : SUSTENANCE

    (A) arbitrary : authority   (B) crafty : deception
    (C) floundering : guidance   (D) affluent : malice
    (E) obstinate : advice

_____ **5.** AFFECTATION : NATURAL

    (A) innovation : original   (B) affliction : painful
    (C) obliteration : illegible   (D) rumor : unreliable
    (E) approximation : accurate

from

My Ántonia

by Willa Cather

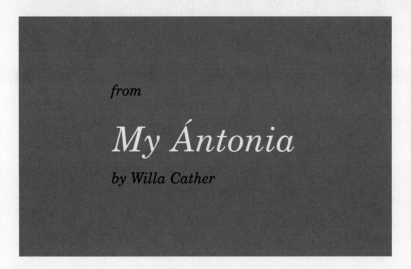

Jim is fond of Ántonia, a pretty immigrant girl he first noticed when they were fellow passengers on the train that brought them to the sparsely settled Nebraska Territory.

Much as I liked Ántonia, I hated a superior tone that she sometimes took with me. She was four years older than I, to be sure, and had seen more of the world; but I was a boy and she was a girl, and I resented her protecting manner. Before the autumn was over, she began to treat me more like an equal and to defer to me in other 5 things than reading lessons. This change came about from an adventure we had together.

One day when I rode over to the Shimerdas' I found Ántonia starting off on foot for Russian Peter's house, to borrow a spade Ambrosch needed. I offered to take her on the pony, and she got up 10 behind me. There had been another black frost the night before, and the air was clear and heady as wine. Within a week all the blooming roads had been despoiled, hundreds of miles of yellow sunflowers had been transformed into brown, rattling, burry stalks. 15

We found Russian Peter digging his potatoes. We were glad to go in and get warm by his kitchen stove and to see his squashes and Christmas melons, heaped in the storeroom for winter. As we rode away with the spade, Ántonia suggested that we stop at the prairie-dog-town and dig into one of the holes. We could find out 20 whether they ran straight down, or were horizontal, like mole-holes; whether they had underground connections; whether the owls had nests down there, lined with feathers. We might get some puppies, or owl eggs, or snakeskins.

25 The dog-town was spread out over perhaps ten acres. The grass had been nibbled short and even, so this stretch was not shaggy and red like the surrounding country, but grey and velvety. The holes were several yards apart, and were disposed with a good deal of regularity, almost as if the town had been laid out in streets and
30 avenues. One always felt that an orderly and very sociable kind of life was going on there. I picketed Dude down in a draw, and we went wandering about, looking for a hole that would be easy to dig. The dogs were out, as usual, dozens of them, sitting up on their hind legs over the doors of their houses. As we approached, they
35 barked, shook their tails at us, and scurried underground. Before the mouths of the holes were little patches of sand and gravel, scratched up, we supposed, from a long way below the surface. Here and there, in the town, we came on larger gravel patches, several yards away from any hole. If the dogs had scratched the sand
40 up in excavating, how had they carried it so far? It was on one of these gravel beds that I met my adventure.

We were examining a big hole with two entrances. The burrow sloped into the ground at a gentle angle, so that we could see where the two corridors united, and the floor was dusty from use,
45 like a little highway over which much travel went. I was walking backward, in a crouching position, when I heard Ántonia scream. She was standing opposite me, pointing behind me and shouting something in Bohemian. I whirled round, and there, on one of those dry gravel beds, was the biggest snake I had ever seen. He
50 was sunning himself, after the cold night, and he must have been asleep when Ántonia screamed. When I turned he was lying in long loose waves, like a letter W. He twitched and began to coil slowly. He was not merely a big snake, I thought—he was a circus monstrosity. His abominable muscularity, his loathsome, fluid
55 motion, somehow made me sick. He was as thick as my leg, and looked as if millstones couldn't crush the disgusting vitality out of him. He lifted his hideous little head, and rattled. I didn't run because I didn't think of it—if my back had been against a stone wall I couldn't have felt more cornered. I saw his coils tighten—
60 now he would spring, spring his length, I remembered. I ran up and drove at his head with my spade, struck him fairly across the neck, and in a minute he was all about my feet in wavy loops. I struck now from hate. Ántonia, barefooted as she was, ran up behind me. Even after I had pounded his ugly head flat, his body
65 kept on coiling and winding, doubling and falling back on itself. I walked away and turned my back. I felt seasick.

Ántonia came after me, crying, "O Jimmy, he not bite you? You sure? Why you not run when I say?"

"What did you jabber Bohunk for? You might have told me there
70 was a snake behind me!" I said petulantly.

"I know I am just awful, Jim, I was so scared." She took my handkerchief from my pocket and tried to wipe my face with it, but I snatched it away from her. I suppose I looked as sick as I felt.

"I never know you was so brave, Jim," she went on comfortingly.
175 "You is just like big mans; you wait for him lift his head and then

you go for him. Ain't you feel scared a bit? Now we take that snake home and show everybody. Nobody ain't seen in this kawn-tree so big snake like you kill."

She went on in this strain until I began to think that I had longed for this opportunity, and had hailed it with joy. Cautiously we went back to the snake; he was still groping with his tail, turning up his ugly belly in the light. A faint, fetid smell came from him, and a thread of green liquid oozed from his crushed head.

"Look, Tony, that's his poison," I said.

I took a long piece of string from my pocket, and she lifted his head with the spade while I tied a noose around it. We pulled him out straight and measured him by my riding-quirt; he was about five and half feet long. He had twelve rattles, but they were broken off before they began to taper, so I insisted that he must once have had twenty-four. I explained to Ántonia how this meant that he was twenty-four years old, that he must have been there when white men first came, left on from buffalo and Indian times. As I turned him over, I began to feel proud of him, to have a kind of respect for his age and size. He seemed like the ancient, eldest Evil. Certainly his kind have left horrible unconscious memories in all warm-blooded life. When we dragged him down into the draw, Dude sprang off to the end of his tether and shivered all over—wouldn't let us come near him.

We decided that Ántonia should ride Dude home, and I would walk. As she rode along slowly, her bare legs swinging against the pony's sides, she kept shouting back to me about how astonished everybody would be. I followed with the spade over my shoulder, dragging my snake. Her exultation was contagious. The great land had never looked to me so big and free. If the red grass were full of rattlers, I was equal to them all. Nevertheless, I stole furtive glances behind me now and then to see that no avenging mate, older and bigger than my quarry, was racing up from the rear.

The sun had set when we reached our garden and went down the draw toward the house. Otto Fuchs was the first one we met. He was sitting on the edge of the cattle-pond, having a quiet pipe before supper. Ántonia called him to come quick and look. He did not say anything for a minute, but scratched his head and turned the snake over with his boot.

"Where did you run onto that beauty, Jim?"

"Up at the dog-town," I answered laconically.

"Kill himself yourself? How come you to have a weepon?"

"We'd been up to Russian Peter's, to borrow a spade for Ambrosch."

Otto shook the ashes out of his pipe and squatted down to count the rattles. "It was just luck you had a tool," he said cautiously. "Gosh! I wouldn't want to do any business with that fellow myself, unless I had a fence-post along. Your grandmother's snake-cane wouldn't more than tickle him. He could stand right up and talk to you, he could. Did he fight hard?"

Ántonia broke in: "He fight something awful! He is all over

Jimmy's boots. I scream for him to run, but he just hit and hit that
snake like he was crazy."

Otto winked at me. After Ántonia rode on he said: "Got him in
130 the head first crack, didn't you? That was just as well."

We hung him up to the windmill, and when I went down to the
kitchen, I found Ántonia standing in the middle of the floor, telling
the story with a great deal of color.

Subsequent experiences with rattlesnakes taught me that my
135 first encounter was fortunate in circumstance. My big rattler was
old, and had led too easy a life; there was not much fight in him.
He had probably lived there for years, with a fat prairie-dog for
breakfast whenever he felt like it, a sheltered home, even an owl-
feather bed, perhaps, and he had forgot that the world doesn't owe
140 rattlers a living. A snake of his size, in fighting trim, would be
more than any boy could handle. So in reality it was a mock adventure; the game was fixed for me by chance, as it probably was for
many a dragon-slayer. I had been adequately armed by Russian
Peter; the snake was old and lazy; and I had Ántonia beside me,
145 to appreciate and admire.

That snake hung on our corral fence for several days; some of the
neighbors came to see it and agreed that it was the biggest rattler
ever killed in those parts. This was enough for Ántonia. She liked
me better from that time on, and she never took a supercilious air
150 with me again. I had killed a big snake—I was now a big fellow.

Line 11. *black frost:* frost so intense as to blacken vegetation
Line 31. *draw:* dry bed of a stream

UNDERSTANDING THE SELECTION

Exercise 7.1: Close Reading

In the blank space, write the *letter* of the choice that best completes the statement
or answers the question.

1. Which of the following is NOT true? _____

    (A) Jim used to resent Ántonia's superior attitude.
    (B) Ántonia used to consider herself superior to Jim in everything.
    (C) After the snake episode, Ántonia had a higher regard for Jim.
    (D) Jim was Ántonia's reading teacher.

2. The snake was obviously _____.

    (A) of average size for the region
    (B) fully aware of Jim's approach
    (C) a rattlesnake
    (D) in prime physical condition

3. The passage suggests that _____.

    (A) Jim's success with the snake made him totally reckless of danger
    (B) Ántonia's language handicap prevented her from describing Jim's feat effectively
    (C) The region had been open to settlers for less than a quarter of a century
    (D) Jim hated hero worship

4. The episode in the passage took place in the _____.

    (A) fall
    (B) winter
    (C) spring
    (D) summer

5. In the conversation with Otto, _____.

    (A) Jim talked freely of his adventure
    (B) Otto implied that the snake was harmless
    (C) Ántonia did all of the talking
    (D) Jim said little

IMPROVING YOUR COMPOSITION SKILLS: USING COMPLEX SENTENCES

QUESTION 1: *What is a complex sentence?*

A ***complex sentence*** consists of one independent clause and one or more dependent clauses.

Although Jim liked Ántonia, he hated her superior tone.
    dependent clause   *independent clause*

INDEPENDENT CLAUSE: *he hated her superior tone*
(This could be a sentence if it stood alone.)

DEPENDENT CLAUSE: *Although Jim liked Ántonia*
(This cannot stand by itself as a sentence.)

Here are some further examples of complex sentences:

COMPLEX SENTENCE	INDEPENDENT CLAUSE	DEPENDENT CLAUSE(S)
As we approached, they barked, shook their tails at us, and scurried underground.	they barked, shook their tails at us, and scurried underground	As we approached
The sun had set when we reached our garden and went down the draw toward the house.	The sun had set	when we reached our garden and went down the draw toward the house

| If he asks, I will tell him what has happened. | I will tell him | 1. If he asks
2. what has happened |
| We decided that Ántonia should ride Dude home, and I would walk. | We decided | 1. that Ántonia should ride Dude home
2. (that) I would walk |

QUESTION 2: *Why is the complex sentence important?*

Compare the following ways of expressing the same ideas:

(A) I was walking backward, in a crouching position. I heard Ántonia scream.
[two simple sentences]

(B) I was walking backward, in a crouching position, and heard Ántonia scream.
[simple sentence with compound verb *was walking* and *heard*]

(C) I was walking backward, in a crouching position, and I heard Ántonia scream.
[compound sentence]

(D) I was walking backward, in a crouching position, when I heard Ántonia scream.
[complex sentence]

Note that *A* (two simple sentences) expresses the two ideas without showing the relationship between them.

B (simple sentence with compound verb) and *C* (compound sentence) express the two ideas by merely adding one to the other with the conjunction *and*. They, too, fail to express the relationship between the ideas.

Only *D* (complex sentence) shows that relationship. It is a *time* relationship: the walking backward and Ántonia's scream occurred at virtually the same time. Obviously the complex sentence is superior for expressing relationships.

I was walking backward, in a crouching position,
WHEN I heard Ántonia scream.

You should know all of the acceptable ways to express your ideas so that you may choose the way that best expresses your meaning, or enables you to vary your style.

In the above instance, Willa Cather chose the complex sentence as the best way.

About half of the sentences in print are complex sentences. As you develop skill in writing, you will be relying more and more on the complex sentence.

Exercise 7.2:   Writing Complex Sentences

Combine each pair of sentences into a complex sentence. Do this by changing the italicized sentence into a dependent clause beginning with one of these conjunctions:

after	as if	before	so that	while
although	because	if	when	until

SAMPLE: *Jackson was far behind.* He did not drop out of the race.

Although Jackson was far behind, he did not drop out of the race.

(Note that a comma usually follows a dependent clause that introduces a sentence.)

SAMPLE: Francine did not order the copier. *It was too expensive.*

Francine did not order the copier **because it was too expensive.**

(No comma is usually necessary after an independent clause that introduces a sentence.)

1. Turn on the light. *You can see where you are going.*

_____

_____

2. *Alice was not well.* She came to take the examination.

_____

_____

3. *You do not have the exact fare.* You will not be allowed to board the bus.

_____

_____

4. It is futile to lock the stable. *The horses have been stolen.*

_____

_____

5. *Spring arrives.* We begin to spend more time outdoors.

_____

_____

6. She asked me to hold her books. *She tried to unlock the door.*

_____

_____

7. Salesclerks are on duty daily from 10 A.M. *The shop closes at 5:45.*

_____

_____

8. I have to go now. *My class is about to start.*

_____

_____

9. *We begin the day's work.* We should have a nutritious breakfast.

_____

_____

10. You glided through the water effortlessly. *You were a fish.*

_____

_____

QUESTION 3: *Where in the sentence may a dependent clause be used?*

In some complex sentences, the dependent clause may come either at the beginning or at the end of the sentence:

DEPENDENT CLAUSE AT END:

You can help us carry the packages *if you come along.*

DEPENDENT CLAUSE AT BEGINNING:

If you come along, you can help us carry the packages.

(*Reminder:* a comma usually follows an introductory dependent clause.)

Exercise 7.3: Moving the Dependent Clause

If the dependent clause begins the sentence, move it to the end. If it ends the sentence, move it to the beginning.

SAMPLE: *Until the doors opened*, they had to wait outside.

They had to wait outside **until the doors opened.**

SAMPLE: Investigate the facts *before you accuse anyone.*

Before you accuse anyone, investigate the facts.

1. If you had come to the dance, you would have had a good time.

_____

_____

2. Everyone ran for cover when the downpour started.

_____

_____

3. The manager is willing to take my personal check since she knows me as a customer.

_____

_____

4. Unless you make your payments on time, you will be charged a late fee.

_____

_____

5. Turn down the flame after the water boils.

_____

_____

Note that you now have another way to vary the beginnings of your sentences: you can begin with a _dependent clause_, if you choose.

Exercise 7.4:   Improving a First Draft

Improve the paragraph entitled "An Unusual Experience" (which follows) by rewriting it in the space provided, making these changes:

I. Find an adverb in S1 and start the sentence with it.

II. Combine S2 and 3 into a complex sentence by reducing S3 to a dependent clause introduced by _since_.

III. Combine S4 and 5 into a complex sentence by reducing S4 to a dependent clause introduced by _while_.

IV. Find a participial phrase in S6 and start the sentence with it. Make no changes in S7, 8, and 9.

V. Find a prepositional phrase in S10 and start the sentence with it.

VI. Rearrange S11 so that it begins with its dependent clause.

An Unusual Experience

[1]I had an unusual experience yesterday. [2]I had decided to start my outdoor cleanup. [3]It was a beautiful spring afternoon. [4]I was raking leaves along the fence. [5]I became suddenly aware of what appeared to be a small animal at my left foot. [6]The furry form, barely missed by my rake, huddled defenselessly beneath me. [7]Its big eyes stared vacantly into space. [8]Nothing moved. [9]I do not know who was the more startled, the rabbit or I. [10]Both of us, for a breathless interval, were paralyzed. [11]Like a streak of lightning, the creature bolted from the spot before I had time to recover.

An Unusual Experience (Improved)

_____

_____

_____

_____

_____

_____

_____

_____

_____

_____

_____

_____

_____

_____

_____

_____

_____

_____

USING DEPENDENT CLAUSES TO ACHIEVE VARIETY OF SENTENCE OPENING

Notice how Willa Cather achieved variety of sentence opening in the following passage by beginning two of her sentences (S2 and 6) with a dependent clause.

[1]We decided that Ántonia should ride Dude home, and I would walk. [2]_As she rode along slowly_, her bare legs swinging against the pony's sides, she kept shouting back to me about how astonished everybody would be. [3]I followed with the spade over my shoulder, dragging my snake. [4]Her exultation was contagious. [5]The great land had never looked to me so big and free. [6]_If the red grass were full of rattlers_, I was equal to them all.

Exercise 7.5: Writing a Composition: A Second Chance

In a paragraph of about 100 to 125 words, explain how you would do something altogether differently if you had a second chance. Of course, you will also have to relate what it was that you did wrong when you had your first chance, mentioning the time, the place, and the other people who were involved.

IMPORTANT: Make sure that at least two of the sentences in your final draft begin with a dependent clause.

Final Draft: A Second Chance

_____

_____

_____

_____

_____

_____

_____

_____

_____

_____

_____

_____

LEARNING NEW WORDS

Line	Word	Meaning	Typical Use
54	**abominable** (*adj.*) ə-ˈbäm-ə-nə-bəl	deserving or causing loathing or hatred; detestable; very unpleasant	The *abominable* grin on Jerry's Halloween mask disgusted everyone who saw it.
		(*ant.* **laudable, delightful**)	We must increase production, which is *laudable*, but without increasing pollution, which is *abominable*.
103	**contagious** (*adj.*) kən-ˈtā-jəs	communicable by contact; catching	Anyone who has influenza may transmit the germs to another by coughing or sneezing; it is a *contagious* disease.
5	**defer** (*v.*) di-ˈfər	1. give in to the opinion or wish of another; yield (followed by *to*)	Although she thought she was right, she *deferred to* her teacher's opinion because of his expert knowledge.

		2. put off to a future time; delay; postpone	Because of poor weather, the picnic was *deferred to* the following Sunday.
103	**exultation** (*n.*) ˌeks-əl-ˈtā-shən	act of *exulting* (being extremely joyful); triumphant joy; jubilation; rejoicing	Having won the game, our team left the field in a mood of *exultation*.
		(*ant.* **dejection**)	*Dejection* was plainly evident on the faces of the losers.
106	**furtive** (*adj.*) ˈfərt-iv	done in a stealthy way, as if to hinder discovery; sly; secret; sneaky	The watchfulness of the proctors discouraged any would-be cheater from *furtive* glances at a neighbor's paper.
		(*ant.* **forthright, straightforward**)	Instead of furtively trying to discover our plans for the weekend, be *forthright*; ask us where we are going.
83	**ooze** (*v.*) ˈüz	1. flow slowly through, as if through small openings; leak out	A sticky liquid *oozed* from the injured bark of the tree.
		2. give off; exude	The players were steadied by the presence of their coach, whose manner *oozed* optimism.
70	**petulantly** (*adv.*) ˈpech-ə-lənt-lē	in a *petulant* (ill-humored) manner; irritably; peevishly	"Watch where you're going!" I shouted *petulantly*, when Dan accidentally stepped on my painful toe.
30	**sociable** (*adj.*) ˈsō-shə-bəl	inclined to seek the company of others; enjoying companionship; friendly; gregarious	At lunch, most of us sit with our friends; we are *sociable*.
		(*ant.* **unsociable**)	If you eat your lunch in a corner all by yourself, others may think you are *unsociable*.
134	**subsequent** (*adj.*) ˈsəb-si-kwənt	following or coming later or after; succeeding (*ant.* **previous**)	The down payment on the car is $5999; the *subsequent* payments are $399 a month for the next three years.
149	**supercilious** (*adj.*) sü-pər-ˈsil-ē-əs	haughtily disdainful; expressing contempt; haughty; contemptuous	Some seniors, carried away by their self-importance, take a *supercilious* attitude toward the rest of the student body.

Exercise 7.6: Sentence Completion

Which of the two choices makes the sentence correct? Write the *letter* of the correct answer in the space provided.

1. Evelyn's mirth is contagious; when she laughs, we ____.

   A. feel sick   B. laugh with her

2. He behaved in a furtive manner, as if he ____.

   A. were spying on us   B. had lost something

3. ____ oozed from the leaky drum.

   A. Noise   B. Oil

4. Anyone who consistently ____ the company of others is unsociable.

   A. seeks   B. avoids

5. I ____ the program; it was abominable

   A. disliked   B. enjoyed

6. When Irma answers you petulantly, you can tell that she is in ____ humor.

   A. bad   B. good

7. A ____ is no cause for exultation.

   A. promotion   B. setback

8. A supercilious person treats almost everybody as an ____.

   A. inferior   B. equal

9. When you defer to someone, you are ____.

   A. showing impatience   B. giving in

10. Besides seeing Mary in the hospital on May 18th and 19th, the physician treated her in subsequent office visits on the ____ of the same month.

    A. 4th and 15th   B. 26th and 30th

Exercise 7.7:   Name-the-Person Quiz

Read all the statements in the boxes. Then enter the required names in sentences 1 to 10, below.

Not only did Yolanda defeat her rival Elsie in the tennis tournament, but she was also designated as "scholar of the month."

Reading Selection 7: My Ántonia   135

as really listening to our conversation when he
e reading a newspaper.

Andy turned his nose up at us when he went by and made us feel very inferior.

every test, Terry kept saying that she would surely fail.

osie's quitting at a time when we were depending on her is something that all of us detest.

Slater asked the judge to change the date of his hearing from April 14 to April 21.

Joan was almost always with friends; you very seldom saw her by herself.

First Aaron had the cold; then his younger sister Marguerite caught it from him.

Pamela's first story was a success, but nothing else that she has written has equaled it.

"Why don't you mind your own business!" Henry blurted at me angrily when I asked about his new job.

1. _____ is suspected of furtive behavior.

2. _____ exuded pessimism.

3. _____ requested a deferment.

4. _____ had ample cause for exultation.

5. _____ acted superciliously.

6. _____ spread contagion.

7. _____ was quite gregarious.

8. _____ made a petulant comment.

9. _____'s subsequent work has been disappointing.

10. _____ is alleged to have behaved abominably.

Exercise 7.8: Concise Writing (Use Fewer Words)

Replace the italicized words in each sentence below with a single word from the following list.

sociable	defer	exultation	subsequent	furtively
supercilious	ooze	contagious	abominable	petulantly

1. They keep complaining *in an ill-humored manner* about one thing after another. _____

2. Is it possible to *put off* the operation *to a future time?* _____

3. As far as we know, mental illness is not *communicable by contact.* _____

4. Rita showed improvement on this test and should do even better on our *still-to-come* quizzes. _____

5. The whole affair is *very unpleasant.* _____

6. Gail is not too *inclined to seek the company of others* _____

7. I do not like your *haughtily disdainful* attitude. _____

8. The hero was borne through the crowd on the shoulders of his teammates in a scene of *triumphant joy.* _____

9. The excess moisture will *flow slowly* through the openings at the base of the flowerpot. _____

10. The suspect did not look people in the face but glanced at them *in a stealthy way.* _____

Exercise 7.9: Using Synonyms and Antonyms

A. Avoid repetition by replacing the italicized word or expression with a SYNONYM from the following list.

succeeding	contagious	defer	ooze	straightforward
gregarious	irritably	dejection	supercilious	laudable

1. After you agreed to *put off* our meeting to the 16th, I put it on my calendar. _____

2. Joan must have been peeved by my question because she answered *peevishly.* _____

3. The *contemptuous* manner in which they dealt with us shows that they hold us in contempt. _____

4. I thought the blood would stop flowing, but it continued to *flow slowly* through the bandage. _____

5. Since a cold is *communicable by contact,* it can easily be communicated to others. _____

B. Complete the sentence by inserting an ANTONYM of the italicized word from the above list.

6. Cheer up; it is a time for *exultation,* not _____. _____

7. Everyone thought Bernice's performance was _____, but she says it was *abominable.* _____

two of our classmates are *unsociable;* all

obviously _____.   _____

8. erson might have proceeded in a *furtive* man-

your dealings were entirely _____.   _____

evious years, we ended with a small surplus, but we

pe to do even better this year and in _____ years.   _____

LEARNING SOME ROOTS AND DERIVATIVES

Each capitalized word below is a *root*. The words under it are its *derivatives*.

ABOMINATE (*v.*)	The Hindus *abominate* flesh-eaters.
abomination (*n.*)	To them the killing of animals is an *abomination.*
abominable (*adj.*)	Even the killing of an insect is, in their eyes, *abominable.*
abominably (*adv.*)	As far as the treatment of animals is concerned, they believe that the rest of the world behaves *abominably.*
CONTAGION (*n.*)	Cover your mouth and nose with a handkerchief when you cough or sneeze; don't spread *contagion.*
contagious (*adj.*)	Smallpox is a highly *contagious* disease.
contagiously (*adv.*)	After being reported in the port city, the flu spread *contagiously* to the rest of the island.
DEFER (*v.*) ("put off")	The repair of the roof is urgent; it cannot be *deferred.*
deferral (*n.*)	*Deferral* of the repair may result in further costly damage to the building and its contents.
deferment (*n.*)	Since the instructor has already granted me an extra week to complete my report, I hesitate to ask her for an additional *deferment.*
DEFER (*v.*) ("yield")	I would have preferred to watch the ball game, but I *deferred* to my father and turned to the news program.
deference (*n.*)	I switched to the news program out of *deference* to my father.
deferential (*adj.*)	The players respect their coach, and when she speaks they listen with *deferential* attention.
deferentially (*adv.*)	They listen to her *deferentially.*
EXULT (*v.*)	The ticket holder *exulted* on learning he had won the lottery.
exultant (*adj.*)	He was *exultant* over his good fortune.

exultantly (*adv.*)	The news photo shows him smiling *exultantly*.
exultation (*n.*)	He is shown embracing his family in *exultation* ov~~e~~ affluence. ~~udden~~
FURTIVE (*adj.*)	No one saw him leave; he must have made a *furtive* ex~~.~~ rear door. ~~he~~
furtively (*adv.*)	He must have left *furtively* while our attention was foc~~.~~ elsewhere.
furtiveness (*n.*)	Because of his *furtiveness*, we shall have to watch him mor~~e~~ closely in the future.
PETULANT (*adj.*)	I was surprised by Nora's *petulant* tone, as I had never known her to be cranky.
petulantly (*adv.*)	"I don't want to talk about it," she said *petulantly*, when I asked what was wrong.
petulance (*n.*)	I took no offense at her *petulance* because I realized that something was irritating her.
SOCIABLE (*adj.*)	Feeling betrayed, Silas kept to himself; he was not *sociable*.
sociably (*adv.*)	The townspeople remarked that Silas did not behave *sociably*.
sociability (*n.*)	Once his name was cleared, Silas gave up his solitary ways and showed more *sociability*.
SUBSEQUENT (*adj.*)	When she got a D on her first paper, Ingrid resolved to do better on *subsequent* essays.
subsequently (*adv.*)	*Subsequently*, she earned a B and two A's.
SUPERCILIOUS (*adj.*)	With a *supercilious* look at the customer who offered less than the asking price, the merchant replaced the article on the shelf.
superciliously (*adv.*)	Vain persons keep themselves *superciliously* aloof in their association with most people.
superciliousness (*n.*)	As a child, Tim suffered from the *superciliousness* of the older boys, who would not let him play because of his size and age.

Exercise 7.10:   Using Roots and Derivatives

Fill each blank with the above root or derivative that best fits the meaning of the sentence.

1. I first met your cousin at our graduation, and I saw her _____ at your sister's wedding.

2. The Mulligans are known for their _____; they have a wide circle of friends.

3. Alice glanced _____ at the open marking-book on the teacher's desk while she was throwing something into the wastebasket.

4. The birth of a daughter gave the proud mother reason to _____.

the possibility of _____ by eliminating the breeding

5. We can and mosquitoes.

place did not smoke during the dinner out of _____ to his non-

6. The guests.

re lovers _____ the use of chemical sprays and insecticides.

7. ad to _____ paying my dues, as I had no funds with me.

Most of the players greeted me when I joined the team, but one or two glared at me _____ from a distance.

10. Young children are sometimes cranky and _____ at a late hour when they are overtired.

SPELLING REVIEW: TURNING ADJECTIVES INTO NOUNS BY ADDING *-ITY*

He was not merely a big snake, I thought—he was a circus *monstrosity*. His abominable *muscularity*, his loathsome, fluid motion, somehow made me sick.

Note how, in the above, Willa Carter has turned adjectives into nouns by adding the suffix -ITY, meaning "condition or state."

ADJECTIVE + SUFFIX = NOUN

monstrous + ity = monstrosity (condition of being monstrous; something monstrous)

muscular + ity = muscularity (state of being muscular)

Rules for Forming -ITY Nouns

Rule 1: Do not drop any letters. However, drop silent *e* before -ITY.

regular	+ ity	=	regularity
vital	+ ity	=	vitality
rigid	+ ity	=	rigidity

But

mature + ity = maturity

Rule 2: If the adjective ends in -BLE, change *le* to *il* before adding -ITY.

sociable	+ ity	=	sociability
possible	+ ity	=	possibility

Rule 3: Some -OUS adjectives lose the letter *u*.

ADJECTIVE		NOUN
monstrous	→	monstrosity
curious	→	curiosity
generous	→	generosity
pompous	→	pomposity

Exceptions to the Rules

Exception 1: A few adjectives add -TY only.

loyal	→	loyalty	subtle	→	subtlety
novel	→	novelty	jolly	→	jollity
cruel	→	cruelty			

Exception 2: The following adjectives lose an *e* but add -IETY.

improper	→	impropriety
proper	→	propriety
sober	→	sobriety

Additional Exceptions: Finally, learn these irregularities:

anxious	→	anxiety	gay	→	gaiety *or* gayety
notorious	→	notoriety	humble	→	humility
brief	→	brevity	poor	→	poverty
clear	→	clarity	vain	→	vanity

Exercise 7.11: Converting Adjectives Into Nouns

Turn each adjective into a noun, as in the sample below:

ADJECTIVE	NOUN		ADJECTIVE	NOUN
fertile	**fertility**			
1. real	_____		11. brutal	_____
2. sincere	_____		12. sober	_____
3. generous	_____		13. sane	_____
4. original	_____		14. brief	_____
5. rigid	_____		15. vain	_____
6. novel	_____		16. subtle	_____
7. obese	_____		17. extreme	_____
8. abnormal	_____		18. impossible	_____
9. improper	_____		19. cruel	_____
10. poor	_____		20. obscure	_____

Converting Nouns Into Adjectives

Exercise 7.1

Turn each [noun] into an adjective, as in the sample below.

NOUN	ADJECTIVE		NOUN	ADJECTIVE
stupid[ity]	**stupid**			
1. form[ality]	_____		11. ability	_____
2. ind[ividuality]	_____		12. neutrality	_____
3. a[nxi]ety	_____		13. humility	_____
4. [cu]riosity	_____		14. monstrosity	_____
[5.] [im]maturity	_____		15. security	_____
[6]. insanity	_____		16. loyalty	_____
7. jollity	_____		17. clarity	_____
8. futility	_____		18. feasibility	_____
9. sensitivity	_____		19. notoriety	_____
10. hostility	_____		20. gaiety	_____

IMPROVING YOUR WRITING SKILLS: AVOIDING SENTENCE FRAGMENTS

A *sentence fragment* results from punctuating a *fragment* (piece) of a sentence as if it were a complete sentence.

Some of the commonest sentence fragments are dependent clauses, participial phrases, and prepositional phrases wrongly punctuated as complete sentences. Study the following examples:

Sentence Fragment	*Fragment Removed*
1. DEPENDENT CLAUSE WRONGLY PUNCTUATED AS A SENTENCE:	DEPENDENT CLAUSE INTEGRATED INTO THE SENTENCE:
When I saw what had happened. I wanted to cry.	When I saw what had happened, I wanted to cry.
We sat in adjoining seats. *Because we wanted to be together.*	We sat in adjoining seats because we wanted to be together.
2. PARTICIPIAL PHRASE WRONGLY PUNCTUATED AS A SENTENCE:	PARTICIPIAL PHRASE INTEGRATED INTO THE SENTENCE:
Seeing that I was waiting for the phone. The person using it maliciously prolonged her conversation.	Seeing that I was waiting for the phone, the person using it maliciously prolonged her conversation.

Nancy deposited half of her salary in her savings account. *Retaining the rest for current expenses.*

Nancy deposited half of her salary in her savings account, retaining the rest for current expenses.

3. PREPOSITIONAL PHRASE WRONGLY PUNCTUATED AS A SENTENCE:

PREPOSITIONAL PHRASE INTEGRATED INTO THE SENTENCE:

From the day I first met you. I knew that you were obstinate.

From the day I first met you, I knew that you were obstinate.

Elinor invited all of her friends. *To the ceremony and the reception.*

Elinor invited all of her friends to the ceremony and the reception.

Sometimes part of a compound predicate is wrongly punctuated as a complete sentence.

Sentence Fragment

Fragment Removed

4. Dan protested that he was not hungry. *And proceeded to eat more than anyone else.*

Dan protested that he was not hungry and proceeded to eat more than anyone else.

Exercise 7.13:   Correcting Sentence Fragments

Completely rewrite each item that contains a sentence fragment. (Refer to the sentences in the *Fragment Removed* column as your models.) If the item contains no sentence fragment (there are two such items), write "correct."

1. By the middle of the first act. I was able to predict how the play would end.

_____

_____

_____

2. The receptionist made a note that you had called. But completely forgot to bring it to my attention.

_____

_____

_____

_____

3. Jeanne was disappointed. At the very least, she had expected to reach the semifinals.

_____

_____

_____

4. Hearing that his rent would be raised. My cousin began looking for another apartment.

_____

_____

_____

5. Late in the afternoon the electrician arrived. Without the parts necessary to complete the job.

_____

_____

_____

_____

6. If you want to come with us Saturday afternoon. We can easily make room for you in the car.

_____

_____

_____

_____

7. Bruce waited outside the library while I went in to return a book. Then we walked home together.

_____

_____

_____

8. A trailer truck overturned. Tying up traffic for miles and miles.

_____

_____

_____

9. Ski-trail operators are having a disastrous season. Because the weather has been too mild.

_____

_____

_____

_____

10. At the last minute she changed her mind. And asked us to refund her money.

_____

_____

_____

_____

Exercise 6.11: Analogies

At the left, write the *letter* of the pair of words related to each other in the same way as the words of the capitalized pair.

_____ 1. ABOMINATION : LOATHING

    (A) catastrophe : rejoicing   (B) affliction : suffering
    (C) thaw : spring   (D) liberation : bondage
    (E) peevishness : trait

_____ 2. GREGARIOUS : COMPANIONSHIP

    (A) listless : work   (B) distracted : attention
    (C) underpaid : morale   (D) unforgiving : revenge
    (E) unenthusiastic : zeal

_____ 3. SUBSEQUENT : PREVIOUS

    (A) libelous : defamatory   (B) hospitable : receptive
    (C) sundry : miscellaneous   (D) barbarous : inhumane
    (E) troubled : tranquil

_____ 4. OOZE : FLOW

    (A) skim : read   (B) gulp : drink
    (C) shout : whisper   (D) stroll : walk
    (E) take : seize

_____ 5. EXULT : JUBILANT

    (A) imitate : creative   (B) hesitate : confident
    (C) censure : commendatory   (D) compromise : obstinate
    (E) defer : courteous

from

Black Boy

by Richard Wright

Is there anything that can equal the terror of children who fear that if they step out on the street, they may be attacked by a neighbor-hood gang?

Hunger stole upon me so slowly that at first I was not aware of what hunger really meant. Hunger had always been more or less at my elbow when I played, but now I began to wake up at night to find hunger standing at my bedside, staring at me gauntly. The
5 hunger I had known before this had been no grim, hostile stranger; it had been a normal hunger that had made me beg constantly for bread, and when I ate a crust or two I was satisfied. But this new hunger baffled me, scared me, made me angry and insistent. When-ever I begged for food now my mother would pour me a cup of tea
10 which would still the clamor in my stomach for a moment or two; but a little later I would feel hunger nudging my ribs, twisting my empty guts until they ached. I would grow dizzy and my vision would dim. I became less active in my play, and for the first time in my life I had to pause and think of what was happening to me.
15 "Mama, I'm hungry," I complained one afternoon.
"Jump up and catch a kungry," she said, trying to make me laugh and forget.
"What's a *kungry?*"
"It's what little boys eat when they get hungry," she said.
20 "What does it taste like?"
"I don't know."
"Then why do you tell me to catch one?"
"Because you said that you were hungry," she said, smiling.
I sensed that she was teasing me and it made me angry.

146

"But I'm hungry. I want to eat."   25

"You'll have to wait."

"But I want to eat now."

"But there's nothing to eat," she told me.

"Why?"

"Just because there's none," she explained.   30

"But I want to eat," I said, beginning to cry.

"You'll just have to wait," she said again.

"But why?"

"For God to send some food."

"When is He going to send it?"   35

"I don't know."

"But I'm hungry!"

She was ironing and she paused and looked at me with tears in
her eyes.

"Where's your father?" she asked me.   40

I stared in bewilderment. Yes, it was true that my father had not
come home to sleep for many days now and I could make as much
noise as I wanted. Though I had not known why he was absent, I
had been glad that he was not there to shout his restrictions at me.
But it had never occurred to me that his absence would mean that   45
there would be no food.

"I don't know," I said.

"Who brings food into the house?" my mother asked me.

"Papa," I said. "He always brought food."

"Well, your father isn't here now," she said.   50

"Where is he?"

"I don't know," she said.

"But I'm hungry," I whimpered, stomping my feet.

"You'll have to wait until I get a job and buy food," she said.

As the days slid past, the image of my father became associated   55
with my pangs of hunger, and whenever I felt hunger I thought of
him with a deep biological bitterness.

My mother finally went to work as a cook and left me and my
brother alone in the flat each day with a loaf of bread and a pot of
tea. When she returned at evening she would be tired and dispir-   60
ited and would cry a lot. Sometimes, when she was in despair, she
would call us to her and talk to us for hours, telling us that we now
had no father, that our lives would be different from those of other
children, that we must learn as soon as possible to take care of ourselves, to dress ourselves, to prepare our own food; that we must   65
take upon ourselves the responsibility of the flat while she worked.
Half frightened, we would promise solemnly. We did not understand what had happened between our father and our mother and
the most that these long talks did to us was to make us feel a
vague dread. Whenever we asked why father had left, she would   70
tell us that we were too young to know.

One evening my mother told me that thereafter I would have to
do the shopping for food. She took me to the corner store to show
me the way. I was proud; I felt like a grownup. The next afternoon
I looped the basket over my arm and went down the pavement   75

toward the store. When I reached the corner, a gang of boys grabbed me, knocked me down, snatched the basket, took the money, and sent me running home in panic. That evening I told my mother what had happened, but she made no comment; she sat down at once, wrote another note, gave me more money, and sent me out to the grocery again. I crept down the steps and saw the same gang of boys playing down the street. I ran back into the house.

"What's the matter?" my mother asked.

"It's those same boys," I said. "They'll beat me."

"You've got to get over that," she said. "Now, go on."

"I'm scared," I said.

"Go on and don't pay any attention to them," she said.

I went out of the door and walked briskly down the sidewalk, praying that the gang would not molest me. But when I came abreast of them someone shouted.

"There he is!"

They came toward me and I broke into a wild run toward home. They overtook me and flung me to the pavement. I yelled, pleaded, kicked, but they wrenched the money out of my hand. They yanked me to my feet, gave me a few slaps, and sent me home sobbing. My mother met me at the door.

"They b-beat m-me," I gasped. "They t-t-took the m-money."

I started up the steps, seeking the shelter of the house.

"Don't you come in here," my mother warned me.

I froze in my tracks and stared at her.

"But they're coming after me," I said.

"You just stay right where you are," she said in a deadly tone. "I'm going to teach you this night to stand up and fight for yourself."

She went into the house and I waited, terrified, wondering what she was about. Presently she returned with more money and another note; she also had a long heavy stick.

"Take this money, this note, and this stick," she said. "Go to the store and buy those groceries. If those boys bother you, then fight."

I was baffled. My mother was telling me to fight, a thing that she had never done before.

"But I'm scared," I said.

"Don't you come into this house until you've gotten those groceries," she said.

"They'll beat me; they'll beat me," I said.

"Then stay in the streets; don't come back here!"

I ran up the steps and tried to force my way past her into the house. A stinging slap came on my jaw. I stood on the sidewalk, crying.

"Please, let me wait until tomorrow," I begged.

"No," she said. "Go now! If you come back into this house without those groceries, I'll whip you!"

She slammed the door and I heard the key turn in the lock. I shook with fright. I was alone upon the dark, hostile streets and gangs were after me. I had the choice of being beaten at home or away from home. I clutched the stick, crying, trying to reason. If I were beaten at home, there was absolutely nothing that I could do about it; but if I were beaten in the streets, I had a chance to fight and defend myself. I walked slowly down the sidewalk, coming closer to the gang of boys, holding the stick tightly. I was so full of fear that I could scarcely breathe. I was almost upon them now.

"There he is again!" the cry went up.

They surrounded me quickly and began to grab for my hand.

"I'll kill you!" I threatened.

They closed in. In blind fear I let the stick fly, feeling it crack against a boy's skull. I swung again, lamming another skull, then another. Realizing that they would retaliate if I let up for but a second, I fought to lay them low, to knock them cold, to kill them so that they could not strike back at me. I flayed with tears in my eyes, teeth clenched, stark fear making me throw every ounce of my strength behind each blow. I hit again and again, dropping the money and the grocery list. The boys scattered, yelling, nursing their heads, staring at me in utter disbelief. They had never seen such frenzy. I stood panting, egging them on, taunting them to come on and fight. When they refused, I ran after them and they tore out for their homes, screaming. The parents of the boys rushed into the streets and threatened me, and for the first time in my life I shouted at grownups, telling them that I would give them the same if they bothered me. I finally found my grocery list and the money and went to the store. On my way back I kept my stick poised for instant use, but there was not a single boy in sight. That night I won the right to the streets of Memphis.

UNDERSTANDING THE SELECTION

Exercise 8.1: Close Reading

In the blank space, write the *letter* of the choice that best completes the statement or answers the question.

1. Which of the following adjectives is the most appropriate to describe the mother in the passage? ____

   (A) cruel
   (B) devoted
   (C) selfish
   (D) cheerful

2. The hunger that the narrator experienced ____.

   (A) weakened him but did not alarm him
   (B) made him hate his father but not his mother
   (C) bothered him at night but not during the day
   (D) embittered him toward his mother but not his father

3. All of the following statements about the gang are true, except _____.

(A) it consisted solely of boys
(B) its members lived in the neighborhood
(C) it used no weapons
(D) it was frightened on catching sight of the stick

4. The narrator showed no fear when he _____.

(A) single-handedly defeated the gang
(B) first learned he would have to do the shopping
(C) was given a long heavy stick
(D) listened to his mother's long talks

5. The passage suggests that in the future _____.

(A) the parents of the gang members will not allow the narrator to shop for food
(B) the absent father will return
(C) the narrator will not be attacked by the gang
(D) the mother will be able to spend more time with her children

IMPROVING YOUR COMPOSITION SKILLS: USING THE COMPOUND-COMPLEX SENTENCE

QUESTION: *What is a compound-complex sentence?*

A *compound-complex* sentence consists of at least two independent clauses and at least one dependent clause.

When they refused,   I ran after them   and   they tore out for their homes, screaming.
dependent clause   *independent clause*   *independent clause*

> DEPENDENT CLAUSE: *When they refused*
> (This cannot stand by itself as a sentence.)

> INDEPENDENT CLAUSES: (1) *I ran after them*
> (This could be a sentence if it stood alone.)
>
> (2) *they tore out for their homes, screaming*
> (This, too, could be a sentence if it stood alone.)

If Richard Wright had not used the dependent clause *When they refused*, he would have had a compound sentence:

I ran after them and they tore out for their homes, screaming.

By adding the dependent clause *When they refused*, he made the sentence compound-complex.

Here are some further examples of the compound-complex sentence:

COMPOUND-COMPLEX SENTENCE	INDEPENDENT CLAUSES	DEPENDENT CLAUSE(S)
Hunger had always been more or less at my elbow when I played, but now I began to wake up at night to find hunger standing by my bedside, staring at me gauntly.	1. Hunger had always been more or less at my elbow 2. now I began to wake up at night to find hunger standing by my bedside, staring at me gauntly.	when I played
Whenever I begged for food now my mother would pour me a cup of tea which would still the clamor in my stomach for a moment or two; but a little later I would feel hunger nudging my ribs, twisting my empty guts until they ached.	1. my mother would pour me a cup of tea 2. a little later I would feel hunger nudging my ribs, twisting my empty guts	1. Whenever I begged for food now 2. which would still the clamor in my stomach for a moment or two 3. until they ached

Exercise 8.2:   Writing Compound-Complex Sentences

Each item below contains a compound sentence and a simple sentence. Combine them into a compound-complex sentence. *Hint:* Change the simple sentence to a dependent clause beginning with one of the following words:

although	as	because	since	that
though	when	which	while	who

SAMPLE: Debra did the driving, and Frank napped on the back seat. *He had been up most of the night.*

Debra did the driving, and Frank napped on the back seat, *since he had been up most of the night.*

1. It was raining. The game continued, and most of the spectators remained in the stands.

_____

_____

_____

2. I returned the damaged blouse, but the salesgirl could not find another one in my size. They had all been sold.

_____

_____

_____

3. The papers were handed back. Most of the students were pleased with their grades, but a few remained to talk to the instructor.

_____

_____

_____

4. The patrolman would not answer any of our questions, but he referred us to the desk sergeant. He gave us the information.

_____

_____

_____

5. The grass has come up, and buds are beginning to swell on the fruit trees. We planted them last spring.

_____

_____

_____

QUESTION: *What are some advantages of using compound-complex sentences?*

Advantage 1:

The compound-complex sentence can help you eliminate choppiness.
Richard Wright did *not* write:

> They refused. I ran after them. They tore out for their homes.
> They screamed.

Such piling on of one short sentence after another would have produced a choppy effect. Also, it would not have made clear the relationships of the ideas—for example, the relationship between *They refused* and *I ran after them.*
Instead, he used a compound-complex sentence:

> "When they refused, I ran after them and they tore out
> for their homes, screaming."

Exercise 8.3: Eliminating Choppiness

Rewrite each group of three sentences below as a compound-complex sentence.

Hint: Use two of the sentences as independent clauses joined by *and* or *but;* and change the third into a dependent clause.

SAMPLE: Yolanda and Richard were at the picnic. Everett had to miss it. He could not get the day off.

Yolanda and Richard were at the picnic, but Everett had to miss it because he could not get the day off.

Note that the first two sentences have become independent clauses joined by *but,* while the third has been turned into a dependent clause introduced by *because.*

1. Howard works after school in the pharmacy. His sister baby-sits occasionally for the Fletchers. They like her very much.

   _____

   _____

   _____

2. Marjorie has no telephone. I wrote to her about the change in our plans. She did not get the letter in time.

   _____

   _____

   _____

3. One employee manned the checkout counter. Another was unpacking some crates of melons. They had just been delivered.

   _____

   _____

   _____

4. I had practiced the new step with Alice. She became nervous on the dance floor. I had to explain it to her all over again.

   _____

   _____

   _____

5. A dog darted across the road. Stephanie jammed on the brakes. The car screeched to a halt.

   _____

   _____

   _____

Advantage 2:

The compound-complex sentence can help you vary your sentence structure.

Reread the following paragraph, noting the different kinds of sentences that Richard Wright has used:

> [1]One evening my mother told me that thereafter I would have to do the shopping for food. [2]She took me to the corner store to show me the way. [3]I was proud; I felt like a grownup. [4]The next afternoon I looped the basket over my arm and went down the pavement toward the store. [5]When I reached the corner, a gang of boys grabbed me, knocked me down, snatched the basket, took the money, and sent me running home in panic. [6]That evening I told my mother what had happened, but she made no comment; she sat down at once,

Reading Selection 8: Black Boy

wrote another note, gave me more money, and sent me out to the grocery again. [7]I crept down the steps and saw the same gang of boys playing down the street. [8]I ran back into the house.

Analysis

S1—complex	S5—complex
S2—simple	S6—compound-complex
S3—compound	S7—simple
S4—simple	S8—simple

You, too, can vary your writing—and make it more effective—by occasionally using a compound-complex sentence.

Exercise 8.4:   Writing a Composition: A Frightening Experience

Recall a childhood experience, such as being lost, or being menaced by a dog, or realizing that the house was on fire, or being nearly drowned, or—like Richard Wright—being set upon by a gang. Describe that experience in a paragraph of at least eight sentences. Include at least one compound sentence and one compound-complex sentence.

_____

_____

_____

_____

_____

_____

_____

_____

_____

_____

_____

_____

_____

_____

_____

_____

_____

_____

LEARNING NEW WORDS

Line	Word	Meaning	Typical Use
10	**clamor** (*n.*) ′klam-ər	vigorous and insistent protest or demand; noisy shouting; uproar	The *clamor* over the Mayor's proposal to reduce our sports program has not yet quieted down.
60	**dispirited** (*adj.*) dis-′pir-ət-əd	disheartened; marked by gloom of spirit; depressed; discouraged (*ant.* **encouraged**)	Louise is in a *dispirited* mood after her humiliating defeat, and it may be a long time before she will feel *encouraged* to compete again.
144	**frenzy** (*n.*) ′fren-zē	temporary madness; wild, frantic outburst; mania	In their *frenzy* over our victory, some of our jubilant fans charged onto the field and knocked down the goalposts.
5	**grim** (*adj.*) ′grim	cruel; savage; fierce; hard and unyielding; admitting of no compromise (*ant.* **lenient***)	José knew that he could expect no mercy from his *grim* foe. Judges are more *lenient* with first offenders than with hardened criminals.
5	**hostile** (*adj.*) ′häs-təl	of or relating to an enemy; antagonistic; showing ill will; inhospitable (*ant.* **friendly**)	By his cleverness and skill as a speaker, Mark Antony changed a *hostile* crowd into a *friendly* audience.
89	**molest** (*v.*) mə-′lest	annoy; disturb; persecute with hostile intent	The older children used to break up our games and chase us from the field, until they were warned to stop *molesting* us.
78	**panic** (*n.*) ′pan-ik	sudden unreasoning terror causing headlong flight; fear; terror; fright	In the mistaken belief that invaders had landed from Mars, thousands fled their homes in *panic*.
44	**restriction** (*n.*) ri-′strik-shən	something, as a rule or law, that *restricts* (restrains or limits); confinement within limits or bounds; limitation	There is a one-hour limitation on parking, except on weekends, when there are no *restrictions*.

137	**retaliate** (*v.*) ri-ˈtal-ē-ˌāt	return like for like to get revenge; pay back injury for injury	When Tybalt killed Romeo's best friend, Romeo *retaliated* by slaying Tybalt.
67	**solemnly** (*adv.*) ˈsäl-əm-lē	in a *solemn* (serious) manner; seriously; earnestly; gravely	On taking office, I *solemnly* pledged to do my best, and I intend to live up to that pledge.

APPLYING WHAT YOU HAVE LEARNED

Exercise 8.5:   Sentence Completion

Which of the two choices makes the sentence correct? Write the *letter* of the correct answer in the space provided.

1. Normally, when you campaign in hostile territory, you should be prepared to meet with ____.

   A. ridicule and disruption B. support and encouragement

2. You would not expect someone who has just received a ____ to look dispirited.

   A. promotion B. bad news

3. The committee, ____, entered the conference room solemnly.

   A. smiling and joking with reporters B. determined to resolve the crisis

4. The spectators ____; there was no panic.

   A. trampled on one another in their rush to the exits B. gathered their belongings and filed quickly out of the theater

5. In the clamor I could ____.

   A. not hear what my neighbor was saying B. have heard a pin drop

6. Asked to leave at once, Bruce retaliated by ____.

   A. apologizing for his rudeness B. slamming the door on his way out

7. You may swim ____; there are no restrictions.

   A. anywhere along the beach B. in protected areas only

8. When you are ____ by a score of 10–0, the outlook is grim.

   A. trailing B. leading

9. The youngster molested the newborn puppy by ____.

   A. pulling its tail B. protecting it from harm

10. You saw me in a moment of frenzy when I was ____.

   A. completely aware of what I was doing B. in a rage over the umpire's ruling

Exercise 8.6: Concise Writing (Using Fewer Words)

Replace the italicized word or expression in each sentence below with a single word from the following list.

frenzy	molested	panic	retaliation	clamor
solemnly	grim	dispirited	restricted	hostilely

1. *Sudden unreasoning fear* gripped us. _____

2. Spending that is not *confined within limits or bounds* usually leads to bankruptcy. _____

3. To a pessimist the future always looks *hard and unyielding*. _____

4. The board did not want to propose a tax increase for fear of the *vigorous and insistent protest* it might unleash. _____

5. I cannot believe that any zoo visitor could have *persecuted* the animals *with hostile intent*. _____

6. Your accusation was so unjust that you drove her into a *temporary madness*. _____

7. The dealer assured us *in a serious manner* that the merchandise would arrive on time. _____

8. Since you have nothing to worry about, we cannot understand why your outlook is so *marked by gloom of spirit*. _____

9. Scott is not one to accept criticism without *returning like for like*. _____

10. They glared at us *in an antagonistic manner*. _____

Exercise 8.7: Name-the-Person Quiz

Read all the statements in the boxes. Then enter the required names in sentences 1 to 10, below.

> Max was in the habit of pushing or punching anyone younger or weaker who could be expected not to fight back.

> Despite the deadlock, Joyce saw a chance for compromise.

> Helen was saddened that so many should be ready to support her rival while nobody dared speak out for her.

> Sandy whispered humorous remarks to Betty and me during the sermon.

> Irving had asked so many questions when Peggy had the floor that she interrupted several times when he was speaking.

> The blue jays unleashed their piercing noises when Felix came near their nest.

> Werner said he would turn the dogs on Sue if she set foot on his property again.

1. _____ was disrespectful on a solemn occasion.

2. _____ panicked in an emergency.

3. _____ provoked a clamor.

4. _____ seemed to be in a frenzy.

5. _____ molested others.

6. _____ felt dispirited.

7. _____ did not want to violate a restriction.

8. _____ made a hostile remark.

9. _____ felt the situation was not entirely grim.

10. _____ did not hesitate to retaliate.

Exercise 8.8:   Using Synonyms and Antonyms

A. Avoid repetition by replacing the italicized word or expression in 1 to 5 below with a SYNONYM from the following list:

lenient	solemn	dispirited	panicked	frenzy
retaliate	unmolested	clamor	hostile	limited

1. Peter is obviously suffering from depression, but he refuses to tell anyone why he is *depressed*.   _____

2. We are not *antagonistic* to you; in fact we have no antagonism to anybody.   _____

3. Perfectly sane people may be overcome by a *temporary madness* and behave as if they were really mad.   _____

4. Being vengeful, they will probably seek an early opportunity to *take revenge*.   _____

5. We heard their *vigorous and insistent protest* but could not tell what they were protesting about.   _____

B. Complete each sentence in 6 to 10 below by inserting an ANTONYM of the italicized word from the above list.

6. Water use, once totally *unrestricted*, has to be

           , or shortages may develop.

7. The captain's *grim* devotion to duty prevented him from

   being   to the youthful offender.

8. Most of us *remained calm*, but a few   .

9. In some lands dissenters were *persecuted;* in others they

   were   .

10. The *jovial* atmosphere of the gathering turned

    when news of the air disaster was heard on TV.

LEARNING SOME ROOTS AND DERIVATIVES

Each capitalized word below is a *root*. The words under it are its *derivatives*.

CLAMOR (*n.*)	The sudden increase in food prices has produced a *clamor* of protest.
clamor (*v.*)	Consumers *are clamoring* for lower prices.
clamorous (*adj.*)	Their *clamorous* outcries have led to a federal investigation of the pricing policies of major distributors.
clamorously (*adv.*)	They had not been expected to protest so *clamorously*.
DISPIRIT (*v.*)	Andy raised our hopes and *dispirited* the opposition by slamming the first pitch for a home run.
dispirited (*adj.*)	Our opponents looked *dispirited*.
dispiritedly (*adv.*)	They watched *dispiritedly* as Andy trotted around the bases.
FRENZY (*n.*)	In a fit of *frenzy* over being denied the use of the car, Cindy abruptly left the dinner table.
frenzied (*adj.*)	Moments later, when her composure had returned, she apologized for her *frenzied* behavior.
GRIM (*adj.*)	The besieged city offered to negotiate a truce, but the *grim* attackers refused.
grimly (*adv.*)	They *grimly* insisted on the city's unconditional surrender within twenty-four hours.
grimness (*n.*)	Only then did the inhabitants fully realize the *grimness* of their situation.
HOSTILE (*adj.*)	I thought you were my friend. Why are you so *hostile?*
hostilely (*adv.*)	Why have you been acting so *hostilely?*
hostility (*n.*)	What is the reason for your *hostility?*

MOLEST (*v.*)	A hoodlum who had been *molesting* youngsters by beating them and stealing their bicycles has been arrested.
molester (*n.*)	The *molester* was identified to the police by two of his victims.
molestation (*n.*)	Since his arrest, there have been no further reports of *molestation*.
PANIC (*n.*)	The cry of "Fire" in the darkened theater led to a *panic*.
panic (*v.*)	At first, most people remained calm, but a few *panicked* and rushed for the exits.
panicky (*adj.*)	Such *panicky* persons can cause a great deal of trouble.
RESTRICT (*v.*)	Admission to the pool *is restricted* to residents who have purchased season tickets.
restriction (*n.*)	Children under 16 must leave the pool at 5 P.M. This *restriction* is necessary to make the pool available to adults returning from work.
restrictive (*adj.*) unrestricted (*adj.*)	Some feel that his policy is too *restrictive*, but others point out that children have *unrestricted* use of the pool from 10 A.M. to 5 P.M.
RETALIATE (*v.*)	The champion opened with a right to the head, and the challenger *retaliated* with several short jabs to the ribs.
retaliation (*n.*)	For the first three rounds, the fight was a draw; each punishing blow brought swift and effective *retaliation*.
retaliatory (*adj.*)	After the champion was staggered with a left to the jaw in the fourth, his *retaliatory* punches seemed to have lost their sting.
SOLEMN (*adj.*)	The fans were in a jovial mood, but when the fullback was injured, they became *solemn*.
solemnly (*adv.*)	Everyone watched *solemnly* as the club physician examined the fallen player.
solemnity (*n.*)	The instant the athlete rose to his feet unaided, there were loud cheers from the stands and the mood of *solemnity* was shattered.

Exercise 8.9: Using Roots and Derivatives

Fill each blank with the above root or derivative that best fits the meaning of the sentence.

1. The _____ between the two families stems from an old feud.

2. Laws that _____ the freedom of religion are unconstitutional.

3. At one point, the discussion was so _____ that it was almost like a shouting spree.

4. A stampede is likely to occur when cattle _____.

5. If Sharon's playmates took any of her toys, she used to _____ by scratching or biting.

6. I thought he had gone mad when I saw him gesturing in a(an) _____ manner.

7. Remember that you took a(an) _____ oath to tell the truth, the whole truth, and nothing but the truth.

8. At the noise of the explosion, the crowd became _____ and ran for cover.

9. Cheerleaders keep us from becoming _____ when our teams are not doing too well.

10. Have you ever felt the prospect of failure staring _____ in your face?

SPELLING REVIEW: ADDING SUFFIXES TO WORDS ENDING IN *-IC*

RULE 1:

Before adding -ED, -ING, -ER, or -Y to a word ending in -IC, insert the letter *k*.

picnic	+	ed	=	picnic*k*ed
frolic	+	ed	=	frolic*k*ed
mimic	+	ing	=	mimic*k*ing
panic	+	ing	=	panic*k*ing
picnic	+	er	=	picnic*k*er
traffic	+	er	=	traffic*k*er
panic	+	y	=	panic*k*y

The *k* keeps the *c* from being pronounced as *s*.

RULE 2:

Before adding -LY to a word ending in -IC, insert AL.

frantic	+	ly	=	frantic*al*ly
drastic	+	ly	=	drastic*al*ly

RULE 3:

When removing a suffix from a word ending in -IC, drop any extra letters that have been inserted.

frolicked	−	ed	=	frolic (*k* dropped)
tragically	−	ly	=	tragic (*al* dropped)

Exercise 8.10:   Adding a Suffix to, or Dropping a Suffix From, -IC words.

Perform the operation indicated.

SAMPLES: picnic + er = **picnicker**
frolicking – ing = **frolic**

1. picnic + ed = _____
2. terrific + ly = _____
3. mimicked – ed = _____
4. economic + ly = _____
5. traffic + ing = _____
6. specifically – ly = _____
7. fantastic + ly = _____
8. frolicker – er = _____
9. heroic + ly = _____
10. picnic + ing = _____
11. basic + ly = _____
12. panicky – y = _____
13. hectically – ly = _____
14. traffic + er = _____
15. romantic + ly = _____
16. electronically – ly = _____
17. artistic + ly = _____
18. mimic + er = _____
19. sarcastically – ly = _____
20. comic + ly = _____
21. panicking – ing = _____
22. tragically – ly = _____
23. realistic + ly = _____
24. frolic + ed = _____
25. patriotically – ly = _____
26. scientific + ly = _____
27. mimic + ing = _____
28. dramatically – ly = _____
29. panicked – ed = _____
30. frolic + ing = _____

IMPROVING YOUR USAGE: MAKING LOGICAL COMPARISONS

In making a comparison, there are two principles you should follow:

PRINCIPLE 1: Be sure that you are comparing things that are comparable.

WRONG: The price of the TV set is lower than the refrigerator.

Note that the above compares a *price* with a *refrigerator.* The two are not comparable, and therefore the sentence is illogical.

IMPROVED: The price of the TV set is lower than the price of the refrigerator.

This sentence is better because it compares two comparable things (the *price of the TV set* and the *price of the refrigerator*), but it contains repetition.

RECOMMENDED: The price of the TV set is lower than *that* of the refrigerator.

The above not only compares two comparable things, but it eliminates repetition of *the price* by using the pronoun *that.*

Let us now consider the following comparison:

WRONG: Our lives would be different from other children.

IMPROVED: Our lives would be different from *the lives* of other children.

RECOMMENDED: Our lives would be different from *those* of other children.

We have taken the recommended version from Richard Wright (see line 63, page 147). Note that he avoided repeating *the lives* by using the pronoun *those*.

Important: The pronouns *that* and *those* help make comparisons logical, and they make repetition unnecessary.

PRINCIPLE 2: Include the adjective **other** when comparing a person or thing with the rest of the group to which that person or thing belongs.

WRONG: Emily is younger than any of the girls.

RIGHT: Emily is younger than any of the *other* girls.

The adjective *other* is needed because Emily is being compared with the rest of her group. Note that *other* is not required in the following:

RIGHT: Emily is younger than any of the boys.

Exercise 8.11: Making Comparisons

In the space provided, rewrite each sentence containing a faulty comparison. If the sentence is correct, write "correct."

1. The industrial output of the United States is greater than any other nation.

_____

_____

2. His interests are not the same as other boys.

_____

_____

3. Angela was brighter than any pupil in her biology class.

_____

_____

4. The climate in New York cannot compare with Florida.

_____

_____

5. We found Hemingway's stories more interesting than those of other writers.

_____

_____

6. The tomatoes from your garden were tastier than any local supermarket.

_____

_____

7. Henry earned more money last summer than any of the boys.

_____

_____

8. People here are not so friendly as my old neighborhood.

_____

_____

9. Fred can type faster than any of the girls.

_____

_____

10. The pay of a major is higher than a captain.

_____

_____

Exercise 8.12:   Analogies

At the left, write the *letter* of the pair of words related to each other in the same way as the words of the capitalized pair.

_____ **1.** PANIC : FLEE

    (A) anxiety : relax   (B) moisture : shrivel
    (C) inattention : err   (D) heat : shiver
    (E) obstinacy : compromise

_____ **2.** DISPIRITED : ENCOURAGEMENT

    (A) floundering : footing   (B) covetous : jealousy
    (C) frenzied : madness   (D) exultant : triumph
    (E) supercilious : contempt

_____ **3.** CLAMOR : EAR

    (A) beverage : thirst   (B) exercise : health
    (C) commendation : morale   (D) dessert : dinner
    (E) glare : eyes

_____ **4.** ANTAGONISM : UNFRIENDLINESS

    (A) intimacy : unfamiliarity   (B) liberation : bondage
    (C) sociability : gregariousness (D) admonition : error
    (E) benevolence : inhumanity

_____ **5.** GRIM : KINDNESS

    (A) crafty : deception   (B) sullen : resentment
    (C) afflicted : suffering   (D) unbiased : prejudice
    (E) malicious : spite

Review 2.1: Composition

Rewrite each paragraph in the space provided, following the instructions below.

A Complaint

[1]Carol entered the Principal's office to complain about something. [2]It was upsetting her very much. [3]She hoped that no other student would be present since it was a matter that concerned her personally. [4]She saw an opportunity to talk with the Principal. [5]She went up to his desk.

Combine S1 and 2 into a complex sentence, changing S2 to an adjective clause.

In S3 reduce the adjective clause *that concerned her personally* to an adjective.

Change S4 to a participial phrase and combine it with S5.

_____

_____

_____

_____

_____

_____

_____

_____

[6]He looked up. [7]She tried to speak. [8]Tears momentarily choked off her words. [9]She regained her composure. [10]She proceeded to pour out her feelings.

Combine S6, 7, and 8 into a compound-complex sentence, changing S6 to a dependent clause.

Change S9 to a participial phrase and combine it with S10.

_____

_____

_____

_____

_____

_____

¹¹She was disappointed. ¹²She had not been chosen for the drama award. ¹³She had been applauded yesterday for doing a scene as Blanche Du Bois in *A Streetcar Named Desire*. ¹⁴Mrs. Jones had called it the finest bit of acting that had been seen in the class in a long time. ¹⁵She was also highly regarded by Mr. Esposito. ¹⁶He had selected her for roles of importance in three school plays.

Combine S11 and 12 into a complex sentence.

Find an adverb in S13 and begin the sentence with it.

In S14 reduce the adjective clause *that had been seen* to one word.

Combine S15 and 16 into a complex sentence; also, change the prepositional phrase *of importance* to an adjective.

_____

_____

_____

_____

_____

_____

_____

_____

_____

_____

¹⁷She had been awarded the drama prize in junor high school. ¹⁸She was expecting to win the high school prize, too. ¹⁹Her hopes of becoming an actress were now ruined. ²⁰Someone else was getting the prize.

Combine S17 and 18 into a complex sentence, changing S17 to a dependent clause.

Find an adverb in S19 and begin the sentence with it; then, with a semicolon, combine S19 and 20 into a compound sentence.

_____

_____

_____

_____

_____

²¹Carol had finished. ²²The Principal explained the work of the Awards Committee. ²³It had gone over the records of several outstanding students, including hers. ²⁴She had not been chosen. ²⁵That should not keep her from studying for an acting career in college. ²⁶She knows that she has acted successfully in the past. ²⁷She should, in his opinion, look to the future with confidence in her talent.

Combine S21, 22, and 23 into a complex sentence, changing S21 and 23 to dependent clauses.

Combine S24 and 25 into a compound sentence.

Change S26 to a participial phrase and combine it with S27.

_____

_____

_____

_____

_____

_____

_____

_____

_____

_____

²⁸Carol felt somewhat better. ²⁹She left. ³⁰She was still unhappy about not getting the prize.

Combine S28, 29, and 30 into a compound-complex sentence, changing S29 to a dependent clause.

_____

_____

_____

Review 2.2:   Correct Usage

Each numbered item below presents three ways of expressing the same idea. Which way is the best way, A, B, or C? Write the *letter* of your answer in the space provided at the left.

_____ 1. (A) There are thousands of people without homes.
(B) There are thousands of people who have no homes.
(C) There are thousands of homeless people.

_____ 2. (A) We were on the way home. We were in a happy mood. It began to pour.
(B) We were on the way home, in a happy mood, when it began to pour.
(C) We were on the way home, in a happy mood, and it started to pour.

_____ 3. (A) She went out into the downpour without a raincoat or an umbrella.
(B) She went out into the downpour. Without a raincoat or an umbrella.
(C) She went out into the downpour. She had neither a raincoat nor an umbrella.

_____ 4. (A) The speed of light is far greater than sound.
(B) The speed of light is far greater than the speed of sound.
(C) The speed of light is far greater than that of sound.

_____ 5. (A) I left for the pool, and I forgot to take a towel.
(B) I left for the pool, forgetting to take a towel.
(C) I left for the pool. Forgetting to take a towel.

Review 2.3: Name-the-Situation Quiz

Each sentence below describes a situation that can be summed up in one word. Select that word from the list below, and write it in the space provided.

panic	affectation	harvest	deference
sustenance	jubilation	petulance	sullenness
corpulence	retaliation	contagion	covetousness

1. _____ An eye for an eye, a tooth for a tooth.

2. _____ His cultured accent seemed artificial and did not fit in with the rest of his personality.

3. _____ Oh, if she could have had her neighbor's fine clothes and jewels!

4. _____ Ask somebody else, why don't you? Can't you see I'm busy? I don't want to be bothered!

5. _____ Supplies of fresh water and food were flown in daily.

6. _____ For the past three weeks, farmers—with the help of hired labor—have been gathering in their corn.

7. _____ When word of the rescue arrived, there was dancing in the streets.

8. _____ Because he was not chosen for the social committee, he sat gloomily through the rest of the meeting and said not a word.

9. _____ I gave in to my friends and accompanied them to the beach, though I would have preferred the pool.

10. _____ An unfounded rumor of a sugar shortage sent shoppers flocking to their supermarkets, and soon there was not a pound on the shelves.

Review 2.4: Vocabulary and Spelling

Each group of words below can be replaced by a one-word synonym. Find that word in the list at the bottom of the exercise, complete its spelling, and insert it in the WORD column.

GROUP OF WORDS   WORD

1. something, as a law, that restrains   _____

2. gave support to   _____

3. great desire or longing   _____

4. temporary madness   _____

5. full of good humor   _____

6. persistent pain   _____

7. returned like for like   _____

8. sudden unreasoning terror   _____

9. gathered in   _____

10. persecuted with hostile intent   _____

11. shrank and became wrinkled   _____

12. noisy shouting   _____

13. skillful at deceiving others   _____

14. gave in to the opinion of another   _____

15. marked by gloom of spirit   _____

16. very great   _____

17. in a serious manner   _____

18. flowed slowly through   _____

19. enviously desired   _____

20. in an ill-humored manner   _____

GNAW__ __G   __ __LEMNLY

SH__ __VELED   CRAVI__ __

COVE__ __D   MOL__ __TED

FR__ __ZY   CLAM__ __

R__ __TRICTION   DEF__ __RED

C__ __FTY   SUST__ __NED

EXT__ __ME   PAN__ __

__ __VIAL   __ __ZED

H__ __VESTED   DISP__ __ITED

PETU__ __NTLY   RET__ __IATED

Review 2.5:   Synonyms and Antonyms

For each italicized word, write a SYNONYM in column A and an ANTONYM in column B. Choose all synonyms and antonyms from the list at the bottom of the exercise.

SYNONYM   ANTONYM

Column A   *Column B*

_____   **1.** slowly *withdrew*   _____

_____   **2.** on *succeeding* days   _____

_____   **3.** a time of *rejoicing*   _____

_____   **4.** *kept* everything   _____

_____   **5.** *inhospitable* attitude   _____

_____   **6.** *sly* dealings   _____

_____   **7.** *portly* bartender   _____

_____   **8.** *fierce* rival   _____

_____   **9.** *alleviated* our concern   _____

_____   **10.** *detestable* idea   _____

intensified	straightforward	abominable	relinquished
subsequent	lean	hostile	grim
advanced	lenient	allayed	dejection
friendly	receded	obese	previous
retained	exultation	furtive	laudable

Review 2.6:   Concise Writing (Using Fewer Words)

Express the thought of each of the following sentences in *no more than four words*, as in 1, below.

1. Others enviously desired to have the position that I held.
Others coveted my position. _____

2. The clouds up in the sky are becoming more and more distant.

_____

3. Isn't the cold that you have communicable to others by contact?

_____

4. We have a strong dislike of those who are haughtily disdainful of others.

_____

5. For what reason was graduation put off to another date?

_____

6. Some people are not inclined to seek the company of others.

_____

Review 2.7: Analogies

At the left, write the _letter_ of the pair of words related to each other in the same way as the words of the capitalized pair.

_____ **1.** INTERNET : INFORMATION

    (A) foundation : concrete   (B) forethought : error
    (C) sustenance : starvation   (D) immunization : polio
    (E) comedy : laughter

_____ **2.** PROTEIN : NUTRIENT

    (A) peninsula : island   (B) clue : solution
    (C) gnawing : pain   (D) cauliflower : fruit
    (E) astrology : science

_____ **3.** ADJOINING : TOUCH

    (A) trite : fascinate   (B) grim : yield
    (C) flimsy : support   (D) tedious : bore
    (E) menacing : ignore

_____ **4.** SLY : FURTIVE

    (A) haughty : supercilious   (B) petulant : content
    (C) sullen : cheerful   (D) portly : lean
    (E) dispirited : jubilant

_____ **5.** HOSTILE : FRIENDLINESS

    (A) ingenious : cleverness   (B) humane : malice
    (C) tranquil : serenity   (D) vain : conceit
    (E) blissful : obstinacy

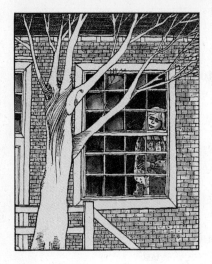

from

The Red Badge of Courage

by Stephen Crane

Henry Fleming has just quit school to enlist in the Union Army.

From his home he had gone to the seminary to bid adieu to many schoolmates. They had thronged about him with wonder and admiration. He had felt the gulf now between them and had swelled with calm pride. He and some of his fellows who had
5 donned blue were quite overwhelmed with privileges for all of one afternoon, and it had been a very delicious thing. They had strutted.

A certain light-haired girl had made vivacious fun at his martial spirit, but there was another and darker girl whom he had gazed
10 at steadfastly, and he thought she grew demure and sad at the sight of his blue and brass. As he had walked down the path between the rows of oaks, he had turned his head and detected her at a window watching his departure. As he perceived her, she had immediately begun to stare up through the high tree branches at
15 the sky. He had seen a good deal of flurry and haste in her movement as she changed her attitude. He often thought of it.

On the way to Washington his spirit had soared. The regiment was fed and caressed at station after station until the youth had believed that he must be a hero. There was a lavish expenditure of
20 bread and cold meats, coffee, and pickles and cheese. As he basked in the smiles of the girls and was patted and complimented by the old men, he had felt growing within him the strength to do mighty deeds of arms.

After complicated journeyings with many pauses, there had
25 come months of monotonous life in a camp. He had had the belief that real war was a series of death struggles with small time in

between for sleep and meals; but since his regiment had come to the field the army had done little but sit still and try to keep warm.

He was brought then gradually back to his old ideas. Greeklike struggles would be no more. Men were better, or more timid. Secular and religious education had effaced the throat-grappling instinct, or else firm finance held in check the passions.

He had grown to regard himself merely as a part of a vast blue demonstration. His province was to look out, as far as he could, for his personal comfort. For recreation he could twiddle his thumbs and speculate on the thoughts which must agitate the minds of the generals. Also, he was drilled and drilled and reviewed, and drilled and drilled and reviewed.

The only foes he had seen were some pickets along the river bank. They were a sun-tanned, philosophical lot, who sometimes shot reflectively at the blue pickets. When reproached for this afterward, they usually expressed sorrow, and swore by their gods that the guns had exploded without their permission. The youth, on guard duty one night, conversed across the stream with one of them. He was a slightly ragged man, who spat skillfully between his shoes and possessed a great fund of bland and infantile assurance. The youth liked him personally.

"Yank," the other had informed him, "yer a right dum good feller." This sentiment, floating to him upon the still air, had made him temporarily regret war.

Various veterans had told him tales. Some talked of gray, bewhiskered hordes who were advancing with relentless curses and chewing tobacco with unspeakable valor; tremendous bodies of fierce soldiery who were sweeping along like the Huns. Others spoke of tattered and eternally hungry men who fired despondent powders. "They'll charge through hell's fire an' brimstone t' git a holt on a haversack, an' sech stomachs ain't a-lastin' long," he was told. From the stories, the youth imagined the red, live bones sticking out through slits in the faded uniforms.

Still, he could not put a whole faith in veterans' tales, for recruits were their prey. They talked much of smoke, fire, and blood, but he could not tell how much might be lies. They persistently yelled, "Fresh fish!" at him, and were in no wise to be trusted.

However, he perceived now that it did not greatly matter what kind of soldiers he was going to fight, so long as they fought, which fact no one disputed. There was a more serious problem. He lay in his bunk pondering upon it. He tried to mathematically prove to himself that he would not run from a battle.

Previously he had never felt obliged to wrestle too seriously with this question. In his life he had taken certain things for granted, never challenging his beliefs in ultimate success, and bothering little about means and roads. But here he was confronted with a thing of moment. It had suddenly appeared to him that perhaps in a battle he might run. He was forced to admit that as far as war was concerned he knew nothing of himself.

A sufficient time before, he would have allowed the problem to kick its heels at the outer portals of his mind, but now he felt compelled to give serious attention to it.

80 A little panic-fear grew in his mind. As his imagination went forward to a fight, he saw hideous possibilities. He contemplated the lurking menaces of the future, and failed in an effort to see himself standing stoutly in the midst of them. He recalled his visions of broken-bladed glory, but in the shadow of the impending tumult

85 he suspected them to be impossible pictures.

He sprang from the bunk and began to pace nervously to and fro. "Good Lord, what's th' matter with me?" he said aloud.

He felt that in this crisis his laws of life were useless. Whatever he had learned of himself was here of no avail. He was an un-

90 known quantity. He saw that he would again be obliged to experiment as he had in early youth. He must accumulate information of himself, and meanwhile he resolved to remain close upon his guard lest those qualities of which he knew nothing should everlastingly disgrace him. "Good Lord!" he repeated in dismay.

95 After a time the tall soldier slid dexterously through the hole. The loud private followed. They were wrangling.

"That's all right," said the tall soldier as he entered. He waved his hand expressively, "You can believe me or not, jest as you like. All you got to do is to sit down and wait as quiet as you can. Then

100 pretty soon you'll find out I was right."

His comrade grunted stubbornly. For a moment he seemed to be searching for a formidable reply. Finally he said: "Well, you don't know everything in the world, do you?"

"Didn't say I knew everything in the world," retorted the other sharply. He began to stow various articles snugly into his

105 knapsack.

The youth, pausing in his nervous walk, looked down at the busy figure. "Going to be a battle, sure, is there, Jim?" he asked.

"Of course there is," replied the tall soldier. "Of course there is. You jest wait 'til tomorrow, and you'll see one of the biggest battles

110 ever was. You jest wait."

"Thunder!" said the youth.

"Oh, you'll see fighting this time, my boy, what'll be regular out-and-out fighting," added the tall soldier, with the air of a man who is about to exhibit a battle for the benefit of his friends.

115 "Huh!" said the loud one from a corner.

"Well," remarked the youth, "like as not this story'll turn out jest like them others did."

"Not much it won't," replied the tall soldier, exasperated. "Not much it won't. Didn't the cavalry all start this morning?" He glared

120 about him. No one denied his statement. "The cavalry started this morning," he continued. "They say there ain't hardly any cavalry left in camp. They're going to Richmond, or some place, while we fight all the Johnnies. It's some dodge like that. The regiment's got orders, too. A feller what seen 'em go to headquarters told me a lit-

125 tle while ago. And they're raising blazes all over camp—anybody can see that."

"Shucks!" said the loud one.

The youth remained silent for a time. At last he spoke to the tall soldier. "Jim!"

"What?" 130

"How do you think the reg'ment 'll do?"

"Oh, they'll fight all right, I guess, after they once get into it," said the other with cold judgment. He made a fine use of the third person. "There's been heaps of fun poked at 'em because they're new, of course, and all that; but they'll fight all right, I guess." 135

"Think any of the boys 'll run?" persisted the youth.

"Oh, there may be a few of 'em run, but there's them kind in every regiment, 'specially when they first goes under fire," said the other in a tolerant way. "Of course it might happen that the hull kit-and-boodle might start and run, if some big fighting came first- 140 off, and then again they might stay and fight like fun. But you can't bet on nothing. Of course they ain't never been under fire yet, and it ain't likely they'll lick the hull rebel army all-to-oncet the first time; but I think they'll fight better than some, if worse than others. That's the way I figger. They call the reg'ment 'Fresh fish' 145 and everything; but the boys come of good stock, and most of 'em 'll fight like sin after they oncet git shootin'," he added, with a mighty emphasis on the last four words.

"Oh, you think you know—" began the loud soldier with scorn.

The other turned savagely upon him. They had a rapid alterca- 150 tion, in which they fastened upon each other various strange epithets.

The youth at last interrupted them. "Did you ever think you might run yourself, Jim?" he asked. On concluding the sentence he laughed as if he had meant to aim a joke. The loud soldier also 155 giggled.

The tall private waved his hand. "Well," said he profoundly, "I've thought it might get too hot for Jim Conklin in some of them scrimmages, and if a whole lot of boys started and run, why, I s'pose I'd start and run. And if I once started to run, I'd run like the 160 devil, and no mistake. But if everybody was a-standing and a-fight-ing, why, I'd stand and fight. By jiminey, I would. I'll bet on it."

"Huh!" said the loud one.

The youth of this tale felt gratitude for these words of his com-rade. He had feared that all of the untried men possessed a great 165 and correct confidence. He now was in a measure reassured.

Line 1. *seminary:* secondary school
Line 31. *secular:* nonreligious
Line 32. *effaced:* wiped out
Line 58. *haversack:* bag similar to a knapsack but worn over one shoulder

Line 78. *portals:* gates
Line 95. *dexterously:* skillfully
Line 102. *formidable:* awe-inspiring
Line 152. *epithets:* abusive names

Exercise 9.1:   Close Reading

In the blank space, write the *letter* of the choice that best completes the statement or answers the question.

1. Henry was most disturbed by the _____.

   (A) memory of the dark-haired girl
   (B) treatment he got from the veterans
   (C) fear that he might panic under fire
   (D) possibility that his regiment might not do well in battle

2. The term "fresh fish" (lines 64 and 145) is meant to suggest a lack of _____.

   (A) experience
   (B) common sense
   (C) respect for one's elders
   (D) courage

3. The passage indicates that Henry _____.

   (A) is close to the front but has done no fighting
   (B) has already participated in a few battles
   (C) is far removed from the enemy lines
   (D) has had no personal contact whatsoever with the enemy

4. Which statement about the tall soldier is NOT supported by the passage? _____

   (A) He dislikes being contradicted.
   (B) He is truthful in replying to Henry's questions.
   (C) He has an exaggerated opinion of his own bravery.
   (D) His past predictions have not proved accurate.

5. The expression "Yank, yer a right dum good feller" _____.

   (A) is spoken by a veteran of Henry's regiment to tease him
   (B) makes Henry feel offended
   (C) puzzles Henry
   (D) arouses brotherly feelings in Henry for his foe

IMPROVING YOUR COMPOSITION SKILLS: USING ADVERBS

QUESTION: *What is an adverb?*

An **adverb** is a word that modifies a verb, an adjective, another adverb, or an entire clause or sentence.

He . . . began to pace *nervously* (line 86)
(adverb *nervously* modifies verb *to pace*)

. . . a *slightly* ragged man (line 46)
(adverb *slightly* modifies adjective *ragged*)

. . . *pretty* soon (line 100)
(adverb *pretty* modifies adverb *soon*)

. . . *perhaps* in a battle he might run (lines 74–75)
(adverb *perhaps* modifies entire clause)

. . . *Previously* he had never felt obliged to wrestle seriously
with this question. (lines 70–71)
(adverb *Previously* modifies entire sentence)

QUESTION: *What questions does an adverb answer?*

An *adverb* usually answers one of the following questions:

QUESTION	EXAMPLE
How or *in what manner?*	He . . . began to pace *nervously* . . . (adverb *nervously* tells how he paced)
When?	. . . he had *never* felt obliged . . . (adverb *never* tells when he felt obliged)
Where?	But *here* he was confronted . . . (adverb *here* tells where he was confronted)
How much?	. . . the army had done *little* . . . (adverb *little* tells how much the army had done)

Exercise 9.2:   Locating Adverbs in Reading Selection 9

Which adverb modifies the following word or expression in Reading Selection 9?
Write that adverb in the blank space at the right.

SAMPLE: *were overwhelmed* in line 5 on page 172   <u>   **quite**   </u>

1. *delicious* in line 6   _____

2. *had begun* in lines 13–14   _____

3. *to stare* in line 14   _____

4. *thought* in line 16   _____

5. *was brought* in line 30   _____

6. *timid* in line 31   _____

7. *expressed* in line 43   _____

8. *liked* in line 48   _____

9. *yelled* in line 63   _____

10. *seriously* in line 70   _____

QUESTION: *Can phrases* and *clauses* be used as adverbs?

Yes. Compare the following:

(A) He began to pace *nervously.*
(B) He began to pace *in a nervous manner.*
(C) He began to pace *as if he were nervous.*

Note that the idea of the adverb *nervously* in sentence A can be expressed also through the prepositional phrase *in a nervous manner* in sentence B, or through the clause *as if he were nervous* in sentence C.

ADVERB PHRASE:

> A prepositional phrase used as an adverb is known as an ***adverb phrase.***
> In sentence B, above, *in a nervous manner* is an adverb phrase.

ADVERB CLAUSE:

> A clause used as an adverb is known as an ***adverb clause.*** In sentence C, above, *as if he were nervous* is an adverb clause.

To make your writing more varied and more interesting, you should be able to use all three ways of expressing an adverbial idea—the simple adverb, the adverb phrase, and the adverb clause.

AVOIDING MONOTONY IN EXPRESSING ADVERBIAL IDEAS

Note the following:

> "His comrade grunted *stubbornly. For a moment* he seemed to be searching for a formidable reply. *Finally* he said . . ."

Suppose, in place of *For a moment*, Stephen Crane had written *Momentarily.* Notice how monotonous it would have been to have three -LY adverbs—*stubbornly, momentarily,* and *finally*—in so short a passage.
The author avoided monotony by using the adverb phrase *For a moment.*

Note also:

> "*As he perceived her*, she had immediately begun to stare up through the high tree branches at the sky. He had seen a good deal of flurry and haste in her movement *as she changed her attitude.* He often thought of it.
> *On the way to Washington* . . ."

Imagine the monotonous effect if, instead of *On the way to Washington*, Crane had written *As he made his way to Washington*. That would have given us three adverb clauses beginning with *as* uncomfortably close to one another. Crane varied his writing here by using the adverb phrase *On the way to Washington*.

Exercise 9.3: Using Adverb Phrases

Rewrite each sentence, replacing the italicized adverb with an adverb phrase from the list at the end of the exercise.

SAMPLES: *Seldom* is she wrong.
     In few instances is she wrong.

1. *Temporarily*, the machine is out of order.

_____

2. You cannot remain *here*.

_____

3. *Finally*, our turn came.

_____

4. He was now *somewhat* reassured.

_____

5. I see her *occasionally*.

_____

6. *Gradually* things changed.

_____

7. They attended *unwillingly*.

_____

8. *Incidentally*, how are you?

_____

9. *Often* there were complaints.

_____

10. You have *always* been dependable.

_____

Adverb Phrases

at last	on many occasions	at all times	at times
in few instances	against their will	in a measure	by the way
by degrees	in this place	for the time being	

Exercise 9.4: Replacing an Adverb Clause With an Adverb Phrase

Replace the italicized adverb clause with an equivalent adverb phrase.

SAMPLES: *When the sun goes down,* the flag is taken in.
At sundown, the flag is taken in.

She dove from the high board *as though she were a swan.*
She dove from the high board *like a swan.*

1. The mist begins to lift *when the sun rises.*

   _____

2. *As we were coming home,* we met your cousin.

   _____

3. He questioned us *as if he were a detective.*

   _____

4. She received the news *while she was at school.*

   _____

5. I paid *though it was against my will.*

   _____

6. *When I got to the middle of the book,* I found some dull passages.

   _____

7. Everyone leaves for lunch *as the clock strikes twelve.*

   _____

8. He played the outfield *as though he were a veteran.*

   _____

9. *When you get to the entrance,* you must show your card.

   _____

10. Some of us were worried *as we began the climb.*

    _____

Exercise 9.5:   Review of Ways to Express Adverbial Ideas

Fill in the blanks, as in the sample.

ADVERB	ADVERB PHRASE	ADVERB CLAUSE
Luckily I got another chance.	*Through luck* (or *By a stroke of luck*) I got another chance.	*Since* (or *As*) *I was lucky,* I got another chance.
1. You left the switch on *carelessly.*	You left the switch on *through* _____.	You left the switch on *because you* _____.
2. He yelled at us _____.	He yelled at us *like a savage.*	He yelled at us *as if* _____ _____.
3. They worked _____.	They worked *with* _____.	They worked *as though they were enthusiastic.*
4. *First* our country was known as the Thirteen Colonies.	_____, our country was known as the Thirteen Colonies.	*When our country* _____ _____, it was known as the Thirteen Colonies.
5. They served _____.	They served *against their will.*	They served *although they* _____.
6. _____, we would have had a parade.	*In* _____ _____, we would have had a parade.	*If times had been normal,* we would have had a parade.
7. She does the step *effortlessly.*	She does the step _____ _____.	She does the step *as if it requires* _____.
8. We accept your challenge _____.	We accept your challenge *without fear.*	We accept your challenge *because we* _____.
9. Should we have dinner _____?	Should we have dinner *after* _____?	Should we have dinner *when the show is over?*
10. Sandy *always* knows the answer.	Sandy knows the answer _____.	Sandy knows the answer *whenever anyone* _____.

The Red Badge of Courage is considered a *psychological* novel because it shows us what is happening in the *mind* of Henry Fleming. For example:

> It had suddenly appeared to him that perhaps in a battle he might run. He was forced to admit that as far as war was concerned he knew nothing of himself.

How well do you know yourself? How, for instance, do you think you would behave in one of the following situations?

1. You are in the bank to cash a check for $115. After you leave the teller's window, you count the money and realize that you have been given $150.

2. You are driving along a highway at 55 miles per hour. All of a sudden a small animal darts in front of your car. Instantly you realize that the car behind you will almost certainly crash into you if you apply the brakes.

3. It is two days before the final examination in a subject with which you are having trouble. If you fail, you may not graduate. A student you hardly know offers to sell you a copy of the final for $100.

4. You hear cries for help. An elderly person is being mugged by someone apparently not much older than yourself. A half dozen other passersby are attracted by the cries, but not one of them interferes.

Exercise 9.6: Writing a Composition: How I Might React

Choose *one* of the above situations. Describe how you would react to that situation on the basis of what you know—or think you know—of yourself. Write about 150 words, dividing your composition into three paragraphs, as in the following model. Also, in expressing your adverbial ideas, use some adverbs, some adverb phrases, and some adverb clauses. *Hint:* If you begin your composition with an *if*-clause, you will be beginning with an adverb clause.

Model Composition: How I Might React

[1]If the teller handed me $150 instead of $115, I would be tempted for a moment to keep it. [2]In all probability, I would immediately count it again to make sure I was not dreaming. [3]Unquestionably the thought of what I could do with the extra $35 would flash into my mind. [4]I would be lying if I did not admit that.

[5]But then my conscience would begin to bother me. [6]I would wonder who might suffer if I kept the money. [7]Perhaps the teller would have to make it up out of her own salary. [8]She might even lose her job when the error was discovered. [9]All of these thoughts would race through my brain.

[10]Though I could certainly use the extra money, I would go back to the teller and ask her to count the money again.

Analysis

ORGANIZATION. The writer explores both courses of action in paragraphs of about equal length (paragraphs 1 and 2) and reaches a conclusion in a very brief concluding paragraph (paragraph 3).

Paragraph 1 (S1–4) considers keeping the money.
Paragraph 2 (S5–9) considers returning the money.
Paragraph 3 (S10) states the writer's decision.

EXPRESSION OF ADVERBIAL IDEAS

Adverbs: immediately (S2); again (S2); Unquestionably (S3); then (S5); Perhaps (S7); even (S8); certainly (S10); again (S10)

Adverb Phrases: for a moment (S1); In all probability (S2); into my mind (S3); out of her own salary (S7); through my brain (S9)

Adverb Clauses: If . . . $115 (S1); if . . . that (S4); if . . . money (S6); when . . . discovered (S8); Though . . . money (S10)

Note that, in the model composition, adverb clauses were introduced by *if*, *when*, and *though*. You may also begin such clauses with *as*, *as if*, *because*, *since*, *whenever*, and *while*.

My Composition: How I Might React

_____
_____
_____
_____
_____
_____
_____
_____
_____
_____
_____
_____
_____
_____
_____
_____
_____
_____
_____
_____
_____

Line	Word	Meaning	Typical Use
150	**altercation** (*n.*) ˌȯl-tər-ˈkā-shən	noisy or angry dispute; heated argument; quarrel; wrangle (*ant.* **accord**)	If I had not settled the *altercation* between the two sides, they surely would have come to blows. By getting each side to compromise a bit, I helped them reach an *accord*.
21	**compliment** (*v.*) ˈkäm-plə-ˌment	congratulate; express esteem or admiration to; pay a *compliment* (commendation) to	Lola should be *complimented* for insisting that her passengers fasten their seat belts—not criticized.
88	**crisis** (*n.*) ˈkrī-səs	time of great danger and instability; emergency; turning point	The company was confronted with a financial *crisis* when some of its customers did not pay their bills on time.
84	**impending** (*adj.*) im-ˈpend-iŋ	threatening to occur soon; imminent; about to happen; approaching	The *impending* dairy strike caused shoppers to stock up on milk.
19	**lavish** (*adj.*) ˈlav-ish	1. using, spending, or giving more than is necessary; extravagant (*ant.* **sparing**) 2. more than enough; very abundant; unlimited; profuse	Be *sparing*, not *lavish*, in your use of electricity; turn off the lights when you don't need them. We had a very meager lunch but a *lavish* dinner.
25	**monotonous** (*adj.*) mə-ˈnät-ən-əs	tiresomely uniform; lacking in variety; unvarying (*ant.* **interesting**)	Vacationing in the same place year after year can become *monotonous*.
62	**prey** (*n.*) ˈprā	1. animal hunted for food by another animal 2. person unable or helpless to resist attack; victim	When the soil is moist, robins dig for earthworms, their favorite *prey*. Right-handed batters were Jack's *prey;* he struck out six of them in the first four innings.

7	**strut** (*v.*) 'strət	walk in a stiff, pompous way, as if to impress observers; parade with a show of pride; swagger	To the strains of martial music, the uniformed marchers *strutted* past the reviewing stand.
72	**ultimate** (*adj.*) 'əl-tə-mət	last; furthest; final; coming at the end; most remote	The candidate has stated that his ambition is to serve the people as Governor for the next four years; but some people say that his *ultimate* goal is the White House.
54	**valor** (*n.*) 'val-ər	boldness or determination in facing great danger; personal bravery in combat; courage (*ant.* **cowardice**)	Thanks to the *valor* of the helicopter pilots, dozens of stranded flood victims were airlifted to safety.

APPLYING WHAT YOU HAVE LEARNED

Exercise 9.7: Sentence Completion

Which of the two choices makes the sentence correct? Write the *letter* of the correct answer in the space provided.

1. As soon as Alice was _____, her parents began to discuss her impending marriage.

   A. born   B. engaged

2. Pirates considered _____ vessels as their prey.

   A. naval   B. merchant

3. Usually _____ as their prey.

   A. freshmen consider seniors   B. seniors consider freshmen

4. From the _____, you can tell that the neighbors are having another altercation.

   A. threats and shouting   B. music and dancing

5. Business is _____ because most of the customers are lavish spenders.

   A. lagging   B. flourishing

6. The train's _____ is its ultimate destination.

   A. last stop   B. route

7. Since we were ahead by a score of _____, Andy's error in the ninth inning that permitted our opponents to score twice did not precipitate a crisis.

   A. 2–0   B. 8–0

8. If you strut, you will give the impression of being ____.

    A. humble   B. conceited

9. The firefighters have been cited for valor because they ____.

    A. have not missed a day's work in   B. rescued a trapped tenant from the roof
        ten years of service   of a burning building

10. The housing development consists of a monotonous array of homes, each of ____ size, shape, and design.

    A. varying   B. similar

Exercise 9.8:   Name-the-Person Quiz

Read all the statements in the boxes. Then enter the required names in sentences 1 to 10, below.

Juan's article may not get into the next issue unless Elaine approves it; she is editor-in-chief.

Barbara keeps her air-conditioning on all the time, even when she is not home.	Grant threw the first punch, but Sam should not have called him a coward.

We voted for John since Cynthia had said he is very dependable.	Lt. Gomez succeeded in defusing the explosive device just seconds before it was set to go off.

When called to receive his award, Donald walked across the platform in a stiff, pompous manner.

As usual, Quentin repeated some of his old jokes; nobody laughed.	Joan is still in a coma, but her physician expects her to recover.	Ann and Joel are now at the airport, waiting to greet Pat.

In the finals, Dolores will again face Betty Sue, who has beaten her soundly in previous tournaments.

    1. _____ was monotonous.

    2. _____ is lavish.

    3. _____ strutted.

    4. _____ complimented someone.

    5. _____ has the ultimate word.

    6. _____'s arrival is impending.

    7. _____ started an altercation.

    8. _____ showed valor.

9. _____ has been an easy prey.

10. _____ is going through a crisis.

Exercise 9.9: Using Synonyms and Antonyms

A. Avoid repetition by replacing the italicized word or expression in 1–5 below with a SYNONYM from the following list:

sparing	imminent	monotonous	accord	crisis
cowardice	first	swagger	victim	congratulate

1. The bullies preyed on the weak and defenseless, often choosing elderly or handicapped persons as their *prey*. _____s

2. After her show, people from whom she had never expected a complimentary word hastened to *compliment* her. _____

3. There is no longer need for emergency aid because the *emergency* is over. _____

4. Putting on his new outfit, he strutted in front of us like a peacock until he grew tired of *strutting*. _____ing

5. We were told something unusual was *about to happen*, but it has not happened yet. _____

B. Complete each sentence in 6–10 below by inserting an ANTONYM of the italicized word from the above list:

6. The parties in this *altercation* are so hostile to each other that they are unlikely to reach a(an) _____. _____

7. It is unthinkable for a person of exceptional *valor* to be suspected of _____. _____

8. Now we are much more _____ in the use of our resources; formerly, we were altogether too *lavish*. _____

9. To eat the same foods day after day is _____; variety is necessary if meals are to become *interesting*. _____

10. Our _____ stop will be Chicago: our *ultimate* destination is Manila in the Philippines. _____

Exercise 9.10: Concise Writing (Using Fewer Words)

Replace the italicized word or expression in each sentence below with a single word from the following list.

strut	crisis	prey	altercation	lavish
impending	ultimate	monotonous	valor	compliment

1. If you go north, the *most remote* point you can reach is the North Pole.

   _____

2. Reporters are usually on the scene when important events are *about to happen.*

   _____

3. Tomorrow, the Little Leaguers in their new uniforms will *parade with a show of pride* down Main Street.

   _____

4. The taxicab driver and his passenger were having a(an) *angry dispute.*

   _____

5. The management provides its guests with a(an) *very abundant* supply of towels.

   _____

6. I must *express my admiration to* you on your good judgment.

   _____

7. For her *boldness in facing great danger*, the officer has been recommended for promotion.

   _____

8. In a(an) *time of great danger and instability*, we must not panic.

   _____

9. We had to listen to a succession of candidates with *tiresomely uniform* speeches.

   _____

10. People who know little about buying property may become the *helpless victims* of fraudulent land dealers.

   _____

LEARNING SOME ROOTS AND DERIVATIVES

Each capitalized word below is a *root*. The words under it are its *derivatives*.

COMPLIMENT (*n.*)   My coach paid me a *compliment* when he said I was doing well.

compliment (*v.*)   He *complimented* me on my improvement.

complimentary (*adj.*)   I was pleased by his *complimentary* remark.

uncomplimentary (*adj.*)   Once, when I dropped two throws in a close game, I was given the *uncomplimentary* name of "Butterfingers."

CRISIS (*n.*)   Some communities are undergoing a financial *crisis*.

critical (*adj.*)   They are faced with a *critical* shortage of funds.

critically (*adv.*)   They are *critically* short of money.

IMPEND (*v.*)   Several mayors are warning of the crisis that *impends* because of a lack of funds to meet expenses.

impending (*adj.*)   They are issuing warnings of an *impending* crisis.

LAVISH (*adj.*)	Our government usually welcomes visiting heads of state with *lavish*, red-carpet hospitality.
lavish (*v.*)	We *lavish* attention on important guests.
lavishly (*adv.*)	We entertain them *lavishly* with parades, receptions, and banquets.
lavishness (*n.*)	This *lavishness* is considered necessary for good international relations.

MONOTONOUS (*adj.*)	Any TV or radio commercial repeated too often becomes *monotonous*.
monotonously (*adv.*)	Listeners often "tune out" *monotonously* familiar advertisements.
monotony (*n.*)	Some advertisers keep changing their commercials to avoid *monotony*.

| PREY (*n.*) | The great white shark regards anything that swims as its *prey*—even other sharks. |
| prey (*v.*) | It *preys* on sea life. |

| STRUT (*v.*) | Behind the marching band *strutted* a company of goose-stepping troops. |
| strut (*n.*) | They marched with a straight-legged, stiff-kneed *strut*. |

ULTIMATE (*adj.*)	The strike is a union's *ultimate* weapon.
ultimately (*adv.*)	Violations of a union contract, unless corrected, may *ultimately* result in a strike.
ultimatum (*n.*)	The union has stated its final position in an *ultimatum*: it will go on strike unless contract violations are stopped at once.

VALOR (*n.*)	Reports of the sinking contained compliments for the *valor* of the captain and crew.
valorous (*adj.*)	The *valorous* captain was the last to leave the ship.
valorously (*adv.*)	The captain *valorously* stayed aboard until the last of the passengers and crew were evacuated.

Exercise 9.11:   Using Roots and Derivatives

Fill each blank with the above root or derivative that best fits the meaning of the sentence.

1. If you know how to shop, you can be well dressed at little cost; it is not necessary to _____ money on clothes.

2. The invaders issued a(an) _____ directing the inhabitants to lay down their arms.

3. The defenders fought _____, refusing to surrender.

4. When Marcia said that I have a good voice, I thanked her for the _____.

5. Word of her coming promotion has made her hold her head high and walk with something of a(an) _____.

6. Why do you bore us by _____ repeating the same old ideas?

7. Since we are now passing through the most _____ phase of the emergency, we need all the help we can get.

8. Professional athletes cannot compete forever; _____, they must retire.

9. Spiders _____ on insects.

10. Are you aware of the disasters that _____ unless we clean up our environment?

SPELLING REVIEW: *COMPLIMENT* AND *COMPLEMENT*

The VERBS *compliment* and *complement* are *homonyms*, words pronounced alike but different in meaning.

The corresponding NOUNS *compliment* and *complement* are also homonyms, and so, too, are the ADJECTIVES *complimentary* and *complementary*.

Study the uses of these words so that you will be able to spell them correctly.

Used as Verbs

1. (A) To *compliment* means "to praise."

> Let me *compliment* you on your improvement.

> "As he . . . was patted and *complimented* by the old men." (line 20)

(B) To *complement* means "to make complete, fill in what is lacking, or round off."

> The singer and her accompanist are a team; each *complements* the other.

> The gown is beautiful, and I have just the right shoes to *complement* it.

Used as Nouns

2. (A) The noun *compliment* means "commendation or praise."

> Your former employer writes that you are conscientious and intelligent; that is a very fine *compliment*.

> The plural *compliments* means "regards or best wishes."

> My sister Sandra sends you her *compliments*.

> Enclosed is a discount coupon with the *compliments* of your local druggist.

(B) The noun *complement* means "something that completes or makes perfect."

A tasty dessert is the *complement* to a good dinner.

Used as Adjectives

3. (A) The adjective *complimentary* means "expressing praise or commendation."

People are flocking to see the new movie that has received several *complimentary* reviews.

Another meaning of *complimentary* is "given free as a courtesy or favor."

We did not pay admission, as I had *complimentary* tickets.

(B) The adjective *complementary* means "completing"; also, "mutually making up what is lacking."

The two regions have *complementary* economies; one specializes in industry, and the other in farming.

The adjective *complementary* is often used in describing angles and colors.

Two angles are *complementary* if they together add up to a right angle (90 degrees).

Two colors are *complementary* if, when combined in the proper proportions, they produce white light.

Exercise 9.12: Using COMPLIMENT, COMPLEMENT, and Their Derivatives

Complete the following:

1. I do not appreciate your remarks about my work; they are not very _____.

2. Violet and yellow are _____ colors.

3. When you see Jack, give him my _____.

4. I _____ you on your extraordinary patience.

5. The partners have _____ duties; one supervises production, while the other is in charge of sales.

6. Terry and Mario make a fine dance couple: they _____ each other.

7. Diane thought she looked attractive in her new outfit, but no one paid her a _____.

8. Angles B and C are _____, as their sum is 90 degrees.

9. A dip in the pool is a perfect _____ to an afternoon of tennis.

10. With these _____ tickets, we can get in free.

Do not automatically reach for an adverb ending in -LY every time you need an adverb. English has many adverbs that do *not* end in -LY, and they are quite effective. In fact, Stephen Crane used dozens of them in the short excerpt we studied from his novel. For example, he wrote:

. . . sit *still* (line 28)	instead of sit *quietly*
. . . talked *much* (line 62)	instead of talked *considerably*
. . . bothering *little* (line 72)	instead of *hardly* bothering
. . . *before*, he would have (line 77)	instead of *previously* he would have

It is instructive to note that only seven lines earlier Crane had used the adverb *previously:*

"*Previously* he had never felt . . ." (line 70)

To avoid monotony, Crane did not repeat *previously* in line 77; he instead used *before*.

Here are some adverbs not ending in -LY that can help make your writing vigorous, varied, and interesting:

about	before	first	often	since
afterward	better	just	once	sometimes
almost	enough	little	perhaps	still
aloud	ever	much	right	then
altogether	fast	now	seldom	well

Exercise 9.13: Using Adverbs Not Ending in *LY*

Replace each italicized -LY adverb with the best synonym from the word list above. Do not use any word from that list more than once. See 1, below.

1. He is *merely* an acquaintance.   **just**_____

2. *Possibly* I am wrong. _____

3. I see her *infrequently*. _____

4. You *nearly* fell. _____

5. *Originally* they settled in Maine. _____

6. She is *considerably* better. _____

7. The snow is *rapidly* disappearing. _____

8. Rex is my *constantly* faithful friend. _____

9. Did I do that *properly?* _____

10. *Occasionally* there is a delay. _____

11. "Good Heavens!" he said *audibly*. _____

12. *Currently* she works in an office. _____

13. Do you exercise *sufficiently?* _____

14. You give up? *Consequently* I win. _____

15. It weighs *approximately* a ton. _____

16. They returned *subsequently.* _____

17. *Previously* I was unlucky. _____

18. That child cannot lie *quietly.* _____

19. It rains *frequently.* _____

20. She was *formerly* an actress. _____

21. We were *completely* confused. _____

22. I left, *hardly* knowing what to expect. _____

23. We knew them *closely.* _____

24. They were *superiorly* equipped. _____

25. She *subsequently* changed her mind. _____

Exercise 9.14: Analogies

At the left, write the *letter* of the pair of words related to each other in the same way as the words of the capitalized pair.

_____ **1.** COMPLIMENT : BELITTLE

(A) concoct : devise   (B) libel : defame
(C) wallow : flounder   (D) retain : relinquish
(E) yield : compromise

_____ **2.** EXTRAVAGANCE : LAVISH

(A) caution : reckless   (B) conceit : vain
(C) confidence : dispirited   (D) leniency : grim
(E) frankness : crafty

_____ **3.** QUARRELSOME : ALTERCATION

(A) panicky : judgment   (B) illiterate : education
(C) unsociable : companionship (D) negligent : accident
(E) timid : valor

_____ **4.** STRUT : WALK

(A) boast : talk   (B) smile : laugh
(C) whisper : scream   (D) eat : devour
(E) nap : sleep

_____ **5.** MONOTONOUS : VARIETY

(A) abominable : loathing   (B) ingenious : originality
(C) menacing : anxiety   (D) flimsy : solidity
(E) nutritious : nourishment

Reading Selection 10

from

"An American Doctor's Odyssey"

by Victor Heiser, M.D.

Imagine yourself in the city of Johnstown, Pennsylvania, on the day the dam broke. What would have been your chances of survival?

All during the latter part of May, 1889, a chill rain had been descending in torrents upon the Conemaugh Valley. The small city of Johnstown, walled in by precipitous Pennsylvania hills, was invaded by high water which stood knee deep in front of my
5 father's house on Washington Street.

Nobody seemed particularly concerned at the time over the dam which rich Pittsburghers had maintained high up on the South Fork to provide water for their fishing streams. When the earthen dam had first been constructed, there had been some apprehen-
10 sion. There was a ninety foot head of water behind the embankment, and only a small spillway had been provided. But the dam had never burst and, with the passage of time, the townspeople, like those who live in the shadow of Vesuvius, grew calloused to the possibility of danger. "Some time," they thought, "that dam will
15 give way, but it won't ever happen to us."

During the afternoon of the thirty-first the overflow from the river crept steadily higher, inch by inch, through the streets of the town. Although it had not yet reached the stable, which stood on higher ground than the house, my father became concerned over
20 the safety of his fine pair of horses which were tied in their stalls, and suggested that I make a dash for the stable and unfasten them. The rain was falling so hard that I was almost drenched as I plowed my laborious way through the two feet of water.

I had loosed the horses and was about to leave the shelter of the
25 doorway when my ears were stunned by the most terrifying noise

194

I had ever heard in my sixteen years of life. The dreadful roar was punctuated with a succession of tremendous crashes. I stood for a moment, bewildered and hesitant. I could see my mother and my father standing at an upper window in the house. My father, frantic with anxiety over my safety, was motioning me urgently toward the top of the building. Fortunately, I had made a passageway only a few days before to the red tin roof, so that some necessary repairs could be made. Thus it was only a matter of seconds before I was up on the ridge.

From my perch I could see a huge wall advancing with incredible rapidity down the diagonal street. It was not recognizable as water; it was a dark mass in which seethed houses, freight cars, trees, and animals. As this wall struck Washington Street broadside, my boyhood home was crushed like an eggshell before my eyes, and I saw it disappear.

I wanted to know how long it would take me to get to the other world, and in the split second before the stable was hit, I looked at my watch. It was exactly four-twenty.

But, instead of being shattered, the big barn was ripped from its foundations and began to roll, like a barrel, over and over. Stumbling, crawling, and racing, I somehow managed to keep on top.

In the path of the revolving stable loomed suddenly the house of our neighbor, Mrs. Fenn. To avoid being hurled off by the inevitable collision, I leaped into the air at the precise moment of impact. But just as I miraculously landed on the roof of her house, its walls began to cave in. I plunged downward with the roof, but saved myself by clambering monkey-like up the slope, and before the house gave way completely, another boiled up beside me. I caught hold of the eaves and swung dangling there, while the weight of my body drained the strength from my hands.

For years thereafter I was visited by recurring dreams in which I lived over and over again that fearful experience of hanging with my fingernails dug deep into the water-softened shingles, knowing that in the end I must let go.

When my grip finally relaxed, I dropped sickeningly into space. But once again I was saved. With a great thud I hit a piece of the old familiar barn roof, and I clutched with all my remaining power at the half-inch tin ridges. Lying on my belly, I bumped along on the surface of the flood, which was crushing, crumbling, and splintering everything before it. The screams of the injured were hardly to be distinguished above the awful clamor; people were being killed all about me.

In that moment of terrible danger I saw the Italian fruit dealer Mussante, with his wife and two children, racing along on what seemed to be their old barn floor. A Saratoga trunk was open beside them, and the whole family was frantically packing a pile of possessions into it. Suddenly the whole mass of wreckage heaved up and crushed them out of existence.

I was borne headlong toward a jam where the wreckage was already piling up between a stone church and a three-story brick building. Into this hurly-burly I was catapulted. The pressure was terrific. A tree would shoot out of the water; a huge girder would come thundering down. As these trees and girders drove booming into the jam, I jumped them desperately, one after another. Then suddenly a freight car reared up over my head; I could not leap that. But just as it plunged toward me, the brick building gave way, and my raft shot out from beneath the freight car like a bullet from a gun.

In a moment more I was in comparatively open water. Although no landmark was visible, I could identify the space as the park which had been there only a short while before. I was still being swept along, but the danger had lessened. I had opportunity to observe other human beings in equally perilous situations. I saw the stoutish Mrs. Fenn astride an unstable tar barrel which had covered her with its contents. Rolling far over to one side, then swaying back to the other, she was making a desperate but grotesque struggle to keep her head above water.

There was nothing I could do for anybody.

UNDERSTANDING THE SELECTION

Exercise 10.1:   Close Reading

In the blank space, write the *letter* of the choice that best completes the statement or answers the question.

1. The passage suggests that _____.

(A) the author was unlucky to be out of his house when the wall of water descended
(B) the pair of horses survived
(C) the author's house was poorly constructed
(D) the author's parents perished

2. The people of Johnstown _____.

(A) did not feel personally endangered by the dam
(B) did not even know that the dam existed
(C) felt that the dam would never give way
(D) constantly worried about the dam

3. The author gives the least emphasis to the wall of water's capacity to _____.

(A) crush   (B) wreck   (C) drown   (D) uproot

4. One structure that apparently was left standing was _____.

(A) Mrs. Fenn's home
(B) the stone church
(C) the three-story brick building
(D) Mussante's barn

5. Which of the following did NOT contribute to the author's survival? ____

(A) His physical fitness.
(B) His knowledge of the area.
(C) Luck.
(D) His sense of timing.

IMPROVING YOUR COMPOSITION SKILLS: USING ADVERB CLAUSES

1. *The Adverb Clause as a Tool for Combining Sentences*

For illustration, let us recall the paragraph where Heiser described how trees and girders (heavy timbers from wrecked buildings) were being driven with a booming noise into a jam, and how he saved himself by jumping from one of these to another.

At this point Heiser did *not* write:

(*A*) These trees and girders drove booming into the jam. I jumped them desperately, one after another.

He wrote:

(*B*) "*As these trees and girders drove booming into the jam*, I jumped them desperately, one after another."

Heiser's version combines the two simple sentences in *A* into a complex sentence. It does this by changing the first one into an adverb clause beginning with *As*.

Note that Heiser's version, *B*, more clearly expresses the relationship between the ideas involved. It is a time relationship—it was AS these trees and girders drove booming into the jam that he jumped them. Version *A* does not state that relationship.

In revising your work, you, too, should be able to combine sentences—and show the relationship between them more clearly—by using an adverb clause.

2. *Characteristics of Adverb Clauses*

Here are further examples of adverb clauses. Notice how each adverb clause answers a question that shows the relationship of the ideas in the sentence.

QUESTION ANSWERED	EXAMPLE
When?	*When my grip finally relaxed*, I dropped sickeningly into space.
	(Adverb clause *When . . . relaxed* tells WHEN I dropped.)
How?	She looked *as if she did not believe me*.
	(Adverb clause *as if . . . me* tells HOW she looked.)
Why?	Fortunately, I had made a passageway only a few days before to the red tin roof, *so that some necessary repairs could be made*.
	(Adverb clause *so that . . . made* tells WHY I had made a passageway.)

Under what circumstances?   *If it rains*, the concert will be given indoors.

(Adverb clause *If . . . rains* tells UNDER WHAT CIRCUMSTANCES the concert will be given indoors.)

As you can see from the above, an adverb clause is always a dependent clause; it is always a *part* of a sentence. Do not make the mistake of writing it as if it were a complete sentence.

> WRONG: *If it rains.* The concert will be given indoors.
> RIGHT: If it rains, the concert will be given indoors.

3. *Introducing Adverb Clauses*

An adverb clause begins with a *conjunction* (connecting word), such as one of the following:

after	as though	since	until
although	because	so that	when
as	before	though	whenever
as if	if	unless	while

4. *Punctuation*

An introductory adverb clause (an adverb clause that begins a sentence) is usually set off from the rest of the sentence by a comma.

> *When the earthen dam had first been constructed,* there had been some apprehension.

If the adverb clause does not begin the sentence, the comma is usually omitted.

> Thus it was only a matter of seconds *before I was up on the ridge.*

Exercise 10.2:   Using the Adverb Clause

Combine the sentences by changing one of them to an adverb clause.

SAMPLES: We cannot make deliveries. Our parcel service is on strike.

We cannot make deliveries *because our parcel service is on strike.*

Thunder was heard in the distance. The lifeguard did not order anyone out of the water.

Though thunder was heard in the distance, the lifeguard did not order anyone out of the water.

1. In these shoes the children felt relaxed and comfortable. They were walking on air.

_____

_____

2. Many nations are limiting their whaling activity. The whale population is decreasing at an alarming rate.

_____

_____

_____

3. Vivian did not have dessert. It appealed to her very much.

_____

_____

4. This wall struck Washington Street broadside. My boyhood home was crushed like an eggshell before my eyes, and I saw it disappear.

_____

_____

_____

_____

5. You drop out of the course now. You will regret it later.

_____

_____

6. Wearing their uniforms for the first time, the young recruits strutted. They were generals.

_____

_____

_____

7. You fasten your seat belt. You turn on the ignition.

_____

_____

8. They eventually paid for the damage. They did it with reluctance.

_____

_____

9. Joan put on her glasses. She could see better.

_____

_____

10. He arrived more than an hour late. He was not permitted to take the examination.

_____

_____

5. *Adverb Clauses and Participial Phrases*

You can eliminate unnecessary words by reducing an adverb clause to a participial phrase.

ADVERB CLAUSE: *When he approached the house*, Frank saw a police car in the driveway.

PARTICIPIAL PHRASE: *Approaching the house*, Frank saw a police car in the driveway.

Caution: Do not reduce an adverb clause unless its subject is the same as that of the independent clause. In the above, both *he* (subject of adverb clause) and *Frank* (subject of independent clause) are the same.

However, note the following:

When *he* approached the house, a *police car* was in the driveway.

Here the adverb clause **cannot** be reduced because there are two different subjects—*he* and *police car*.

Exercise 10.3:   Reducing a Sentence to a Participial Phrase

Rewrite each sentence, reducing the italicized adverb clause to a participial phrase. Make no changes in the rest of the sentence. If the adverb clause cannot be reduced, write *irreducible*.

SAMPLES: The director did not drop Cheryl from the cast *because he expected her to improve.*

The director did not drop Cheryl from the cast, **expecting her to improve.**

As we were exhausted by the heat, we stopped to rest in the shade.

Exhausted by the heat, we stopped to rest in the shade.

When they came out again, the rain had stopped.

IRREDUCIBLE (Why? See *Caution* above.)

1. Bruce did not mention the dance to me *as he thought I would not be interested.*

_____

_____

2. *Since I knew I would not be elected*, I turned down the nomination.

_____

_____

3. Pamela is not going anywhere this weekend *because she is determined to get rid of her cold.*

_____

_____

4. *As the batting champion stepped to the plate*, a roar went up from the stands.

_____

_____

5. *When she checked her battery*, Randi found the water level dangerously low.

_____

_____

6. *While I was waiting for the bus*, I got into a conversation with a girl from the junior class.

_____

_____

7. *Since I realize that there will be more opportunities*, I must try to be patient.

_____

_____

8. *When Sue discovered her error*, there were only nine minutes left in the examination.

_____

_____

9. *Though we expected the performance to be dull*, we paid our admission and went in.

_____

_____

10. Harvey is resigning as president *because he is annoyed by our lack of cooperation*.

_____

_____

Exercise 10.4:   Combining Several Sentences Into One

Each set below consists of three to five sentences. Combine each set into a single sentence, as directed. Study the samples:

FOUR SENTENCES	CHANGE TO
We passed the athletic field.	(adverb clause)
We were on our way home.	(prepositional phrase)
We saw your brother.	
He was trying out for the baseball team.	(participial phrase)

ONE SENTENCE

As we passed the athletic field on our way home, we saw your brother trying out for the baseball team.

Note that the first sentence has become an adverb clause (*As we passed the athletic field*); the second sentence has been reduced to a prepositional phrase (*on our way home*); and the last sentence has been cut down to a participial phrase (*trying out for the baseball team*).

THREE SENTENCES	CHANGE TO
News photographers were taking pictures.	(adverb clause)
Reporters interviewed several people.	
They had witnessed the accident.	(adjective clause)

ONE SENTENCE

While news photographers were taking pictures, reporters interviewed several people who had witnessed the accident.

In the above, the first sentence has been changed to an adverb clause (*While news photographers were taking pictures*) and the third to an adjective clause (*who had witnessed the accident*).

1. I am going along with the plan.
It was adopted at our meeting.   (adjective clause)
I do not think it will work.   (adverb clause)

_____

_____

_____

2. You just speak to him in a friendly way.   (adverb clause)
He will do his best to help you.
There will be no hesitation.   (prepositional phrase)

_____

_____

3. Traffic was very heavy.   (adverb clause)
We got to the theater.
The play had started.   (adverb clause)

_____

_____

4. I shouted and waved to Judy.   (adverb clause)
She was trying to find me.   (adjective clause)
She failed to notice me.
She was not looking in my direction.   (adverb clause)

_____

_____

_____

_____

5. The flood had not yet reached the stable.   (adverb clause)
It stood on higher ground than the house.   (adjective clause)
My father became concerned over the
    safety of his fine pair of horses.
They were tied in their stalls.   (adjective clause)

_____

_____

_____

_____

6. You are not satisfied with the camera.   (adverb clause)
You bought it yesterday.   (adjective clause)
You should return it.
You should ask for an exchange or refund.   (prepositional phrase)

_____

_____

_____

_____

7. I do not particularly care for Inez.   (adverb clause)
I am going to her party.
It is at eight tomorrow evening.   (prepositional phrase)
Most of my friends will be there.   (adverb clause)

_____

_____

_____

_____

8. The officer increased his speed.   (participial phrase)
The officer overtook the vehicle.
It had made a left turn.   (adjective clause)
The light was red.   (adverb clause)

_____

_____

_____

_____

9. You lend me the money.   (adverb clause)
I need it for the down payment.   (prepositional phrase)
I will return it to you.
I get paid next Friday.   (adverb clause)

_____

_____

_____

_____

10. I got off the last car. (adverb clause)
I was carrying my luggage. (participial phrase)
I saw my relatives and friends.
They were waiting for me. (participial phrase)
They were in the center of the platform. (prepositional phrase)

_____

_____

_____

_____

Exercise 10.5: Writing a Composition: A Critical Situation

In about 250 words, describe a critical situation in which you were involved. Use any personal crisis, or develop one of these suggestions:

A. Your rowboat or canoe capsizes and pitches you into the water. Or, while swimming at the beach, you are caught in an undertow.
B. While shopping, you discover that your purse or wallet is gone, and you are left without a cent.
C. You have told your friend that you will be out of town for the weekend, but he (she) sees you the next day in the company of another friend.
D. You are in a hurry to get somewhere, but your car will not start—or you get caught in a traffic jam.
E. You find yourself imprisoned in a room. The doorknob is defective and does not turn. You cannot open the door. Or, you are stranded in an elevator.

In your final draft, use an adverb clause to begin at least three sentences and to end at least two others. Vary your sentence beginnings, your sentence structure—use mainly complex and simple sentences—and your sentence length.

Divide your composition into three paragraphs, as in the following model:

Model Composition: A Critical Situation

¹It was a beautiful afternoon for the beach. ²Bathers kept running gleefully into the surf after each receding wave and racing madly back before the next one pounded the shore. ³As I wanted to swim, I went out beyond the point where the waves were breaking. ⁴I had begun to swim parallel to the beach when I heard the lifeguard's whistle. ⁵Looking up, I saw him gesturing for me to come in. ⁶Though I could not understand what the danger was, I started at once for the shore.

⁷To my surprise, it was hard to get back. ⁸With each stroke I took, the

undertow pulled me twice as far toward a pile of rocks that jutted out from the beach. [9]I was gripped with the fear of being dashed against those rocks. [10]Terrified, I touched bottom; the water was still two feet over my head. [11]But when my toes dug into the sand, I discovered that I could resist the undertow. [12]That gave me an idea. [13]I would take a few swift strokes and then dig in underwater until the undertow momentarily eased. [14]Then I would come up and repeat the process. [15]Soon I was able to stand with my head above water, and from that moment I was confident that I could reach the beach.

[16]When I waded ashore fifteen feet from the rockpile, there stood the life-guard who had been watching me. [17]It was a close call.

Analysis

ORGANIZATION: Paragraph 1 (S1–6) describes the events leading up to the crisis.
Paragraph 2 (S7–15) describes the crisis.
Paragraph 3 (S16–17) briefly sums up the outcome.

ADVERB CLAUSES:

Beginning a sentence—S3 (As . . . swim); S6 (Though . . . was); S16 (When . . . rockpile)
Ending a sentence—S2 (before . . . shore); S4 (when . . . whistle); S13 (until . . . eased)

SENTENCE OPENINGS:

With the subject—S1, 2, 4, 9, 12, 13, and 17
With a dependent clause—S3, 6, 11, and 16
With a participle—S5 and 10
With a prepositional phrase—S7 and 8
With an adverb—S14 and 15

SENTENCE STRUCTURE:

Simple—S1, 5, 7, 9, 12, 14, and 17
Compound—S10
Complex—S2, 3, 4, 6, 8, 11, 13, and 16
Compound-complex—S15

Now write your composition.

My Composition: A Critical Situation

_____

_____

_____

_____

_____

_____

_____

_____

_____

_____

_____

_____

_____

_____

_____

_____

_____

_____

_____

_____

_____

_____

_____

_____

_____

_____

_____

_____

Line	Word	Meaning	Typical Use
13	**calloused** (*adj.*) ˈkal-əst	1. made *callous* (hard or unfeeling); hardened; lacking pity	A surgeon does not faint at the sight of blood, as he is *calloused* to such sights.
		2. having a *callus* (hardened, thickened place) or *calluses*	My palms are *soft* though a mechanic's are usually *calloused*.
		(*ant.* **tender, soft**)	Her *tender* feelings for her grandchildren were in contrast to her *calloused* attitude toward everyone else.
92	**grotesque** (*adj.*) grō-ˈtesk	absurdly awkward; fantastic	Something is wrong with the TV; we are getting distorted heads, elongated bodies, and other *grotesque* images.
85	**identify** (*v.*) i-ˈdent-ə-ˌfī	recognize or establish as being a particular person or thing; establish the *identity* (sameness) of	Pointing to the suspect, the victim *identified* him as the one who had taken her purse.
49	**impact** (*n.*) ˈim-pakt	striking of one body against another; forceful contact; collision	A crowd was attracted to the scene of the crash by the noise of the *impact*.
48	**inevitable** (*adj.*) in-ˈev-ə-tə-bəl	incapable of being avoided; bound to happen; certain; necessary	Since a majority of the Senate is opposed to the bill, its defeat is *inevitable*.
		(*ant.* **avoidable**)	The optimists feel that war is *avoidable*, while the pessimists believe it is *inevitable*.
23	**laborious** (*adj.*) lə-ˈbȯr-ē-əs	requiring hard or toilsome effort; arduous; difficult; hard	Cutting thick branches with hand tools is a *laborious* task, but with a chain saw it is *easy*.
		(*ant.* **easy**)	
7	**maintain** (*v.*) mān-ˈtān	1. keep in operation; keep up; keep	Do not get a car that needs frequent and costly repairs; buy one that is inexpensive to *maintain*.
		2. uphold or defend, as by argument; assert; affirm	The suspect *maintained* that she was innocent.

88	**perilous** (*adj.*) 'per-ə-ləs	full of *peril* (danger); involving risk; dangerous; hazardous (*ant.* **safe**)	The shorter trail to the top of the mountain is steep and *perilous;* the longer one is roundabout but relatively *safe.*
3	**precipitous** (*adj.*) pri-'sip-ət-əs	steep like a precipice (cliff); falling very quickly	As they approach the *precipitous* drop in the road, motorists are warned to slow to 30 miles per hour and to use low gears.
37	**seethe** (*v.*) 'sēth	1. bubble or foam as if boiling; boil	The storm made the ocean *seethe.*
		2. be in a state of excitement or agitation	At the slightest insult he would *seethe* with rage.

APPLYING WHAT YOU HAVE LEARNED

Exercise 10.6:   Sentence Completion

Enter the choice required by the sentence, as in 1, below.

1. Taking the (stairs, elevator) ____stairs____, she made her laborious way to the ninth floor.

2. Since the outcome was (beyond, within) _____ anyone's control, we had to regard it as inevitable.

3. Statistics show the home is a perilous place because (few, most) _____ accidents occur there.

4. Along the road she found a (common, strange) _____ wildflower that was easy to identify.

5. Has the free-admission policy been (discontinued, continued) _____, or is it being maintained?

6. Calloused people show (concern, unconcern) _____ when they see others suffer.

7. You must have been extremely (pleased, dissatisfied) _____ over something when I saw you because you were seething.

8. What can explain the precipitous drop in average daily attendance at home games from 41,500 to (39,500, 16,000) _____?

9. The pilot escaped by parachuting from the plunging craft seconds (after, before) _____ ground impact.

10. The little children looked grotesque in their (holiday, parents') _____ clothes.

Exercise 10.7: Using Synonyms and Antonyms

A. Avoid repetition by replacing the italicized word or expression in 1–7 below with a SYNONYM from the following list:

seethe	arduous	avoidable	steep	calloused
fantastic	hazardous	maintain	identify	impact

1. Not only new recruits but also *hardened* veterans complained about the unusual hardships of the mission. _____

2. The walkers' pace quickened as gravity precipitated them down a *precipitous* stretch of the road. _____

3. If you are shown something beyond recognition, how can you possibly *recognize* what it is? _____

4. The altercation was at the boiling point; both of the opponents were *boiling* with rage. _____

5. When the vehicles collided, the noise of the *collision* shattered the peace of the residential neighborhood. _____

6. Mythology is full of grotesque half-human, half-animal creatures, each one more *grotesque* than the next one. _____

7. After spending thousands on the upkeep of the building, the owner said it was getting too costly to *keep up*. _____

B. Complete each sentence in 8–10 below by inserting an ANTONYM of the italicized word from the above list.

8. She had thought it would be an *easy* project, but it turned out to be quite _____. _____

9. After the Barbary Pirates were defeated, waters that had been _____ for merchant ships became *safe*. _____

10. Unfortunately, earthquakes are *inevitable*, but traffic accidents are usually _____ if we are careful. _____

Exercise 10.8: Concise Writing (Using Fewer Words)

Replace the italicized word or expression in each sentence below with a single word from the following list.

maintain	calloused	laborious	perilous	grotesque
seethe	precipitous	collision	identify	inevitable

1. They are unwilling to undertake anything *requiring hard effort*. _____

2. You look *absurdly awkward* in that costume.   _____

3. Overnight, masses of cool Canadian air will cause a(an) *very quickly falling* drop in temperature.   _____

4. A violinist's fingertips are *made hard* by constant pressure on the strings.   _____

5. Is it costly to *keep* the pool *in operation?*   _____

6. Let him *be in a state of agitation* if he wants to.   _____

7. The catastrophe was *bound to happen.*   _____

8. Should you have sent anyone on a mission *that involves risk?*   _____

9. Glass usually shatters on *forceful contact* with a hard object.   _____

10. I was not able to *recognize* her *as being a particular person.*   _____

Exercise 10.9:   Name-the-Person Quiz

Read all the statements in the boxes. Then enter the required names in sentences 1–10, below.

When the concrete mixer broke down in the middle of the job, Moe finished the rest of the mixing by hand.	Pam is boiling with resentment over her suspension from the squad.

Paul came to the masquerade wearing the head of a lion.

With 95% of the ballots counted, Geraldine has 1,192 votes, Ruth 1,186, and Richard 852.

At first, Janice was opposed to the trip; now she says that she is for it.

Mona's head would have hit the windshield if she had not been wearing her seat belt.

Gregg had to show his driver's license before the manager would accept his check.	Lou is up on the ladder even though he has been told that it is unsteady.

Rhonda's shares have changed little in value, but Jennifer's have gone down by more than fifty percent.	Audrey used to complain to the dentist about the pain of the drilling, but after the third or fourth visit it did not bother her too much.

1. _____ is seething.

2. _____ became calloused.

3. _____'s defeat seems inevitable.

4. _____ avoided a serious impact.

5. _____ completed a laborious task.

6. _____ is not maintaining a fixed position.

7. _____'s assets declined precipitously.

8. _____ looked grotesque.

9. _____'s situation is perilous.

10. _____ identified himself.

LEARNING SOME ROOTS AND DERIVATIVES

Each capitalized word below is a *root*. The words under it are its *derivatives*.

CALLUS (*n.*)	Shoes that do not fit properly may cause corns and *calluses*.
callous (*adj.*)	Some passengers were smoking in *callous* disregard of the "No Smoking" sign.
callously (*adv.*)	The sign was plain to see, but they *callously* disregarded it.
callousness (*n.*)	Can you imagine such *callousness?*
calloused (*adj.*)	They were so *calloused* that stares of the other passengers did not seem to disturb them.
GROTESQUE (*adj.*)	The children who came to the door on Halloween wore *grotesque* outfits.
grotesquely (*adv.*)	One five-year-old was *grotesquely* attired as Father Time in a long gray beard and a tall hat.
grotesqueness (*n.*)	Another arrived completely wrapped in bandages, except for slits for the eyes, nose, and mouth. That was the height of *grotesqueness*.
IDENTIFY (*v.*)	Are you sure you can *identify* the thief?
identifiable (*adj.*)	Besides the scar, what other *identifiable* features do you recall?
identification (*n.*)	Are you sure you can make a positive *identification?*
identifier (*n.*)	Remember that an *identifier* must be absolutely certain not to make a mistake.
INEVITABLE (*adj.*)	We do not believe that our bankruptcy is *inevitable*.
inevitability (*n.*)	We do not believe in the *inevitability* of our bankruptcy.
inevitably (*adv.*)	We do not think that we will *inevitably* go bankrupt.

LABORIOUS (*adj.*)	House painting is very *laborious* work.
laboriously (*adv.*)	With a roller, certain areas can be painted less *laboriously* than with a brush.
laboriousness (*n.*)	The roller, however, has only partly reduced the *laboriousness* of painting.

MAINTAIN (*v.*)	With your salary you should be able to *maintain* a car.
maintenance (*n.*)	The cost of *maintenance* is easily within your means.
maintainable (*adj.*)	With your income, you will find a car *maintainable*.

PERIL (*n.*)	Is our existence as a nation in *peril?*
imperil (*v.*)	Our rights must not be *imperiled*.
perilous (*adj.*)	The American Revolution was a *perilous* undertaking.
perilously (*adv.*)	The Thirteen Colonies came *perilously* close to being defeated.
perilousness (*n.*)	Many at first did not join in the revolt because of its *perilousness*.

PRECIPITOUS (*adj.*)	Prices suffered a *precipitous* decline.
precipitously (*adv.*)	They fell *precipitously*.
precipitousness (*n.*)	Economists attribute the *precipitousness* of the drop in farm prices to overproduction and buyer resistance.

Exercise 10.10:   Using Roots and Derivatives

Fill each blank with the above root or derivative that best fits the meaning of the sentence.

1. The laundry mark is very faint and scarcely _____.

2. That inflammable material is _____ close to the oven.

3. Your first assertion is a sound one—there are many facts to support it—but your second is not _____.

4. A(An) _____ on my left sole is paining me.

5. From my hammock I watched my neighbor _____ washing and polishing his car.

6. A late rally by our opponents _____ our lead.

7. Machines that are not properly maintained _____ break down.

8. While the dance couples swirled around the floor, a comedian waltzed _____ with a broom as a partner.

9. In a matter of seconds, the express elevator _____ descended from the seventy-second to the main floor.

10. When they enter the gate, employees are required to show their badges for

_____.

SPELLING REVIEW: COMPOUND ADJECTIVES

1. A *compound adjective* (an adjective consisting of two or more words) is usually hyphened when it comes before a noun.

    three-story building
    hit-and-run driver

2. When the compound adjective follows a noun, it is not hyphened.

    ADJECTIVE FOLLOWS NOUN   ADJECTIVE PRECEDES NOUN

    The water was *knee deep.*   I was in *knee-deep* water.
         N   ADJ   ADJ   N

    Our methods are *up to date.*   We use *up-to-date* methods.
         N   ADJ   ADJ   N

3. A plural noun becomes singular when used as a part of a compound adjective.

    a delay of two *hours*   [but] a two-*hour* delay
    shoes that cost eighty *dollars* [but] eighty-*dollar* shoes

4. No hyphen is used if the first word of the compound adjective is an -LY adverb.

    fully equipped shop

Note, however, that the hyphen is used in:

    well-equipped shop

Exercise 10.11:   Reducing a Clause or Phrase to a Compound Adjective

Reduce each italicized clause or phrase to a compound adjective.

SAMPLES: an opportunity *that comes once in a lifetime*
         a *once-in-a-lifetime* opportunity

         a fine *of fifty dollars*
         a *fifty-dollar* fine

         applicants *who are poorly trained*
         poorly trained applicants

1. books *that are long overdue*

    _____

2. a play *of three acts*

    _____

3. reporters *who were on the spot*

    _____

4. meat *that is properly cooked*

    _____

5. an apartment *with three bedrooms*

_____

6. results *which are better than average*

_____

7. complaints *that are often heard*

_____

8. members *who were newly admitted*

_____

9. tenants *on the eleventh floor*

_____

10. the coach *at third base*

_____

11. ideas *that are down to earth*

_____

12. a car *that can accommodate six passengers*

_____

13. employees *who were recently hired*

_____

14. the technicians *who work behind the scenes*

_____

15. families *with low incomes*

_____

16. news *that is up to the minute*

_____

17. programs *which are well planned*

_____

18. mountain peaks *covered with snow*

_____

19. a raise of *one hundred dollars a month*

_____

20. planes *that fly low*

_____

IMPROVING YOUR USAGE: USING DIVIDED QUOTATIONS

Use two sets of quotation marks when you divide a quotation, as Heiser did:

"Some time," they thought, "that dam will give way, but it won't ever happen to us."

Carefully note the following:

1. Each part of a divided quotation is enclosed in its own set of quotation marks.

   FIRST PART: "Some time,"
   SECOND PART: "that dam will give way, but it won't ever happen to us."

2. The explanatory words *they thought* are set off from the quotation by a pair of commas.

   "Some time," *they thought*, "that . . ."

3. Commas and periods are always placed *inside* closing quotation marks.

   "Some time," . . .
   ". . . but it won't ever happen to us."

4. If a quotation is a question or an exclamation, the question mark or exclamation point is also placed *inside* the closing quotation marks.

   QUESTION: "Can you tell us," she asked, "how you got the idea?"
   EXCLAMATION: "What fools we are," he exclaimed, "to sit around and do nothing!"

5. One set of quotation marks would have sufficed if Heiser had not divided his quotation. He could have written:

   "Some time that dam will give way, but it won't ever happen to us," they thought.
         Or:
   They thought, "Some time that dam will give way, but it won't ever happen to us."

Exercise 10.12:   Writing Quotations

Each quotation below can be written in three ways, but only one is given. Supply the other two, as in the sample.

EXPLANATORY WORDS AT BEGINNING	DIVIDED QUOTATION	EXPLANATORY WORDS AT END
SAMPLE:		
I finally said, "Mother, I am hungry."	"Mother," *I finally said*, "I am hungry."	"Mother, I am hungry," *I finally said*.
1. _____ _____ _____ _____	"Madame Magloire," said the bishop, "put on another plate."	_____ _____ _____

Reading Selection 10: An American Doctor's Odyssey

2. _____ _____ "Go on and don't pay any
_____ _____ attention to them," she
_____ _____ said.
_____ _____

3. The dealer advised, _____ _____
"Before you use a _____ _____
package of film, read _____ _____
the instructions that _____ _____
come with it. _____ _____
_____ _____

4. _____ "That," he screamed, "is the _____
_____ worst thing you could have _____
_____ done!" _____
_____

5. _____ _____ "I will call you as soon as I
_____ _____ get back," Ruth promised.
_____ _____
_____ _____

6. She protested, "How _____ _____
could I have known _____ _____
that this would hap- _____ _____
pen?" _____ _____

7. _____ "Surely," I said to myself, _____
_____ "we will never have another _____
_____ chance like this." _____
_____ _____
_____

8. _____ _____ "Good Lord, what's the
_____ _____ matter with me?" he said
_____ _____ aloud.
_____ _____

9. Bill warned, "The later you start, the harder it will be to get back." _____ _____

_____ _____

_____ _____

_____ _____

_____ _____

10. _____ "Come now," Jane insisted, "you haven't finished your story." _____

_____ _____

_____ _____

_____ _____

_____ _____

Exercise 10.13: Analogies

At the left, write the *letter* of the pair of words related to each other in the same way as the words of the capitalized pair.

_____ **1.** INEVITABLE : AVOID

(A) improbable : happen   (B) contradictory : deny
(C) imperishable : die   (D) indefensible : maintain
(E) pliable : agree

_____ **2.** CALLOUSED : SOFT

(A) excessive : extreme   (B) tedious : exciting
(C) hostile : inhospitable   (D) arbitrary : dictatorial
(E) sundry : miscellaneous

_____ **3.** PERILOUS : RISK

(A) monotonous : variety   (B) tranquil : agitation
(C) valorous : cowardice   (D) barbarous : benevolence
(E) lavish : extravagance

_____ **4.** ARDUOUS : LABORIOUS

(A) limited : unrestricted   (B) steep : gradual
(C) petulant : irritable   (D) unsociable : gregarious
(E) complimentary : unfavorable

_____ **5.** GROTESQUE : NATURALNESS

(A) affected : genuineness   (B) sly : furtiveness
(C) ingenious : admiration   (D) despicable : criticism
(E) abominable : unpleasantness

from

"Hunger of Memory"

by Richard Rodriguez

The author recalls how education gave him a good start in life, and how a lack of education had handicapped his immigrant parents.

"Your parents must be very proud of you." People began to say that to me about the time I was in sixth grade. To answer affirmatively, I'd smile. Shyly I'd smile, never betraying my sense of the irony: I was not proud of my mother and father. I was embarrassed
5 by their lack of education. It was not that I ever thought they were stupid, though stupidly I took for granted their enormous native intelligence. Simply, what mattered to me was they were not like my teachers.

But, "Why didn't you tell us about the award?" my mother
10 demanded, her frown weakened by pride. At the grammar school ceremony several weeks after, her eyes were brighter than the trophy I'd won. Pushing back the hair from my forehead, she whispered that I had "shown" the *gringos*. A few minutes later, I heard my father speak to my teacher and felt ashamed of his
15 labored, accented words. Then guilty for the shame. I felt such contrary feelings. (There is no simple roadmap through the heart of the scholarship boy.) My teacher was so soft-spoken and her words were edged sharp and clean. I admired her until it seemed to me that she spoke too carefully. Sensing that she was conde-
20 scending to them, I became nervous. Resentful. Protective. I tried to move my parents away. "You both must be very proud of Richard," the nun said. They responded quickly. (They were proud.) "We are proud of all our children." Then this after-thought: "They sure didn't get their brains from us." They all
25 laughed. I smiled.

Tightening the irony into a knot was the knowledge that my parents were always behind me. They made success possible. They evened the path. They sent their children to parochial schools because the nuns "teach better." They paid a tuition they couldn't afford. They spoke English to us. 30

For their children my parents wanted chances they never had—an easier way. It saddened my mother to learn that some relatives forced their children to start working right after high school. To *her* children she would say, "Get all the education you can." In schooling she recognized the key to job advancement. And with the 35 remark she remembered her past.

As a girl new to America my mother had been awarded a high school diploma by teachers too careless or busy to notice that she hardly spoke English. On her own, she determined to learn how to type. That skill got her jobs typing envelopes in letter shops, and it 40 encouraged in her an optimism about the possibility of advancement. (Each morning when her sisters put on uniforms, she chose a bright-colored dress.) The years of young womanhood passed, and her typing speed increased. She also became an excellent speller of words she mispronounced. "And I've never been to col- 45 lege," she'd say, smiling, when her children asked her to spell words they were too lazy to look up in a dictionary.

Typing, however, was dead-end work. Finally frustrating. When her youngest child started high school, my mother got a full-time office job once again. (Her paycheck combined with my father's to 50 make us—in fact—what we had already become in our imagination of ourselves—middle class.) She worked then for the (California) state government in numbered civil service positions secured by examinations. The old ambition of her youth was rekindled. During the lunch hour, she consulted bulletin boards for announcements of 55 openings. One day she saw mention of something called an "anti-poverty agency." A typing job. A glamorous job, part of the governor's staff. "A knowledge of Spanish required." Without hesitation she applied and became nervous only when the job was suddenly hers.

"Everyone comes to work all dressed up," she reported at night. 60 And didn't need to say more than that her co-workers wouldn't let her answer the phones. She was only a typist, after all, albeit a very fast typist. And an excellent speller. One morning there was a letter to be sent to a Washington cabinet officer. On the dictating tape, a voice referred to urban guerrillas. My mother typed (the wrong word, cor- 65 rectly): "gorillas." The mistake horrified the anti-poverty bureaucrats who shortly after arranged to have her returned to her previous position. She would go no further. So she willed her ambition to her children. "Get all the education you can; with an education you can do anything." (With a good education *she* could have done anything.) 70

When I was in high school, I admitted to my mother that I planned to become a teacher someday. That seemed to please her. But I never tried to explain that it was not the occupation of teaching I yearned for as much as it was something more elusive: I wanted to *be* like my teachers, to possess their knowledge, to assume their 75 authority, their confidence, even to assume a teacher's persona.

In contrast to my mother, my father never verbally encouraged his children's academic success. Nor did he often praise us. My mother had to remind him to "say something" to one of his children
80 who scored some academic success. But whereas my mother saw in education the opportunity for job advancement, my father recognized that education provided an even more startling possibility: It could enable a person to escape from a life of mere labor.

In Mexico, orphaned when he was eight, my father left school to
85 work as an "apprentice" for an uncle. Twelve years later, he left Mexico in frustration and arrived in America. He had great expectations then of becoming an engineer. ("Work for my hands and my head.") He knew a Catholic priest who promised to get him money enough to study full time for a high school diploma. But the
90 promises came to nothing. Instead there was a dark succession of warehouse, cannery, and factory jobs. After work he went to night school along with my mother. A year, two passed. Nothing much changed, except that fatigue worked its way into the bone; then everything changed. He didn't talk anymore of becoming an en-
95 gineer. He stayed outside on the steps of the school while my mother went inside to learn typing and shorthand.

UNDERSTANDING THE SELECTION

Exercise 11.1: Close Reading

In the blank space, write the *letter* that best completes the statement or answers the question.

1. Which of the following statements about the writer's father is *not* supported by the passage? ____

    (A) He saw education as a way of escaping all work.
    (B) Poverty prevented him from earning a high school diploma.
    (C) He seldom praised his children.
    (D) He was handicapped by fatigue.

2. At no time does the writer express or hint at any criticism of ____.

    (A) himself
    (B) the value of education
    (C) teachers
    (D) typing as a way to earn a living

3. There is no evidence in the passage that the writer's parents have ____.

    (A) a sense of humor
    (B) in any way suffered because of their lack of education
    (C) derived great satisfaction from their son's success in school
    (D) ever scolded him for being ashamed of them

4. When the writer says, "I took for granted their enormous native intelligence," he means that he ____.

   (A) assumed without proof that his parents were unusually intelligent
   (B) valued too lightly the intelligence they had been born with
   (C) gave them credit for what they had learned in their native Mexico
   (D) was fair to them in judging their intelligence

5. At no time in the passage is the author ____.

   (A) protective of his parents
   (B) embarrassed by his parents
   (C) guilty for feeling ashamed of his parents
   (D) resentful of his parents

IMPROVING YOUR COMPOSITION SKILLS: USING DIRECT QUOTATIONS

One way to make your writing more interesting and dramatic is to use a few carefully chosen direct quotations. Note how effectively Richard Rodriguez did this in lines 21–25:

> "You both must be very proud of Richard," the nun said. They responded quickly. (They were proud.) "We are proud of all our children." Then this afterthought: "They sure didn't get their brains from us." They all laughed. I smiled.

Notice how the author enlivened his writing by quoting the exact words that his teacher and his parents used on this occasion.

Exercise 11.2:   Using Direct Quotations in Composition

Write a composition of 150 to 200 words about a problem you had with another person. Important: Include at least one direct quotation of what the other person said to you, and at least one direct quotation of what you said to the other person. A sample composition follows:

Sample Composition: A Problem With Another Person

Recently, I was looking for a recording of a popular song I was sure I had at home, so you can imagine my frustration when I couldn't find it. Remembering that I had once lent it to Andy, I asked him if he still had it. Andy shocked me by denying that I had ever lent him the recording. "Besides," he added, "if you had lent it to me, I would have returned it right away. That's the way I am."

A month passed. Yesterday, Andy greeted me with a sheepish grin when he saw me on the bus. "Amy," he said, handing me a cassette, "I owe you an apology. This is the tape you lent me. I came across it yesterday in going through my collection. I hope you'll forgive me."

"Thanks, Andy," I said, reassured of my sanity. "Don't feel too bad because I am delighted to get this back."

Your Composition: A Problem With Another Person

_____

_____

_____

_____

_____

_____

_____

_____

_____

_____

_____

_____

_____

_____

_____

_____

LEARNING NEW WORDS

Line	Word	Meaning	Typical Use
2	**affirmatively** (*adv.*) ə-ˈfər-mə-tiv-lē	in an *affirmative* (assenting, positive) manner; by saying or voting "yes."	When we vote yes, we vote *affirmatively*.
	(*ant.* **negatively**)		When we vote no, we vote *negatively*.
19	**condescend** (*v.*) ˌkän-di-ˈsend	assume an air of superiority; patronize	People feel offended when someone *condescends* to them.
74	**elusive** (*adj.*) ē-ˈlü-siv	tending to *elude* (avoid or evade grasp or pursuit); cleverly or skillfully evasive	No one was more *elusive* than the god Proteus; he could assume different shapes at will.

86	**frustration** (*n.*) frəs-ˈtrā-shən	sense of dissatisfaction arising from unresolved problems or unfulfilled needs; disappointment; defeat	Several workers have quit in *frustration* over their failure to win a raise.
57	**glamorous** (*adj.*) ˈgla-mər-əs	full of *glamor* (excitement and adventure); fascinatingly attractive and alluring; captivating; charming	Miniver Cheevy longed for the age of chivalry; which he considered far more *glamorous* than modern times.
65	**guerrilla** (*n.*) gə-ˈri-lə	person who engages in irregular warfare as a member of an independent unit carrying out harassment and sabotage; irregular; partisan	*Guerrillas* slowed the enemy advance by blowing up vital bridges.
15	**labored** (*adj.*) ˈlā-bərd	with difficulty; betraying effort; hard; forced; lacking spontaneity	A *labored* signature suggests the signer may have had little schooling.
41	**optimism** (*n.*) ˈäp-tə-ˌmi-zəm	tendency to take the most hopeful or cheerful view of matters and to expect the best possible outcome	*Optimism* about the future of the United States economy caused many Americans to invest in the stock market.
		(*ant.* **pessimism**)	*Pessimism* about their future in their homeland led millions of families to migrate to America.
54	**rekindle** (*v.*) ri-ˈkin-dəl	kindle (arouse) again; rearouse; ignite anew	Faint signals from the rubble have *rekindled* hope that more victims will be found alive.
65	**urban** (*adj.*) ˈər-ban	of, relating to, or taking place in a city; municipal (*ant.* **rural**)	*Urban* traffic is usually congested, especially in the rush hours; *rural* traffic, by comparison, is usually very light.

Exercise 11.3:   Sentence Completion

Enter the choice required by the sentence, as in 1, below.

1. Russia's success in launching Sputnik 1 rekindled interest in America in the study of math and (*economics, physics*) __physics__.

2. Optimists are usually sure they are going to (*fail, succeed*) _____.

3. Recruits of ordinary appearance usually look glamorous in their (*civilian clothes, military uniforms*) _____.

4. A shopper whose breathing was labored had just come up from the basement to the second floor by way of the (*stairs, escalator*) _____.

5. Asked if she would contribute, our neighbor said no; we were stunned because we had expected (*a negative, an affirmative*) _____ reply.

6. The ambushing of an enemy supply convoy by a group of guerrillas was an act of (*sabotage, vandalism*) _____.

7. The senior used a condescending term when he got the attention of a couple of newly admitted students by saying "Hey (*kids, guys*) _____."

8. When a pitcher is so fast that none of the opposing batters is able to hit the ball, the (*winning, losing*) _____ team experiences frustration.

9. The British thought they had Washington cornered, but he managed to slip away; (*they were, he was*) _____ elusive.

10. A (*mayor, governor*) _____ is an elected municipal official.

Exercise 11.4:   Using Synonyms and Antonyms

A. Avoid repetition by replacing the italicized word or expression in 1–5 below with a SYNONYM from the following list:

patronize	rural	effortless	disappointment	elusive
unglamorous	rekindle	optimism	affirmative	partisan

1. The ballcarrier's great speed and skillfully *evasive* tactics

   enabled him to evade all pursuers.   _____

2. A small number of *guerrillas* skilled in guerrilla warfare

   kept harassing the invaders.   _____s

3. Once interest in the ballet is aroused, it grows and grows;

   it seldom has to be *rearoused*.   _____d

4. When you *condescend to* people, you make them feel infe-

   rior; avoid condescension.   _____

5. Though frustrated by failures, we kept trying; we would not let *frustration* get the better of us. _____

B. Complete each sentence in 6–10 below by inserting an ANTONYM of the italicized word from the above list.

6. Two members asked to change their vote from *negative* to

_____. _____

7. Many *urban* residents prefer to spend the summer months in a(an) _____ area. _____

8. The speech of most new immigrants seems _____ in their native tongue, but quite *labored* in English. _____

9. The *pessimism* among the fans gave way to cautious _____ when the home team regained the lead. _____

10. This building has an *attractive* exterior, but its interior is relatively _____. _____

Exercise 11.5:   Concise Writing (Using Fewer Words)

Replace the italicized words in each sentence below with a single word from the following list.

municipal	condescend	glamorous	guerrilla	affirmatively
frustration	labored	elusive	rekindle	optimism

1. Does your newspaper have a column on *city-related* problems? _____

2. She admits her *tendency to expect the best possible outcome* is sometimes unwarranted. _____

3. I answered *by saying yes*. _____

4. If the fire goes out during the night, it must be *ignited anew*. _____d

5. Robinson Crusoe felt that the life of a sailor was *fascinatingly attractive and alluring*. _____

6. The spy was *able to avoid capture*. _____

7. Surprise night raids by *persons engaged in irregular warfare* slowed the invasion. _____s

8. His *sense of dissatisfaction over unresolved problems* kept him from continuing his education. _____

9. It is no pleasure to read writing that is *lacking in spontaneity*. _____

10. Don't *assume an air of superiority* with me if you want to remain my friend. _____

Exercise 11.6: Name-the-Person Quiz

Read all the statements in the boxes. Then enter the required names in the blanks accompanying questions 1–10, below.

Since Sam had both defended and attacked the motion, we asked him whether he was for or against it, but he wouldn't say exactly what his position was.

A farmer gave asylum to a member of a small independent unit who had been wounded while attempting to sabotage an enemy tank.

When the president said, "All in favor of the motion, say aye," Nicole was one of those who responded.

Many workers from the South found jobs in Detroit after World War II.

Even when prospects were favorable, Dan expected the worst possible outcome.

Though the staff addressed the office manager as Mr. Johnson, he addressed them only by their last names—Goldsmith, Rizzo, Porter, etc.

Four times Harris ran for governor; each time he was narrowly defeated.

Carmela was captivated by the red convertible in the dealer's showroom.

A brilliant performance by the concert guitarist that Louisa heard last Sunday has revived her interest in the guitar, which she had studied as a child.

My nearly illiterate cousin addressed an envelope to send me a birthday card by copying my name and address—one letter at a time—from an address label.

---

1. Who had a condescending attitude? _____

2. Who migrated to an urban area? _____

3. Who found something fascinatingly attractive and alluring? _____

4. Who rekindled something? _____

5. Who voted affirmatively? _____

6. Who experienced frustration? _____

7. Who remained elusive? _____

8. Who performed a labored operation? _____

9. Who sheltered a guerrilla? _____

10. Who was afflicted with pessimism? _____

Each capitalized word below is a *root*. The words under it are its *derivatives*.

AFFIRM (*v.*)	I had said there was some fog at the time, and weather reports filed by my attorney *affirmed* that it was so.
affirmative (*adj.*)	To the question about whether I wear driving glasses, I gave an *affirmative* answer.
affirmatively (*adv.*)	When asked whether I was wearing them at the time of the accident, I also answered *affirmatively*.
CONDESCEND (*v.*)	If you *condescend* to someone, you are implying that the person is inferior to you.
condescending (*adj.*)	Generally, the occupying nations had a *condescending* attitude toward the inhabitants of their colonies.
condescendingly (*adv.*)	In olden times, members of the nobility behaved *condescendingly* to commoners.
condescension (*n.*)	For good interpersonal relations with others, we must at all costs avoid *condescension*.
ELUDE (*v.*)	Ponce de Leon spent a great deal of time searching for the Fountain of Youth, but it *eluded* him.
elusive (*adj.*)	As far as is known, no one has found the fountain; it is still *elusive*.
FRUSTRATE (*v.*)	The failure of our bus to arrive *frustrated* our plans to get to graduation on time.
frustrating (*adj.*)	Trying to get a cab was equally *frustrating;* every taxi we hailed was occupied.
frustration (*n.*)	In the meantime, to add to our *frustration*, it started to rain heavily, and we got all wet.
GLAMOR (*n.*)	In renovating the old restaurant, the new owners went to great expense to add some *glamor*.
glamorous (*adj.*)	They installed attractive new furniture and lighting fixtures to make it a *glamorous* place to dine.
glamorously (*adv.*)	Also, the walls of all the dining areas and the restrooms were *glamorously* equipped with mirrors.
glamorize (*v.*)	In short, the new proprietors have *glamorized* the restaurant.
unglamorous (*adj.*)	Customers admit the old restaurant was *unglamorous*, though they say the food was excellent.

LABOR (*n.*)	Electrical appliances, like dishwashers, have greatly reduced the amount of *labor* in the kitchen.
labor (*v.*)	At harvest time, farmhands *labor* long hours gathering in the crops.
laborious (*adj.*)	Walking uphill is much more *laborious* than coming down a gentle slope.
labored (*adj.*)	When exhausted runners finish a marathon, people who are nearby can hear that their breathing is *labored*.
laboratory (*n.*)	Researchers work in *laboratories*, conducting scientific tests.
OPTIMISM (*n.*)	The critically ill patient is improving; there is reason for *optimism*.
optimistic (*adj.*)	Doctors are cautiously *optimistic* about her chances of recovery.
optimist (*n.*)	Her brother has felt all along that she was going to get well; he has been an *optimist* from the start.
KINDLE (*v.*)	It was hard to *kindle* the fire because the wood we had would not burn easily.
kindling (*n.*)	However, Diane found some dry twigs and other *kindling*, and with this we got the fire started.
rekindle (*v.*)	Once, the fire went out, but luckily we managed to *rekindle* it.
URBAN (*adj.*)	Technological advances have encouraged many people to move to *urban* areas from rural communities.
interurban (*adj.*)	Major cities, like New York and Washington, D.C., are linked by an *interurban* air shuttle.
suburban (*adj.*)	There are usually several *suburban* communities on the outskirts of a large city.
exurbanite (*n.*)	*Exurbanites* reside beyond the suburbs of a city.

Exercise 11.7: Using Roots and Derivatives

Fill each blank with the root or derivative that best fits the meaning of the sentence.

1. It is impossible to start a campfire with wet _____.

2. Making photocopies does not require much _____; machines do almost all the work.

3. You should be _____; there is no cause for pessimism.

4. Janice lives in a quiet _____ community on the outskirts of town.

5. Skilled decorators can make a(an) _____ place into a showplace.

6. By defeating us in the deciding game of the series for the third year in a row, our rivals have again _____d our championship hopes.

7. The suspect managed to _____ capture by mingling with a crowd on a busy street.

8. The bride usually gives a(an) _____ answer when the preacher asks, "Do you take this man to be your lawful wedded husband?"

9. If a candle goes out, it can be _____d with a match, or with the flame from another candle.

10. There can be no spirit of equality between the neighbors if one of them has a(an) _____ attitude.

Exercise 11.8: Analogies

At the left, write the *letter* of the pair of words related to each other in the same way as the words of the capitalized pair.

_____ **1.** LABORED : SPONTANEITY

    (A) concise : brevity   (B) stale : consumption
    (C) furtive : openness   (D) grotesque : absurdity
    (E) abominable : unpleasantness

_____ **2.** GUERRILLA : HARASSMENT

    (A) victim : compensation   (B) infant : attention
    (C) apprentice : experience   (D) invader : panic
    (E) addict : self-control

_____ **3.** GLAMOROUS : ATTRACT

    (A) menacing : ignore   (B) elusive : capture
    (C) obliterated : decipher   (D) inevitable : avoid
    (E) loathsome : repel

_____ **4.** CONDESCEND : RESENTMENT

    (A) frustrate : fulfillment   (B) liberate : rejoicing
    (C) libel : reputation   (D) flounder : direction
    (E) retaliate : conscience

_____ **5.** AFFIRMATION : DENIAL

    (A) admonishment : commendation   (B) climax : culmination
    (C) gnawing : pang   (D) calamity : affliction
    (E) craving : desire

Review 3.1: Composition

Rewrite each paragraph in the space provided, following the instructions below.

JOHN F. KENNEDY

[1]John Fitzgerald Kennedy was born in Brookline, Massachusetts, in 1917. [2]He was to become the thirty-fifth President of the United States.

Combine S1 and 2 into a complex sentence by changing S2 to an adjective clause.

_____

_____

_____

_____

[3]In 1938 he worked as secretary to his father, Ambassador Joseph P. Kennedy, in London. [4]At the time he was still a student at Harvard.

Combine S3 and 4 into a complex sentence by changing S4 to an adverb clause.

_____

_____

_____

_____

[5]He enlisted in the Navy in 1941. [6]He became commander of a P-T boat in the Pacific during World War II. [7]The boat was torpedoed by the Japanese in August, 1943, off the Solomon Islands. [8]Kennedy was credited with rescuing at least one of the crewmen.

Combine S5 and 6 by changing S5 to a participial phrase. Then combine S7 and 8 into a complex sentence, changing S7 to an adverb clause.

_____

_____

_____

_____

_____

_____

_____

[9]He served in the House of Representatives with the Massachusetts delegation beginning in 1947. [10]In 1952 he was elected to the Senate. [11]By a narrow margin he defeated Richard M. Nixon for the office of President in 1960. [12]He became, at age 43, the youngest Chief Executive in the nation's history.

Combine S9 and 10 into a compound sentence. Then combine S11 and 12, changing S11 to a participial phrase.

_____

_____

_____

_____

_____

_____

_____

_____

[13]Kennedy was criticized for his support of the unsuccessful attempt to invade Cuba in 1961. [14]In the Cuban Missile Crisis of October 1962, he was highly praised for his bold confrontation with the Soviet Union. [15]It led to the removal of Soviet nuclear weapons from Cuba.

Combine S13, 14, and 15 into a compound-complex sentence, changing S15 to an adjective clause.

_____

_____

_____

_____

_____

_____

_____

[16]The young President was murdered by an assassin in Dallas, Texas, on November 22, 1963. [17]The nation was shocked.

Combine S16 and 17 into a complex sentence, changing S16 to an adverb clause.

_____

_____

_____

_____

Review 3.2:   Using Adverbs to Make Writing More Concise

Reduce each italicized expression to an *adverb*, choosing your adverbs from the list below.

affirmatively	condescendingly	ingeniously	listlessly	subsequently
arbitrarily	furtively	instinctively	menacingly	superciliously
blissfully	grotesquely	jovially	monotonously	tranquilly
callously	hospitably	laboriously	obstinately	tritely
clamorously	humanely	lavishly	petulantly	ultimately

_____ 1. They performed their duties *as if they had no inclination to exert themselves.*

_____ 2. For years we lived there *in perfect happiness.*

_____ 3. *At a later time*, I may regret what I have said.

_____ 4. That was done *in a clever way.*

_____ 5. She looked at me *in a manner that expressed contempt.*

_____ 6. *With noisy shouting*, they protested the verdict.

_____ 7. "It's as hot as blazes," he remarked *with a lack of originality.*

_____ 8. He shook his bat at the pitcher, *as if to threaten him.*

_____ 9. She replied *without any sign of agitation.*

_____ 10. You should not have dealt with us *like a dictator.*

_____ 11. They resisted *with stubbornness.*

_____ 12. *From natural impulse*, she is kind to animals.

_____ 13. At the shelter, the homeless were treated *with sympathy and consideration.*

_____ 14. You can't continue to spend *at an extravagant rate.*

_____ 15. The same old complaints were repeated *in a tiresomely uniform way.*

_____ 16. You acted *in a manner that showed no pity for the sufferers.*

_____ 17. We saw him slip something into his pocket *as if to hinder discovery.*

_____ 18. *At the end*, they went bankrupt.

_____ 19. Have you ever worked *with hard effort* at anything?

_____ 20. The receptionist answered my questions *as if she were in a bad humor.*

_____ 21. Asked whether she would tell the truth, the whole truth, and nothing but the truth, the witness answered *that she would do so.*

_____ 22. The Santa we saw outside the store greeted passersby *in a jolly way.*

_____ 23. Some people dress *in absurdly awkward costumes* on Halloween.

_____ 24. The host and hostess treated the guests *in a kind and friendly manner.*

_____ 25. It is insulting to talk to others *in a way that makes them feel inferior.*

Review 3.3: Using Adjectives to Make Writing More Concise

Reduce each italicized clause to an *adjective*, choosing your adjective from the following list.

abominable	deferred	hideous	optimistic	sullen
adjoining	dispirited	identifiable	perilous	ultimate
complimentary	floundering	inevitable	precipitous	unsociable
contagious	grim	jovial	seething	urban
covetous	grotesque	nutritious	shriveling	vain

1. results *that were bound to occur*   _____ results

2. people *who are enviously eager to own what belongs to others*   _____ people

3. diseases *which are communicable by contact*   _____ diseases

4. foods *that provide nourishment*   _____ foods

5. surf *that foams as if boiling*   _____ surf

6. a student *who was inclined to avoid the company of others*   a(an) _____ student

7. a woman *who is excessively proud of her appearance*   a(an) _____ woman

8. neighbors *who are full of good humor*   _____ neighbors

9. an exaggeration *that is absurdly awkward*   a(an) _____ exaggeration

10. terms *that are hard and unyielding*   _____ terms

11. the apartment *which is next door to ours*   the _____ apartment

12. claws *that are horribly ugly*   _____ claws

13. remarks *that express admiration*   _____ remarks

14. a beginner *who is struggling awkwardly to obtain footing*   a(an) _____ beginner

15. characteristics *that can be recognized* _____ characteristics

16. the suspect *who was resentfully silent* the _____ suspect

17. leaves *which are shrinking and becoming wrinkled* _____ leaves

18. a mission *that is full of danger* a(an) _____ mission

19. the test *that was put off to a future date* the _____ test

20. a slope *that falls with extreme rapidity* a(an) _____ slope

21. a deed *that deserves loathing* a(an) _____ deed

22. congestion *encountered in the cities* _____ congestion

23. investors *expecting the best possible gains* _____ investors

24. an outlook *marked by gloom of spirit* a(an) _____ outlook

25. the result *that came at the end* the _____ result

Review 3.4: Using Nouns to Make Writing More Concise

Reduce each italicized expression to a one-word *noun*, choosing your nouns from the following list.

altercation	craving	harvest	kindling	prey
anticipation	crisis	hospitality	libel	retaliation
censure	exultation	hostility	liberator	strut
consumer	glamor	impact	panic	thaw
craftiness	gnawing	intimacy	panorama	valor

_____ 1. Do you believe in *paying back injury for injury?*

_____ 2. Nobody is impressed by your *stiff, pompous manner of walking.*

_____ 3. The result was a(an) *sudden unreasoning terror causing headlong flight.*

_____ 4. I can sue you if you print that *false defamatory statement.*

_____ 5. The men look up to him because of his *boldness in facing danger.*

_____ 6. Weren't you surprised by their *show of ill will?*

_____ 7. *Picturing a future event beforehand* sometimes makes me nervous.

_____ 8. Two players became involved in a(an) *heated argument.*

_____ 9. Moses was hailed as a(an) *hero who led people out of bondage.*

_____ 10. How long do we have to wait before the *crop is gathered in?*

_____ 11. Her *harsh criticism* of my brother is not justified.

_____ 12. They are now looking for their next *helpless victims who are unable to resist attack.*

_____ 13. She had a(an) *great desire* for a cool drink.

_____ 14. We are entering a(an) *period of great danger and instability.*

_____ 15. The increased cost of electricity will be borne mainly by the *one who uses it.*

_____ 16. Helen can answer your question because of her *close association* with the problem.

_____ 17. Because of his *skill in deceiving others*, we must be on our guard.

_____ 18. In January we had a brief *period when the snow and ice melted.*

_____ 19. These forces jarred civilization by their *striking one against the other.*

_____ 20. Her parents are known for their *friendliness and kindness to all who come to their home.*

_____ 21. Two of us went to look for some *bits of dry wood for starting a fire.*

_____ 22. Hunger may cause a *persistent pain* in one's stomach.

_____ 23. From this hilltop, we can get a *full and unobstructed view* of the surrounding area.

_____ 24. Never had she experienced such *triumphant joy* as when she won the tournament for the first time.

_____ 25. Many aspiring young actors are drawn to the theater by the *excitement and adventure* of a stage career.

Review 3.5: Using Antonyms

Complete each sentence below by inserting the *antonym* of the italicized word. Choose your antonym from the following list.

accord	barbarous	dispirited	humble	relinquished
adoration	censured	eager	legitimate	rural
affliction	corpulent	easy	original	sparing
allayed	cowardice	exultation	pessimism	tedious
anguish	despised	hideous	previous	tranquil

1. You should have been _____ rather than *commended.*

2. What had appeared to be _____ was in reality an act of *valor.*

3. How can anyone call a play so _____ "*exciting*"?

4. They are opposites: one is *listless* and the other _____.

5. The _____ patient had once had a *lean* figure.

6. Despite the *altercation* at the start, we finally reached a(an) _____.

7. You have always been *lavish* in your promises but _____ in their fulfillment.

8. I consider his speech *trite* rather than _____.

9. She thought the alteration would be _____, but it turned out to be *laborious.*

10. He should have pursued his goal by _____ rather than by *arbitrary* means.

11. They were _____ in their treatment of prisoners; we were *humane.*

12. The property that you *retained* should have been _____ long ago.

13. In a short time, *bliss* turned to _____.

14. The child that was supposed to be the *solace* of his aging parents turned out to be their _____.

15. With the rumor of approaching aid, the _____ populace became *encouraged.*

16. Younger sisters should be *appreciated* rather than _____.

17. On *subsequent* occasions, we made the same error as on _____ ones.

18. You should have _____ our worries, not *intensified* them!

19. _____ turned to *dejection* as the victory that was within grasp slipped away.

20. Experience taught the once-*vain* youth to be more _____.

21. A weekend in _____ surroundings may help soothe a *troubled* mind.

22. At last we have replaced the _____ peeling paint with *attractive* new wallpaper.

23. Fresh dairy products arrive daily from _____ areas to feed hungry *urban* populations.

24. The recent disturbing reports have changed our *cheerfulness* to _____.

25. As the truth became known, the _____ with which the official had been regarded slowly turned to *loathing.*

Review 3.6: Spelling

Each line contains one misspelled word. Spell that word correctly in the space provided.

_____	1. drasticly, suddenness, anxiety, caressed
_____	2. renewable, extravagant, loyality, climactic
_____	3. excusable, disclosure, grotesquely, openess
_____	4. retention, abundent, desirable, heroically
_____	5. curiousity, satisfying, hideous, tranquilly
_____	6. supercilious, idley, frolicking, responsibility
_____	7. joviality, complement, dependible, tyranically
_____	8. possibly, maintenance, dramatically, picnicing
_____	9. eligible, fantastically, abominable, fully-equiped
_____	10. consumeable, equally, subtlety, arbitrariness
_____	11. sociability, believable, flimsily, generousity
_____	12. exposure, tragicly, oozing, exaggeration
_____	13. recede, gaiety, hopefuly, monotonous
_____	14. compliment, seizure, invisable, exposure
_____	15. probaly, incredible, monstrosity, obstinate
_____	16. countenance, realistically, wholly, permissable
_____	17. advisability, callus, icey, mimicking
_____	18. available, meaness, corpulence, urgency
_____	19. truely, conceivable, dramatically, solemn
_____	20. panicky, digestible, sturdyness, retaliate

Review 3.7: Correct Usage

If the underlined expression is correct, write *A* in the space provided. If it is incorrect, choose the best correction of those given and write its *letter* in the blank space.

_____ 1. Emergency crews were alerted for possible action, however, they were not used.

    (A) Correct as is.
    (B) action; However,
    (C) action; however,
    (D) action however

_____ 2. "Can you please tell me," I asked, "how to get to the post office?"

    (A) Correct as is.
    (B) "how to get to the post office."
    (C) how to get to the Post Office?"
    (D) "how to get to the post office"?

_____ 3. "That, she replied, is stated in the contract."

(A) Correct as is.
(B) "That," she replied, "is
(C) "That," She replied, is
(D) "That," she replied, "Is

_____ 4. The congestion in the theater district is worse <u>than any area</u>.

(A) Correct as is.
(B) then any other area.
(C) than any other area.
(D) than that in any other area.

_____ 5. Passengers <u>going to Brooklyn,</u> should change at Jamaica.

(A) Correct as is.
(B) , going to Brooklyn,
(C) going to Brooklyn
(D) , going to Brooklyn

_____ 6. They came by <u>bus. Bringing</u> their lunch.

(A) Correct as is.
(B) bus bringing
(C) bus; bringing
(D) bus, bringing

_____ 7. Marie accepted the <u>invitation and</u> thanked us for thinking of her.

(A) Correct as is.
(B) invitation. And
(C) invitation; and
(D) invitation; And she

_____ 8. The President <u>showing no signs of fatigue,</u> was applauded as he entered the chamber.

(A) Correct as is.
(B) , showing no signs of fatigue,
(C) showing no signs of fatigue
(D) , showing no signs of fatigue

_____ 9. "We got in free," said Joan, "as we had <u>complementary tickets."</u>

(A) Correct as is.
(B) complimentary tickets".
(C) complementary tickets".
(D) complimentary tickets."

_____ 10. The banks were closed on <u>Friday. Because</u> it was Veteran's Day.

(A) Correct as is.
(B) Friday; because
(C) Friday because
(D) Friday. Since

Review 3.8: Concise Writing (Using Fewer Words)

Express the thought of each of the following sentences in *no more than four words*, as in 1, below.

1. This time of great danger and instability could not have been foreseen in advance.
   This crisis was unforseeable.
   _____

2. Those who are engaged in irregular warfare, carrying out harassment and sabotage, tend to evade pursuit.
   _____

3. What was the reason for their walking in a stiff, pompous way?
   _____

4. The assuming of an air of superiority is something that is insulting.
   _____

5. Dissatisfaction resulting from unresolved problems or unfulfilled needs can destroy hope.
   _____

6. The career that Philip had chosen was not fascinatingly attractive and alluring.
   _____

Review 3.9: Analogies

At the left, write the *letter* of the pair of words related to each other in the same way as the words of the capitalized pair.

_____ 1. VALOR : VIRTUE

   (A) superciliousness : fault   (B) cowardice : surrender
   (C) famine : starvation   (D) glamor : attention
   (E) optimism : despair

_____ 2. KINDLING : FIRE

   (A) index : book   (B) seeds : garden
   (C) outage : electricity   (D) recession : employment
   (E) panic : reason

_____ 3. CONSERVE : EXTRAVAGANT

   (A) seethe : agitated   (B) swagger : proud
   (C) sympathize : calloused   (D) devise : inventive
   (E) resent : annoyed

_____ **4.** CARESS : AFFECTION

    (A) altercation : harmony   (B) monotony : boredom
    (C) infection : fever   (D) frustration : success
    (E) clamor : unrest

_____ **5.** GRIM : UNYIELDING

    (A) rational : panicky   (B) covetous : content
    (C) crafty : trustworthy   (D) inhospitable : receptive
    (E) arbitrary : undemocratic

SUBJECT INDEX

adjective, 17, 88, 102
  forming adjectives ending in -ful and -less, 100
  forming adjectives ending in -ing and -ed, 121
adjective clause, 90–91, 108–109
  and prepositional phrase, 91
  a tool for combining sentences, 108–110
  who, whose, and whom in adjective clauses, 108
adverb, 17, 176–177
  conjunctive, 65–66
adverb clause, 178, 197–198
adverb phrase, 178, 180
analogies, 34–35, 55–56
authors and reading selections (see Contents, page vii)

choppiness, 44–45, 152
comma, 23–24, 56–57, 89, 215
comparisons, 162–163
complex sentence, 127–128
composition skills:
  compound sentence from simple sentence, 63
  length, 48
  trite expressions and triteness, 74–76
  using and to combine simple sentences, 44
  varying sentence beginning, 6, 27
compound adjective, 213
compound-complex sentence, 150–154
compound sentence, 63–64
compound subject and compound verb, 43–44
conjunction, 63–64, 129, 198
conjunctive adverb, 65–66

dependent and independent clauses, 90, 127, 130, 150–151
derivative, 13–14

hyphen in compound adjective, 213

noun, 17

participial phrase, 23–24, 56–57, 200
participle, 23
parts of speech, 17–18, 65–66
prepositional phrase, 47, 91
pronoun, 91, 108, 162

quotation marks, 215

reading questions, 4–6
rewriting to eliminate choppiness, 47
root, 13–14

sentence fragments, 142–143
simple sentence, 43, 63–64
spelling:
  -able or -ible, 57–58
  -ability or -ibility, 58
  adjectives into adverbs, 36
  adjectives into nouns with -ity, 140–141
  adverbs into adjectives, 37
  compliment and complement, 190–191
  nouns into adjectives, 99–100
  nouns into verbs, 74
  verbs into adjectives, 120–121
  verbs into nouns, 73
suffix, 15–16

verb, 17
  object of, 17
  subject of, 17

VOCABULARY INDEX